Henry Alexander White

The Origin of the Pentateuch in the Light of the Ancient Monuments

Henry Alexander White

The Origin of the Pentateuch in the Light of the Ancient Monuments

ISBN/EAN: 9783337253202

Printed in Europe, USA, Canada, Australia, Japan

Cover: Foto ©Lupo / pixelio.de

More available books at **www.hansebooks.com**

THE

ORIGIN OF THE PENTATEUCH

IN THE

LIGHT OF THE ANCIENT MONUMENTS.

BY

HENRY ALEXANDER WHITE, M. A., Ph. D., D. D.,
Professor of History in the Washington and Lee University,
Lexington, Virginia.

RICHMOND, VA.:
B. F. JOHNSON PUBLISHING COMPANY.
1894.

THIS VOLUME IS DEDICATED
TO
MY WIFE.

PREFACE.

THE greater part of this volume, in the form of lectures, has been given, during several sessions, to my class in Bible History. The reader of these lectures should keep constantly before his eyes the open pages of the sacred narrative itself. It is hoped that they may be found available in connection with the study of the English Bible as a text-book of history in our colleges and universities.

The best literature available on the various subjects has been consulted. Reference to some of these authorities has been made in the foot-notes. Special acknowledgment must be rendered, in the line of Egyptian and Babylonian history to Brugsch's Egypt Under the Pharaohs (Scribner's); Renouf's Religion of Ancient Egypt; Budge's Dwellers on the Nile; Rawlinson's Ancient Egypt; his Great Monarchies, and his Origin of Nations; Wilkinson's Ancient Egyptians; Kenrick's Egypt; the publications of Ebers; Fergusson on Egyptian Architecture; Dawson's Egypt and Syria; Smith's Ancient History of the East; Sayce's Ancient Empires of the East; his Fresh Light from the Ancient Monuments, and his Assyria, its Princes, Priests and People; Budge's Babylonian Life and History; Layard's Nineveh and Babylon; Keary's Dawn of History, and the various encyclopedias and publications of the Palestine and Egyptian Exploration Funds.

In connection with the Babylonian myths and modern critical theories, the following have been chiefly used: Smith's Chaldean Account of Genesis (Scribner's); Lenormant's Beginnings of History; Records of the Past; Driver's Introduction to the Literature of the Old Testament; Briggs' The Higher Criticism of the Hexateuch; The Bible, the Church and the Reason; Ryle's Early Narratives of Genesis.

In the study of the narrative of the Pentateuch, valuable assistance has been found in The Speaker's Commentary; Delitzsch on Genesis; Ewald's History of Israel; Stanley's History of the Jewish Church, and his Sinai and Palestine; Oehler's *Old Testament Theology.*

HENRY ALEXANDER WHITE.

WASHINGTON AND LEE UNIVERSITY, *September, 1894.*

CONTENTS.

PART I.
THE WITNESS OF THE ANCIENT MONUMENTS.
Introductory.

CHAPTER I.—*The Fall of the Ancient Empires of the East.*
The Tragedy of the Ten Tribes of Israel 14
The Battle of Megiddo 15
The Fall of Nineveh 17
The Captivity of Judah in Babylon 19
The Overthrow of Egypt 20
The Destruction of the Kingdom of Lydia 21
The Fall of Babylon 22
Two Discoveries—The Decree of Cyrus and the Book of the Law of Moses 23

CHAPTER II.—*The Civilization of Ancient Egypt.*
The Land of Egypt 28
The Pyramid Builders 30
The Pharaohs of Thebes 32
The Empire of Thothmes III. 36
Pharaoh Rameses II. 37
The Sun-gods, Ra and Osiris 39

CHAPTER III.—*The Civilization of Babylonia.*
The Land Between the Rivers 45
The Accadians 46
The Moon-god of Ur 48
Assyrian and Babylonian Kings 50
Asshur-bani-pal 52
Nebuchadnezzar 54
Merodach, the Sun-god of Babylon 56

CHAPTER IV.—*Discovery and Interpretation of the Ancient Inscriptions.*
The Library of Asshur-bani-pal 59
The Rosetta Stone 62
The Behistun Inscription 64

PART II.
THE BEGINNINGS OF DIVINE REVELATION CONTRASTED WITH HEATHEN FOLK-LORE.

CHAPTER V.—*The Creation.*
The Chaldean Story of Creation 71
The Story of Creation in the Book of Genesis. 77
Origin of Inorganic Life 78
Origin of Organic Life 79
The Image of God 80
Jehovah is God. 82
The Purpose of the Narrative in Genesis 83

CHAPTER VI.—*The Origin and Progress of Evil.*
The Sacred Tree of Eridu 87
The Babylonian Belief in the Physical Origin of Evil 89
The Fall of Man and His Expulsion from Eden. 90
The Cainites and the Sethites 93
The Documentary Theory of the Origin of this History. 95

CHAPTER VII.—*The Deluge.*
The Babylonian Legend 96
The Greek Legend 99
The Story in Genesis 100
The Covenant with Noah 105
The Destiny of the Sons of Noah. 106

CHAPTER VIII.—*One God and One Race of Men.*
Heathen Views of the Origin of Man. 108
The Dispersion from Babel 109
The Unity of the Human Race 109
The Unity of Human Speech 110
Origin of the Early Genesis Narrative 111

PART III.
DIVINE REVELATION CONTINUED IN OPPOSITION TO HEATHEN NATURE-WORSHIP.

CHAPTER IX.—*Abram Called Out from the Land of the Moon-Worshippers.*
Ur of the Chaldees. 118
Abram's First Call 120
The Second Call 122
The Vision at Sichem 122

CHAPTER X.—*Abram Tempted by the Sun-Worshippers.*
The Famine in Palestine 125
Abram Before the Pharaoh. 126

The Altar at Bethel	128
Abram's Separation from Lot	128
The Home at Hebron	130

CHAPTER XI.—*The Faith of Abraham Confirmed by the Divine Covenants.*

War with Babylonia	132
The Sacrificial Covenant	132
The Egyptian Hagar	138
The Covenant of Circumcision	138
Sodomites and Philistines	143
The Covenant of the Oath	143

CHAPTER XII.—*The Chosen Race Kept Pure.*

The Marriage of Isaac	151
The Birth of Esau and Jacob	152
Jacob's Family's Pride	153
The Descent into Egypt	158
Joseph's Governorship	159
Jacob's Dying Blessing	163

PART IV.

DIVINE REVELATION IN CONFLICT WITH HEATHENISM.

CHAPTER XIII.—*Israel in Egypt.*

The Growth of the People	168
The Store-Cities, Pithom and Raamses	168
Moses and the Pharaoh	173
The Royal University at Heliopolis	174
Moses as a Soldier of the Egyptian Empire	177
Moses the Self-Appointed Deliverer	178

CHAPTER XIV.—*Jehovah Declares His Name.*

Moses in Midian	180
The Burning Bush	182
God's Covenant-Name is Jehovah	183
Moses and Aaron in Egypt as the Representatives of Jehovah	184

CHAPTER XV.—*Jehovah's Name Vindicated in the Presence of the Sun-gods of Egypt.*

Zoan, the Capital of the Delta	188
"Wonders in the Field of Zoan"	189
The Seven Days' Death of the Nile-god	191
The Plague of Frogs	193
The Curse Upon the Soil of the Earth	194
The Atmosphere Breeds a Plague, but Not Upon the Hebrews	196
Curses Upon the Cattle and Upon the People	197
The Pharaoh's Heart Hardened	198

The Darkness that Could be Felt.................... 203
"Judgment Against all the Gods of Egypt"............. 204
    CHAPTER XVI.—*From Heliopolis to Sinai.*
The Sacrifice of the Passover...................... 207
The Gathering at Succoth......................... 208
The Passage of the Red Sea....................... 209
Bread from Heaven.............................. 212
The Rock of Rephidim............................ 215
The Mountain of Fire............................ 216
The Song of Moses.............................. 219

PART V.
THE DIVINE CHARTER OF DELIVERANCE FROM HEATHEN SUPERSTITION.
    CHAPTER XVII.—*The National Covenant.*
The Invisible Redeemer.......................... 223
The Sealing of the National Covenant............... 225
The Tables of the Covenant....................... 229
The Book of the Covenant........................ 232
The Ark of the Covenant......................... 235
Jehovah the Sovereign King....................... 238
    CHAPTER XVIII.—*The National Administration.*
The Kingdom Visible............................. 246
The National Altar.............................. 248
The National Priesthood......................... 253
Ordinances Concerning Holiness................... 255
The Holy Festivals.............................. 257
The Blood of the Atonement...................... 260
    CHAPTER XIX.—*The National Organization.*
The National Assembly........................... 266
The Elders of the Congregation................... 269
The Brazen Serpent.............................. 271
The Spirit of God............................... 273
    CHAPTER XX.—*Jehovah's Ideal for the Nation.*
The Last Messages of Moses....................... 276
"Jehovah, God of your Fathers".................... 276
National Ideals................................. 279
The Everlasting Covenant........................ 284
The Three Legal Codes........................... 287
    CHAPTER XXI.—*Authorship and Inspiration of the Pentateuch.*
Moses Wrote the National Constitution.............. 289
The Culmination of Moses' Work as Prophet.......... 293
The Inspiration of the Pentateuch.................. 299

PART I.

THE WITNESS OF THE ANCIENT MONUMENTS.

INTRODUCTORY.

CHAPTER I.

THE FALL OF THE ANCIENT EMPIRES OF THE EAST.

[*621–521 B. C.*]

A SINGLE century, extending from the year 621 B. C. to 521 B. C., saw the downfall of all the original empires of the East. During this short period the sceptre of the world was transferred from the Hamitic and Semitic to the Aryan races. On the banks of the Tiber the Romans were almost ready to drive out the line of kings and to organize the republic; in Athens Solon was laying the foundations of the Democracy; in Miletus Thales was setting forth the principles of that physical philosophy which was destined to supplant the myths that had come from Babylon to Greece. At the same time the Aryan races of the East under Cyrus, of Persia, were crushing into dust the last of the Semitic kingdoms, and were also gathering strength for the later struggle between Asia and Europe at Marathon and Salamis, in the reigns of Darius and Xerxes.

From the days of Noah until this century of Cyrus and of Solon, five great empires were builded by the sons of Ham and of Shem. First in the order of time, they continued to stand first among organized governments in the order of power. The kingdom of the Egyptian Pharaohs on the river Nile traced its origin back to Mizraim, second son of Ham. Babylon, on the Euphrates, claimed as father Nimrod, the grandson of Ham. Nineveh, on the river Tigris, worshipped as chief god her original founder, Asshur, second son of Shem. The kingdom of Lydia, in western Asia Minor, was the last living fragment of the Hittite empire, founded by Heth, grandson of Ham. The children of Heth in early times sold to Abraham the cave of Machpelah; they probably invaded Egypt under the Hyksos princes and were afterwards forced northward by Babylon and became a part of Lydia. Jerusalem, daughter of Zion, centre of the kingdom of Judah, retained her old position as one of the great powers of the earth. For more than two thousand years had some of these empires lived. The annals of mankind had never yet been illustrated by a single complete national downfall. Into this century these kingdoms entered, still in possession of much of the splendor of their youth. Ere ten decades had past they were all dead and buried at the hands of the Almighty God. With a single exception, those kingdoms remain dead and buried unto this day. After seventy years of burial, there was a great resurrection from the dead in the case of Judah. Persia, the hammer of the nations, who had beaten Babylon to powder reëstablished Jerusalem upon Mount Zion, for a longer term of power. Yet this period of the overthrow of the ancient races marked the first great fulfillment of the prophecy delivered by Jehovah Himself unto Noah that Japheth, father of the Aryan peoples, "shall dwell in the tents of Shem and Canaan shall be his servant."*

The Tragedy of the Ten Tribes of Israel—721 B. C.

Several preludes were furnished before the curtain rose upon the great five-act drama of national overthrow. Exactly one century before the beginning of this continuous tragedy, Samaria, capital of the kingdom of the Ten Tribes, was taken by Sargon, of Assyria, and all the people of that northern portion of Palestine were borne away into captivity beyond the Euphrates. This captivity was a direct punishment from God on account of Israel's practice of idolatry. Jeroboam, the founder of this northern kingdom, had instituted the worship of the golden calves, in imitation of Egyptian idol-worship. Ahab and his wife Jezebel set up altars to Baal and Ashtoreth, gods brought from Babylon by the people of Tyre. Since they scorned Jehovah's protection, He gave these Israelites up to the power of the heathen whose gods were preferred before Him. A great black obelisk from Nineveh, now in the British museum, represents five kings paying tribute to Shalmaneser II. of Assyria. Foremost among these five kings is the figure of "Jehu, the son of Omri." Thus, at a period ante-dating the prophet Jonah, King Jehu was made to feel the scourging hand of the Assyrian. Through the voices of His prophets, Hosea

---

* Gen. 9: 27.

and Amos, God besought Israel to return unto Him in order that He might deliver them from this second bondage, even as in the days of old, He had set free their fathers at the Red Sea. But the kings and the priests and the people all refused to hearken. The last king of Israel, Hoshea, led his nation yet more deeply into the toils. When Shalmaneser IV., of Assyria, demanded a heavy tribute, Hoshea refused to pay and turned to seek aid, not from Jehovah, but from Sebek or So, of Egypt. The expedition organized against Israel by Shalmaneser was at last successful under his successor Sargon, and the Ten Tribes were swept from their allotted habitation " as a man wipeth a dish, wiping it and turning it upside down."*

The Battle of Megiddo—609 B. C.

Another prelude to the great drama was the battle in the pass of Megiddo. This event reveals the false position of the kingdom of Judah in becoming entangled in alliances with heathen nations and in casting off the protection of Jehovah. . Since the fall of Samaria, a century before, Judah had imitated the foreign policy of the northern kingdom. After the conquest of the Ten Tribes, King Sargon advanced to punish Sebek of Egypt for the assistance rendered to Hoshea of Israel. The Pharaoh fled and Sargon took and fortified Ashdod in Philistia, a post that gave him control of the great sea-coast route into the land of Egypt. From that time onward, Assyria and Egypt engaged in deadly conflict for the possession of western Asia, and in particular, for the kingdom of Judah. This struggle was like unto the contest so long continued between France and Germany for the intervening territory of Alsace-Lorraine. The fatal policy adopted by Judah herself was to make alliance with one of these heathen nations in order to resist the other. One glorious exception to this method of national defence illustrated the century prior to the battle of Megiddo. When Sennacherib, the son of Sargon, came up against Judah, King Hezekiah hearkened to the advice of the prophet Isaiah and sought not the help of the king of Egypt, but trusted in the arm of Jehovah. Through the camp of the invading Assyrians passed the angel of Jehovah and smote

---
* II Kings 21: 13.

an hundred and four score and five thousand of the enemies of Judah,

> "And the might of the Gentiles, untouched by the sword,
> Had melted like snow at the blast of the Lord."

This return to the policy advocated by God's prophets was of brief duration. Hezekiah himself ere long showed a strong inclination to enter into alliance with Babylonia, in spite of Isaiah's prophecy that this third power should finally subjugate Judah. Henceforth there are three sides to Judah's political position as connected with those three foreign nations.

The impious and idolatrous king of Judah, Manasseh, son of Hezekiah, rested upon the friendship of Egypt, while he looked on to see Assyria and Babylonia settle their quarrel. But the friendship of Egypt failed to prevent Manasseh's captivity in Babylon at the hands of the Assyrian King Esar-haddon, who made the latter city one of his capitals. The generosity of the Assyrians in restoring Manasseh to his throne, perhaps, inclined the hearts of the people of Judah to turn from the alliance with Egypt to a dependence upon Assyria. Against the urgent entreaties of Jeremiah that they should take Jehovah alone as their defence, the chosen people in the time of King Josiah made ready to assail Pharaoh-Necho of Egypt as he was marching against their old enemies, but now their friends, the Assyrians.

Sais, the capital of Pharaoh-Necho, situated on the western branch of the Nile, near the sea, was the last centre of the power of independent Egypt. The dynasty of Necho had established itself on the throne by the aid of Greek mercenaries. Necho himself had attempted to re-open the ancient canal between the Red Sea and the Mediterranean, a work begun in the time of Moses by Rameses II. From the Red Sea, Necho's fleet had sailed around Africa and entered the Mediterranean at the Pillars of Hercules. Necho was in close sympathy with the religious creed of the Greeks, for after the battle of Megiddo he sent an embassy to the oracle of Apollo at Branchidae, near Miletus, to bear as a votive offering to the god his battle-tunic. Filled with the spirit of Greek enterprise, Necho led up his army against the power of Assyria. Across his path rushed King Josiah. Josiah had instituted a great reform in Judah after the discovery of the Book of the Law. Impelled in part by zeal against the ancient enemies of his people, in part by his inclination to an alliance with Assyria, Josiah marched down from the hills of Judah into the great plain of Esdraelon near Mount Carmel. Along the seashore northwards came Necho. The two kings met in battle at Megiddo. Josiah wore a disguise, for Necho had sent him friendly warning not to withstand his advance. At the first onset, Josiah's soldiers turned and fled, for the king himself was sore wounded by an Egyptian arrow and in his second chariot was borne back dead to Jerusalem. The true patriotism of the people of Judah had been deadened and their hands had been palsied by idolatry and vile heathenish customs. The glory of the line of David departed with Josiah. The tragedy of the king was a forecast of the tragedy of the nation. Soon was this kingdom to fall beneath the power of the foreign empire whose protection had been courted. A type of many future sorrows was this defeat of Josiah unto later prophets.* But at the last, the plain of Megiddo appeared in the vision of John, in Patmos, as the scene of the battle of Ar-Megiddo or Armageddon, where Jesus Christ reverses the ancient tragedy and overthrows finally and forever the enemies of His people.

The Fall of Nineveh—606 B. C.

The first act in the tragedy of dying empires took place in the year 606 B. C., when Nineveh, the capital of Assyria, at the word spoken by the God of Nations, was sealed up forever in the tomb. Conquest and rapine had marked the career of Assyria. Her military power had grown until the sceptre of her kings waved red over Western Asia from the Tigris even as far as to the river Nile. A few years before the coming of the avenger of blood, a scholar-tyrant ruled in Nineveh. Asshur-bani-pal, the Sardanapalus of Greek legend, transformed Nineveh the arsenal to Nineveh the national library. In the rooms of his palace he gathered together all the State and religious and educational records of the two Semitic empires, Assyria and Babylonia. Then was the city of towers and palaces ready for burial along with these written records of her infamy. The destroying

---

* Zechariah 12: 10, 11.

blow came from the hand of a kindred people, the men of Babylonia.

The records from Asshur-bani-pal's library portray the Assyrians as a race whose veins were full of the wine of cruelty. In deeds of slaughter wrought with fire and sword they found their chief joy. For a brief space they sat in ashes at the warning call of the prophet Jonah. "Woe to thee, city of bloods! The fire shall devour thee!"* cried the prophet Nahum, not long after Sargon's capture of Samaria, since Nahum himself was probably one of the captives and died in exile on the Tigris.

"I will punish the fruit of the stout heart of the king of Assyria and the glory of his high looks. For he saith, By the strength of my hand I have done it, and by my wisdom." † Thus spoke the prophet Isaiah in the name of the Lord. By authority of the same Lord of hosts, this prophet declared that fire would be sent to consume the glory of the kings of Nineveh. A foretaste of avenging power was given to Sennacherib as he approached Jerusalem. But in its complete form was vengeance wrought out upon Nineveh by the Babylonians and the Medes.

From three sides at once destruction closed in upon the wicked capital of the Upper Tigris. The last of the Assyrian kings, known to the Greeks as Saracus, was trembling on his throne as Pharaoh-Necho marched northward from the battle of Megiddo. Ere long the victorious spears of the king of Egypt were flashing along the bank of the Euphrates. Necho made that stream for a time the eastern boundary of the empire of the Nile. While Saracus sat powerless in Nineveh, his vassals in Babylonia made ready to throw off their chains. Alliance was made with the fierce mountain-warriors of Media. Nebuchadnezzar, son of the viceroy of Babylonia, drew near the walls of Nineveh with the army of the coalition. In despair the king of Assyria assembled his wives and his treasures in the royal palace. The river Tigris rose to a great height about the walls of the city. At last a column of ascending smoke told the story of a capital fired by its own ruler. Two centuries afterward the Greek historian, Xenophon, at the head of his retreating "Ten Thousand," came upon the ruins of a deserted city

---
* Nahum, ch. 3.   † Isa. 20; 12, 13.

on the banks of the Tigris. Above the site of Nineveh he stood, yet he knew it not. A meaningless name he gave to the place and passed on, leaving the true story of Assyria's glory and destruction buried beneath that desolate mound.

The Captivity of Judah in Babylon—586 B. C.

The second act in the great world-drama was concerned with the kingdom of Judah. Jehovah sent dire calamities upon His chosen race because they trusted no longer in Him but attempted to fortify their kingdom by dependence upon heathen nations and heathen gods. While Babylonia was growing up in strength before the fall of Nineveh, Judah's princes were looking for help to both Assyria and Egypt. "What hast thou to do in the way of Egypt to drink the waters of Sihor [Nile]? or what hast thou to do in the way of Assyria to drink the waters of the river? . . . How, then, art thou turned into the degenerate plant of a strange vine unto me!"* In the name of Jehovah came the prophet Jeremiah thus to remonstrate with Judah. He warned them that God would bring a dry wind from the east to wither up the joy of the people if they turned not from idols and heathen political schemes unto Him. They hearkened not, but when Nineveh fell, King Jehoiakim sought aid from Egypt. Like a withering whirl-wind came Nebuchadnezzar, fresh from the destruction of the Assyrian capital, and more recently from the battle of Carchemish, on the Euphrates, where he defeated Pharaoh-Necho and sent him in flight back to Egypt. In the same year, 605 B. C., he took the city of Jerusalem and bore away the vessels of the house of Jehovah unto the temple of Bel in Babylon.† In his train as captives were led Daniel and his three companions of the seed royal. Jehoiakim, the friend of Egypt, in order to save his throne, renounced the alliance with Pharaoh and swore allegiance to Nebuchadnezzar. But soon this puppet-prince at Jerusalem began to plot against his Babylonian master, and in accordance with Jeremiah's prophecy, was murdered by Chaldean bands of invaders and was "buried with the burial of an ass beyond the gates of Jerusalem." ‡ Jehoiakim now began to rule as

---

*Jeremiah, 2: 18, 21.   †II Chron. 36: 6, 7.   ‡Josephus; Jer., 36: 30.

the vassal of Babylonia, but the poison of political trickery was strong in his Jewish blood. An Egyptian alliance tempted him, and then came Nebuchadnezzar in person to besiege the city. A second train of captives were led away to Babylon, all the princes and all the mighty men of valor. The year 597 B. C. saw this staggering blow delivered.

Zedekiah, another son of Josiah, began now to play the vassal-prince unto Nebuchadnezzar. With the same old weakness and treachery he followed in the path marked out by his predecessors. In reliance upon Pharaoh-Hophra he broke out into open rebellion against Babylonia. He burned the book of Jeremiah's prophecy but could not silence this old patriot and messenger of God. The cup of Judah's iniquity was now full. The prophet sent a message of consolation to the people already captive in Babylon that their bondage should continue only seventy years.*
Then fell the judgment of God at the hands of the heathen conqueror. Fire and sword swept the city that had placed its reliance in fire and sword. Heathen friendship had become heathen cruelty. The house of Jehovah and all the other great houses were burnt and the walls of Jerusalem were leveled to the ground. There was left in Judah only a miserable remnant of the poorest of the land to be the vine-dressers and husbandmen. †

The Overthrow of Egypt—568 B. C.

"Pharaoh, king of Egypt, is but a noise; he hath passed the time appointed."‡ This was the opinion of the prophet Jeremiah concerning the Egyptian kingdom when he saw the chariots of Necho dashing away in flight from the onset of Nebuchadnezzar at Carchemish in 605 B. C. Out of the captivity in Babylon was heard another prophet's voice very soon after the fall of Jerusalem. "Thus saith the Lord God, Behold I am against thee, Pharaoh, king of Egypt, the great dragon that lieth in the midst of his rivers, which hath said, My river is mine own and I have made it for myself.

"But I will put hooks in thy jaws and . . . . . I will bring thee up out of the midst of thy rivers . . . . Behold I will give the land of Egypt unto Nebuchadnezzar, king of Babylon."§

---
*Jer., ch. 29.   †II Kings, 25.   ‡Jer. 46: 28.   §Ezek. 29: 3, 4, 19.

Nearly twenty years after Ezekiel's prophecy, Nebuchadnezzar turned aside from his great work of building and adornment in Babylon to punish the pride of Pharoah-Hophra. This king had furnished assistance to Zedekiah in the last struggle at Jerusalem. Now he fled before the Babylonians to the extreme border of his kingdom, far up the river Nile to Syêne. There the power of Egypt was broken, Hophra was deposed and executed and Amasis was made a vassal-king of Egypt and compelled to pay tribute to Babylonia.* The final blow to Egyptian ascendancy was here given. In 525 B. C. Cambyses, of Persia, came likewise into the Nile country. The strength of the kingdom had been somewhat restored, but was now utterly shattered at the battle of Pelusium by the Persian conqueror. But the eclipse of the ancient glory of the empire of the Pharaohs was due to the coming of Nebuchadnezzar, conqueror of Nineveh and captor of Judah.

The Destruction of the Kingdom of Lydia—546 B. C.

Fragments of various Asiatic tribes came together in Asia Minor to form the kingdom of Lydia. The last and greatest king of the dynasty was Croesus. He brought beneath his control the trading cities of Ionia and became thus, in a measure, a Greek sovereign. His fleets sailed from Ephesus and Smyrna and controlled the commerce of the Mediterranean, and hence arose his princely wealth.

The leading clan in the founding of this kingdom was the Hittite. But long before the establishment of Lydia, the Hittites possessed an empire of their own. Their two ancient capitals were Kadesh on the Orontes and Carchemish on the Euphrates. At one time they ruled nearly all of Western Asia. They fought long and successfully against the empire of Egypt, and were probably the leaders in the Hyksos invasion. But their power was broken by Sargon, of Assyria, a few years after his capture of Samaria. He captured Carchemish and made it the centre of an Assyrian province.

In their last seat of power, Lydia, the Hittites were attacked by Cyrus, founder of the Persian empire. About the year 546 B. C. Cyrus fought a battle with Croesus on

---

*Josephus: Ant. Jud. X. 9, § 7. Wiedemann: Zeitschrift für Ägyptische Sprache, 1878: 2-6 and 87-89.

the banks of the river Halys. Sardis, the capital of Lydia, fell into the hands of the conqueror, and the sons of Heth, as a distinct race, were soon forgotten. Babylonian art and civilization they had, in large measure, in connection with the Phœnicians, transferred to the people of Greece. But just as they laid aside forever the sceptre of power, Babylon's own appointed hour had come.

The Fall of Babylon—538 B. C.

"Babylon shall become heaps, a dwelling-place for dragons"* cried Jeremiah when he saw the last captive Hebrew passing away toward the Euphrates. From the century preceding, Isaiah had thus spoken: "Babylon, wild beasts of the desert shall lie there, and owls shall dwell there . . . . and satyrs shall dance there."†

When Jeremiah uttered his prophecy, King Nebuchadnezzar was building up the strength of Babylon. Soon he made it the centre of an empire stretching from the Tigris and Euphrates to the Nile. Here towered the greatest kingdom that the sons of men had ever yet looked upon. The pride of this king's heart was likewise great, but Daniel, the prophet, was commissioned to humble that pride. In the vision recorded in the Book of Daniel, Nebuchadnezzar saw the stone cut out of the mountain which broke in pieces the image of gold, silver, brass, iron and clay as a prophecy that God would establish His own eternal kingdom upon the ruins of all the kingdoms of the earth. In another vision it was revealed to the king that his own empire should be the first to fall. Daniel himself lived long enough to read the message of Babylon's immediate doom. Into the banquet-hall of Belshazzar, grandson of Nebuchadnezzar, was the prophet summoned. The last of the line of proud kings had impiously used the sacred vessels carried away from the temple at Jerusalem as the implements of his drunken feast. The hand of God appeared to write on the wall: "Thy kingdom is divided and given to the Medes and Persians." ‡ In that same hour, beneath the walls along the recently drained channel of the river, rushed the army of Cyrus, under the leadership of Darius, the Mede. Thus closed the fifth act in the tragedy

---

*Jer. 51: 37. †Isa. 13: 19, 22. ‡Daniel 5.

in which empires were the leading figures. The Semitic race gave way forever, and the Aryan began to rule the world. This century of wonders, at its close, saw Darius ascend the throne of Persia, 521 B. C. The founder of a great dynasty was Darius, the organizer of the first completely centralized government. He divided his empire into twenty-three provinces or satrapies, and among them the will of the king was the fountain of all law. Upon the ruins of the five preceding kingdoms rested the cornerstones of this empire of Persia.

Two Discoveries—The Decree of Cyrus and the Book of the Law of Moses.

Two important events stand as sign-posts at the beginning and at the close of this' era of national decay. The first of these was the discovery of the Book of the Law of Moses in the Temple at Jerusalem by King Josiah in the year 621 B. C. The second was the discovery in the palace at Ecbatana by King Darius of the decree of Cyrus of Persia granting permission to the Jews to return from Babylon in order to rebuild Jerusalem.* The discovery and the re-issue of this decree was the first great act of Darius who came to the throne in 521 B. C.

The decree of Cyrus was the agency employed by Jehovah in raising to life again the buried kingdom of Judah. The prophet Isaiah had long before made this declaration: "I am the Lord that . . . . . saith of Cyrus, He is my shepherd and shall perform all my pleasure;" † moreover, the prophet foretold that this service of Cyrus under Jehovah was to be rendered in the re-establishment of Jerusalem and the holy temple. The first year of Cyrus as king at Babylon was the year 536 B. C. ‡ Then did the Lord stir up Cyrus to make proclamation throughout his empire that God's people should return to Jerusalem to rebuild the house of the Lord. All the sacred vessels carried away by Nebuchadnezzar were given to the first colony of returning captives under Zerubbabel. Much substance besides in gold, silver and beasts of burden was furnished the liberated exiles. In the following year 635 B. C. began these patriotic Hebrews to rebuild the temple. § Just

---
* Ezra 6: 1-3. † Isa. 44: 24-28. ‡ Ezra, 1: 1. § Ezra, 3-8.

seventy years was this event after the first seizure of some of those captives and some of those sacred vessels in 605 B. C. When Cyrus died, his royal decree was annulled by succeeding kings until Darius began to reign. This prince made search in Babylon and in Ecbatana until he found the roll of Cyrus' proclamation, and then the work upon the temple was resumed. In the sixth year of King Darius was the house of the Lord again made complete,* and this year of restoration, 516 B. C., was exactly *seventy* years after the downfall of the Temple in 586 B. C. Thus did God make use of Persia, the destroyer of the previous empires, in restoring the kingdom of His chosen people. That century of imperial overthrow was all of His divine ordering; it was an object-lesson to the Jews and to all succeeding nations that He holds in the hollow of His hand all the kingdoms of the earth. This same divine lesson was taught the Jews in another event that transpired at the very opening of this momentous century, 621 B. C. In the eighteenth year of his reign King Josiah gave orders to repair the house of the Lord. While the work was in progress, Hilkiah, the priest, in a secret recess of the sanctuary, "found the Book of the Law of the Lord given by Moses."†

The documentary theory of the origin of the Pentateuch, held now by many scholars, finds its chief corner-stone in the assumption that the book found in the year 621 B. C. was not the entire Pentateuch, but only the single Book of Deuteronomy. Moreover, the development theory assumes this same position and goes a step farther in asserting that this Book of Deuteronomy had been written only a very short time before its discovery in the Temple; that Deuteronomy was the second document in the order of *development*, the prophetic narrative being the first, and the priestly narrative coming after the return from Babylon. These two theories are based chiefly upon the assumption that Josiah found only the Book of Deuteronomy. This assumption is based upon the two-fold argument (1) that the contents of this book as described in II. Kings answer exactly to the contents of Deuteronomy, and (2) that the law as quoted

---
*Ezra, 6: 15.   †II Chron. 34: 14.

by the writer of the books of the Kings is the law as given in Deuteronomy.*

This position cannot be maintained. It is true that most of the references to Josiah's book accord with the contents of Deuteronomy; but some of them do not. Moreover, we have an additional account in the Chronicles. The command that the priests, assisted by the Levites, should make ready the sacrifice of the Passover; that these ministers should first sanctify themselves; that the flesh of the Passover feast should be roasted in fire,† are details not found in Deuteronomy, but in Exodus and Leviticus. Concerning the second point that the writer of the historical books knew Deuteronomy alone among the books of the Pentateuch, the details of the Passover, celebrated by King Hezekiah, and the reason for that celebration in the ceremonial impurity of priests and people show that he must have had in his possession the books of Exodus and Leviticus as well as the Book of Deuteronomy.‡

It was the Pentateuch, and probably the original autograph of Moses, that was found in the Temple by Hilkiah.

What are the facts upon which this presumption is based? They are those connected with the overthrow of the great kingdoms, whose story has been already given. Time and again in the scripture histories and in the writings of the prophets is it declared that those nations were destroyed because of their violation of the principles of the Law given by Moses. According to the Scripture narrative which treats of this century of doom and the time preceding, what was the Law of Moses? The Book which Moses himself wrote was placed by the priests in the Ark of the Covenant.§ That law was recognized for many centuries as the voice of God Himself. The people chose to disobey, and only at rare intervals they chose to follow that law. But their records are clear in the assertion that during all those years, that book left by Moses was still God's law. Thus came the downfall of the Ten Tribes in 721 B. C. " Because they rejected His *statutes* and His *covenant* that He made with their fathers, and His *testimonies* which He testified unto them. . . . . . Therefore the Lord was very angry with Israel and removed them out of His sight."‖

---
* Ryle in Briggs's Higher Criticism of the Hexateuch, p. 16. † II. Chron. 35, and II. Kings 23. ‡ II. Chron. 29 and 30. § Deut. 31: 26. ‖ II. Kings 17: 7, 15, 18.

God would not destroy a part of His people for disobeying His law before that law in all its completeness had been set before them. Israel had been in possession of the whole Pentateuch for centuries, and she was destroyed for despising that which she fully and clearly knew.

This same "Book of the Law of Moses" was followed by King Hezekiah in his reformation. He arranged the service of the priests and other parts of keeping the feasts as they are commanded in the book of Leviticus.* But King Manasseh rejected "all the law and the statutes and the ordinances given by Moses."† King Ammon followed in the footsteps of his father. During this period of evil-doing, of idolatry, when the Temple of Jehovah was profaned, some priest most probably hid away the temple copy of the law of Moses in the recess where it was discovered in the reign of the reformer, King Josiah. At that time, no surprise at the discovery fell from the lips of Hilkiah, the priest, nor from the scribes, nor from Huldah, the prophetess, nor from the elders of the people, the priests and the Levites. The book was received as a volume well known, for it contained the Lord's "*commandments* and His *testimonies* and His *statutes* . . . . . and the *covenant* of God, the God of their fathers."‡ This outline takes in the spirit of the entire Pentateuch. Entirely arbitrary and altogether too narrow is the interpretation that would confine it to the book of Deuteronomy.

But this law was not long kept. The reformation of Josiah marked the expiring glory of the kingdom of Judah. For her disobedience to God's law was this kingdom doomed. It was concerning Judah that Jeremiah thus spake: "The Lord saith, Because they have forsaken my *law which I set before them*, and have not obeyed my voice, neither walked therein. . . . Therefore I will scatter them also among the heathen."§ Jeremiah foretold also the fall of the heathen because of their scorn for God and His people: "Was not Israel a derision unto thee?"|| cried he concerning Moab. "As Babylon hath caused the slain of Israel to fall, so at Babylon shall fall the slain of all the earth."¶ All the nations that went down to death in the century following the

---

* II. Chron. 29 and 30.   † II. Chron. 33: 1. 13.   ‡ II. Chron. 34: 31. 32.   § Jerem. 9: 13. 16.
|| Jer. 48: 27.   ¶ Jer. 51: 49.

discovery of the Book of the Law of Moses, fell because of their rejection of the principles of that book. The strong presumption is that the book itself was the complete enunciation of God's Law, viz.: the Pentateuch. It is contrary to the teaching of the Scripture that God should utterly destroy great nations without ample and complete warning. The theory that only the book, Deuteronomy, with the bare outline of the history of the Hebrew race in the prophetic narrative, without God's revelations of Himself as shown in the alleged priestly narrative—that these were all the written parts of God's law at that period—is a theory not in conformity with the facts.

The primary assumption underlying the development theory is that the religion of Israel was wrought out by the genius of the people and not spoken once for all by God at Sinai. The natural growth of religious consciousness is made to take the place of God's gradual revelations through His prophets. It is denied that the chosen people were ever guilty of apostasy. It is claimed that they continued steadily to grow up into the realm of spiritual truth.* But this assumption is refuted by the testimony of the ancient monuments that the chosen people did make alliances with heathen nations, and did pay them tribute. This was rank apostasy. The Ten Tribes were made captive in heathendom because of apostasy, and they have never returned. The kingdom of Judah was swept from her ancient seat amid the general crash of empires because she was an apostate and had become as wicked as the heathen kingdoms. At the very opening of the era wherein Judah was to be cast into the pit along with foreign tribes and races, the Word of God in the Pentateuch was brought forth from its hiding place as a final appeal and warning unto God's chosen. But they fell. Out of that great apostasy were to return the few whom the fire of punishment had separated from the dross. All of these were devout and faithful, and when they stood once more in the sacred streets of Jerusalem, they shouted and wept for joy when Ezra read to them this same "Book of the Law of Moses." †

---
*Briggs: The Higher Criticism of the Hexateuch, pp. 124-25. †Nehemiah 8: 1-2.

CHAPTER II.
THE CIVILIZATION OF ANCIENT EGYPT.

WHILE the Temple at Jerusalem was rising out of its ashes in the early years of King Darius, the canon of Old Testament writings was almost completed. Fifteen out of the sixteen prophets had committed their messages to parchment before the year 516 B. C. A century later the last of the inspired scribes of the ancient era was to seal up the sacred records with the Book of Malachi. With this single exception, all of the Old Testament books deal with the history of the Hebrews prior to and contemporaneously with the fall of the great empires of the East. The divine revelation which is set forth as a continuous system in regular order in those books, was given through God's special ambassadors while the Hebrew theocracy was beset on all sides by the power of the Hittite, the Assyrian, the Babylonian and the Egyptian. It may be profitable to glance at the character of those civilizations which came into such close contact with the chosen people of God. Two of these, the Babylonian and the Egyptian, will serve to indicate the leading features of all.

The Land of Egypt.

The Hebrews gave to ancient Egypt the name Mizraim, or "the double land," while the natives themselves in their inscriptions sometimes called it Kamit, "the black land."[*] The latter were thinking of the soil, the former of the geographical divisions of the country. The dark, fertile deposits left year after year by the overflow of the river Nile made the soil a rich hot-bed for the production of plant and grain. The entire land, to quote the phrase of Herodotus, was "the gift of the Nile." A vast population could be supported in the territory of this narrow river valley.

In shape, the Nile region is divided into two distinct parts, Upper Egypt and Lower Egypt. Upper Egypt is the

---
[*] Brugsch, pp. 5, 6.

region of the Nile gorge, where the river is shut in by cliffs on each side. This part of the valley extends for six hundred miles from Assouân, at the border of Ethiopia far up the river, to the apex of the delta. This long vale is from two to eleven miles in width, and as one proceeds down the river from south to north, the ranges of rocky hill and cliff show granite at first, sandstone near the central part and limestone nearer the broad plain at the mouth of the river. One hundred miles from the sea the rocky walls recede toward the desert on the west and the Red sea on the east, and the river spreads itself over the vast triangular plain called the delta, seeking the Mediterranean through seven channels. This is Lower Egypt, and here was the granary of the ancient world, a vast alluvial plain without a single hill. Three crops during the year made the husbandman glad and the shepherd and the boatman rejoiced with him. These three classes made up the body of the people who crowded into this earliest seat of empire. Protected from invasion by the river's rocky walls, by the desert, by the Mediterranean and by the Red sea, and open to access only across the narrow bridge, the isthmus of Suez, the kingdom of Egypt naturally grew strong and became wealthy in this garden of the East. The "double land" was one in interest, a fact typified in the double crown of the monarch, a red crown surmounted by a white one.

The land of Egypt has been compared to "a narrow girdle, divided in the midst by a stream of water and hemmed in on both sides by long chains of mountains." * Again, it has been called a lily, with a crooked stem, the stalk of the lily represented by the long valley and the blossom by the wide plain at the mouth of the Nile; a bud upon the lily-stalk is found in the basin of the Fayoum, just above the apex of the delta. There the Libyan hills break away toward the west, leaving a little valley covered in part by the Birket-el-Keroun ("Lake of the Horn") about four miles wide by thirty-three miles long. † The military key of this land of the Nile is the point where the blossom is united with the stem of the lily. Napoleon recognized this fact when he here won the victory that gave him control of Egypt. Mena, the first king of Egypt, acted upon the same

---
* Brugsch 6.   † Bunsen, II, 335.

principle as Napoleon when he founded his capital, Memphis, at this apex of the delta.

The Egyptians, like the Greeks, claimed that their first kings were a dynasty of gods. After these ruled a race of demigods. Then first in order among the dynasties of men came Mena of Memphis. The traditions concerning this prehistoric period have come down to us chiefly through ancient Greek writers. Herodotus has left on record in the second book and in a part of the third book of his history a strange mixture of fact and fable, which he claims to have received from the Egyptian priests. Diodorus Siculus made additions to the vague folk-lore retailed by Herodotus. Manetho, an Egyptian priest of the third century B. C. wrote, in Greek, a history of the kings of Egypt from the beginning. The original work of this priest is lost, but we have synopses handed down through Africanus and Eusebius, two writers of the second and fourth century A. D. Manetho divided the entire line of kings into thirty dynasties. His chronology is imperfect, since he probably counts as successive, dynasties and individual kings who were really contemporaneous.* As to the real date of Mena, founder of Manetho's first dynasty, there is great diversity of opinion. Böckh asserts that the date was 5702 B. C., Bunsen 3623 B. C., and Wilkinson 2691 B. C. In the midst of such uncertainty we can only say that the scattered tribes of the Nile were all brought into subjection to one central authority at Memphis about 3000 B. C.

The Pyramid Builders.

No authentic history of Mena is extant. The earliest reference to him on the monuments appears on the Tablet of Abydos, made by Seti I. of the nineteenth dynasty.† The classic stories claim that Mena came down the river Nile from the city of This, which stood in the midst of the narrow valley; that he built a dyke to turn aside the stream from its channel near the Libyan hills, and then on the western bank of the Nile, close to the cliffs, he founded the first capital of Egypt. In the centre of the city he built a temple to the father of all the Egyptian gods, Ptah, the counterpart of the architect-god of the Greeks, Hephaistos.

---

*Rawlinson's Egypt, II. 7.   † De Rougé: Recherches, p. 17.

Some historians even think that the classical writers have reproduced on the Nile in the person of Mena the legend of Theseus, founder of Athens.* We find the earliest historical certainty in the inscriptions left by Manetho's fourth dynasty of kings. Here begin to pass before us real personages of flesh and blood, each bearing the royal appellation of Pharoah, "the great house," a title like our modern Czar or Emperor. Three of the kings of this fourth dynasty built the Three Pyramids that stand near the village of Gîzeh, on the edge of the desert just westward from the ancient city of Memphis. In the edge of the sand-waste that stretched away toward the setting sun, the dwellers in Memphis had selected a burial-place for the dead. They believed in the resurrection from that burial, but in some vague way they fancied a continuous union of body and spirit.† Hence, from the earliest times they embalmed the bodies of the dead and laid them away in tombs cut from the solid rock. Most of the kings at Memphis brought limestone from the neighboring hills and red granite from the quarries of Assouân, five or six hundred miles up the river Nile, and with these stones builded themselves great tombs in the sands of their royal necropolis. Inscribed on the inner walls of the largest Pyramid is the name of its builder Khufu, or the Greek Cheops, of the fourth dynasty of the Pharoahs. The height of this "Great Pyramid" is 480 feet and the length of its side at the base 764 feet. Within this massive pile were found three tomb-chambers, and in the largest of these rested the sarcophagus of Khufu.

The second pyramid was built by Khaf-ra, the Chephren of the Greeks, successor to Khufu. This tomb is not quite so tall as the first, and stands near its great compeer. The third was the burial-place of the next king, Men-Kau-ra. His stone sarcophagus was brought out and dispatched to England, but sank with the ship off the coast of Spain.

These three pyramids stood in the city of the dead near Memphis. Just west of Khaf-ra's Pyramid stood the Sphinx —a great monster, the body of a lion with the face of a man. The lion was cut from the solid rock of the Libyan cliff and looked eastward. Between his outstretched feet was a temple. An inscription gave to the Sphinx the name Horem-

---
* Rawlinson's Egypt. II.: 27.   † Brusch. p. 34.

khu, or "Horus on the horizon," the designation of the rising sun. An additional inscription declares that the Sphinx was known to Khufu, and hence we infer that it was constructed before the building of the Great Pyramid. Dedicated to the returning sun, this great statue stood on guard in that house of the dead as a symbol of the resurrection. Around the Sphinx were upreared the pyramids of this early time. About seventy are yet standing on the Nile in the neighborhood of Memphis. The Fifth Dynasty followed the fourth in royal power at this first capital, and then the centre of empire was transferred to a point further up the river Nile.

This ancient civilization, which began at Memphis under the Fourth and Fifth Dynasties was, in some respects, of a high order. The mechanical skill required in cutting and placing the stones of the Pyramids; the knowledge of geometry in establishing their dimensions; the use of letters in making the inscriptions—all these show an advanced stage of cultivation. The belief in the resurrection, the worship of a definite system of gods in the numerous temples then erected, point us to an early origin of the wisdom and religion of the Egyptians. The construction of such vast piles of masonry, on the other hand, indicates the despotic character of the Pharaohs who handed down their own names at the expense of the toil and blood of their subjects. With such apparently lofty theories and tyrannical practices began the civilization of the Nile country more than 3,000 years before Christ.

The Pharaohs of Thebes.

The line of ancient kings of Memphis came to an end with the Fifth Dynasty.* With the accession of the Sixth Dynasty the centre of power was shifted up the Nile to Middle Egypt. Perhaps at Abydos ruled these monarchs who now for the first time controlled a united kingdom. The Memphian kings had not been able to extend their sceptre with supreme authority very far toward the Ethiopian borders.

When the strong monarchs of the Sixth Dynasty passed away, the Kingdom of Egypt suffered disintegration. The

---
* Brugsch, p. 46.

old civilization lost its hold. A period of darkness, so far as historical records are concerned, enveloped the land during the reign of the next five of Manetho's dynasties. There were three capitals instead of one.

With the coming of the Twelfth Dynasty we find Thebes in the seat of imperial power. Pharaohs, bearing the names Amen-em-hat and Usurtasen, made this city the centre of the world's learning, art and commerce. Upon both sides of the Nile, where the river swept through a great plain ten miles wide and forty miles long, was built this second capital, Thebes. Here was developed a new civilization. Usurtasen I. erected the first great obelisk at Heliopolis as a sign of his authority in the delta, and there it stands to this day. On this shaft of rose-colored granite, sixty-six feet in height, Usurtasen carved his name with the title: "The King of the Upper and the Lower lands . . . . the Lord of the double crown, the ever-living golden Horus." * Although this King recognized Horus and Ptah, gods of Memphis, yet at Thebes he constructed in part the great temple to Ammon, patron deity of this Upper district. The Romans identified this god with their own chief deity and called him Jupiter-Ammon.

Pharaoh Amen-em-hat III. constructed in the Fayoum valley an artificial basin which Herodotus called Lake Moeris. † A canal drew off water from the Nile to fill the lake, and this became a reservoir for irrigating the other parts of the Fayoum.

Other kings of this dynasty conquered the Ethiopians and also the people of the Sinaitic peninsula. The copper mines in the Sinaitic hills were worked and commerce was carried on with Arabia and Palestine, and perhaps with India. This new civilization was utilitarian in character. The former kings at Memphis had sacrificed their people in gratifying their own vanity. The kings of Thebes sought the good of their subjects. They were satisfied with humble sepulchres, and spent their time in the development of commerce and in the construction of public works. The Nile was carefully measured. The obelisk took the place of the pyramid. But in boldness and vigor the architecture and sculpture of this period was inferior to that of the

---

* Brugsch, 59.   † Herod II.: 101, 149.

Memphis era. Moreover, with the monarchs of the Theban regime arose the custom of identifying the Pharaoh with some god. If the kings of the Twelfth Dynasty did not build themselves pyramid-tombs they deified themselves. In this custom do we see a great deterioration in their religion. The earlier simplicity was abandoned. Ammon, the head of the tribe of gods at Thebes, became identified with many of the former chief gods as Ra, the sun-god, from whom at first he was entirely distinct. This was a long step toward the confusion and debasement of the wretched polytheism of later periods.

The Hyksos Invasion.

With the close of the Twelfth Dynasty, the Old Empire of Egypt, which had grown up around the two capitals, Memphis and Thebes, passed away. The Middle Empire followed the Old through the course of the next Five Dynasties in the lists of Manetho. This period is the dark age of Egyptian history. Nearly all contemporary monuments have been swept away and hopeless confusion marks the chronology. Revolts and assassinations were the order of the day, and the power of the Theban kings was ere long snatched away by numbers of petty princes. Toward the close of this period the Seventeenth Dynasty of the eastern delta was composed of a race of foreign invaders, the Hyksos or Shepherd-Kings from Syria and Arabia. It seems most probable that these Hyksos were the Hittites, who afterwards gave trouble to the Pharaohs of the New Empire. The god of the Hittites was Set, the principle of evil, and the worship of Set was established in the region of the delta about this time.

The Hittites, in common with other dwellers in Canaan and Syria, were of Hamitic or Cushite extraction, but in the very earliest times they seem to have used the Semitic form of speech. The tablet recently found (1892) at the site of ancient Lachish in Southern Palestine by Mr. Bliss, contains a letter in the Babylonian dialect dating back so far as 1400 B. C. This official document indicates that the Babylonian language was in use in western Asia not very long after the reign of the Hyksos in Egypt. But the dwellers in the hill and desert regions west of the Euphrates were either of Cushite or of mixed Semitic and Cushite extraction, like Ishmael, son of Abram, and the Egyptian wife. Like Ishmael, all these Highlanders and Lowlanders, spoke the Semitic language, which may in part explain the fact that the Ishmaelites were firebrands among the nations.* Blood and speech were antagonistic within the race itself.

Perhaps of this composite character were the Hittites, leaders of the nomads, who ruled over Egypt for more than two centuries. At Memphis, Avaris and Tanis, in Lower Egypt, they established royal courts. They controlled all Egypt and yet permitted a line of native princes to rule at Thebes.

The names of two of these foreign kings have been preserved—Apepi and Nub. In connection with the latter, the approximate date of the dynasty has been determined. In Tanis, the capital of the Hyksos, a memorial stone has been found, erected by the Pharaoh Rameses II. to the honor of his father Seti I. The memorial begins thus: "In the year 400, on the fourth day of the month Mesori, of King Nub." From other evidence we estimate the probable date of Rameses II. as 1350 B. C. Four hundred years before this time would bring us to the year 1750 B. C. as the possible date of the Hyksos King Nub.

Further than this, it is probable that the Hebrew Exodus took place in the time of Meneptah II., son of Rameses II.—about 1300 B. C. By adding 430 years, the length of the sojourn of the Hebrews in Egypt, we find 1730 B. C. as the approximate date of Jacob's migration to Egypt. This would place the governorship of Joseph in the time of one of the Hyksos kings, and would indicate 1950 B. C. as the time of Abram's visit to this same Hyksos court.† The writings of Georgius Syncellus and an inscription at El-Kab corroborate this supposition, by indicating that Joseph ruled at the court of the Hyksos King, Apepi, at Tanis, where the Semitic language was used.

Like the Moors in Spain, the Hyksos were soon driven out by the founder of a New Empire. But the native kings of the Eighteenth Dynasty learned many lessons from the government of the Hyksos. These wanderers of the desert had a complete military organization and established a

---

*Gen. 16: 12. † Brugsch, p. 120. Lenormant: Manuel d'Histoire Ancienne I.: 363.

strong centralized government. The kings of the next period inherited from them a united monarchy, which was to extend the boundaries of Egypt to the Euphrates river. These invaders had likewise given an impetus to literature, and the new era that followed was prolific in inscriptions. On the other hand, their worship of the god of Evil, Set, was thrown into the boiling caldron of Egyptian creeds as an additional impulse toward a degraded religion.

The Empire of Thothmes III.

The paralysis that had seized the princes of Thebes was shaken off by Aahmes, "child of the moon," who led the native forces in insurrection, drove out the Shepherd Kings and established the greatest of all the Egyptian dynasties—the Eighteenth. The third king of this line, Thothmes I., followed the track of the retreating nomads and passed eastward in the first great Egyptian invasion of Asia. Fire and sword he carried into Syria and across the Euphrates into the mid-river region of Babylonia and Assyria, and returned with much booty and many captives.

Sixth in the line came Thothmes III., chief monarch in this family of conquerors and builders. As soon as he had grasped the sceptre, Thothmes put his army in motion to invade Asia. At Megiddo, the future battle-field of Necho and Josiah, the Pharaoh met a great army under the King of Kadesh, one of the capitals of the Hittites, on the river Orontes.* War-chariots to the number of 924, with vast treasures in precious metals, and also flocks and herds, were taken in triumph to Thebes. A prolonged festival was celebrated in honor of Ammon-Ra; concerning these ceremonies the king left long inscriptions.†

Another expedition carried him beyond the Euphrates and Tigris and made him master of all Assyria. For many years he continued to carry off booty and to receive annual tribute from all the nations between Egypt and the Tigris, including Mesopotamia and Syria. About the year 1600 B. C. Thebes, under Thothmes III., was the military and commercial capital of the world.

Thothmes made Thebes likewise the literary and artistic centre of the whole earth. The great temple to Ammon,

---

*Birch: Ancient Egypt, p. 116. †Records of the Past, II.: sections 53, 55.

begun long before, was completed in magnificent style. To the east of the temple he upreared the great Hall of Pillars as a memorial to the god and also to the deified ancestors of his own royal house. Before one of the wings of the temple were placed large stone statues of some of these deified Pharaohs. On the southern side he erected immense obelisks, one of which now stands in Rome. In a chamber connected with the pillared hall was the "Great Tablet of Karnak," an inscription relating Thothmes' view of the whole line of Pharaohs from the time of the third dynasty.

The obelisks erected by this monarch near the temple of the Sun at Heliopolis now stand in Rome, in London and in New York. At Memphis, Abydos and other places he built temples and monuments, and from one end of the land to the other was recorded in stone the story of the great empire of the Nile in the time of Thothmes III.

The great works of this monarch were carried on by captives taken in war. Pictorial representations of this reign show us captives making brick under the direction of taskmasters armed with great sticks. This has led some scholars to assert that these toiling slaves were the Hebrew children in the time of oppression.[*] But the weight of authority holds that Hebrew forms and faces are not delineated on these monuments. The mode of treating captives is here set forth, but during the reign of Thothmes III. the tribes of Israel were probably left to live in peace in the eastern delta.

Pharaoh Rameses II.

On a wall of the temple at Karnak (Thebes) are ranged six battle paintings descriptive of the first war of the Nineteenth Dynasty. Seti I., second king of the line, but first great warrior, goes forth to meet Egypt's ancient foe, the Hittite. At that time the Hittite empire filled all of western Asia and was about to cross the isthmus once more to seize the pasture-lands of the delta. The New Empire had to fight for its life. In his war-chariot King Seti rode out to battle against the shepherds, and he stayed not his victorious march until he had captured their capital Kadesh.

---

[*] Hengstenberg: Aegypten und Mose. Scribner's Magazine, Jan., '94.

By a treaty he extended his sway over nations as far north as Cappadocia, in Asia Minor. * All this vast kingdom was left to his son Rameses II., who received above all other Pharaohs the title of "The Conqueror." But his military prowess was exercised in restraining the rebellious impulses of the subjected Hittites rather than in making advances to new conquests. These enemies hovered continually like a great war-cloud just beyond his eastern boundaries. The fear that the Hebrew people in Goshen would increase in numbers and form alliance with the Semitic-tongued Hittites, led Rameses to those stern measures which have given him the title, "The Pharaoh of the Hebrew Oppression." In Greek legend he is known as the great Sesostris. The Boulak Museum at Cairo, Egypt, holds in a glass case the mummy of Rameses II. Since the year 1881 A. D. the men of science have rejoiced over this captive treasure exhumed from his burial-place amid the lime-stone cliffs just west of the site of ancient Thebes. There in the very heart of a mountain of rock, in the Westminister Abbey of the Pharaohs, in a small chamber, had his body rested for centuries by the side of his father Seti I., and the bodies of many other kings and priests of ancient Egypt. In numerous winding-sheets was each body wrapped. Upon the outer sheet and just over the region of the breast of the most striking figure among these dead kings was written the name of Rameses II. Likewise "in black ink, written upon the mummy-case by the high-priest and King Pinotem," is the record affirming that this casket holds the body of the *grand monarque*, Rameses, the son of Seti. "The face of the mummy gives a fair idea of the face of the living king. The expression is unintellectual, perhaps slightly animal; but even under the somewhat grotesque disguise of mummification there is plainly to be seen an air of sovereign majesty, of resolve and of pride. . . . The corpse is that of an old man, but of a vigorous and robust old man." †

This Louis Quatorze, of Egypt, lives before us again in the literary remains of his time. As far as Kadesh, on the Orontes, to his father's battle-ground, he advanced in the war against the Hittites, and his personal bravery

---

* Brugsch, 248.   † The Century Magazine, May, 1887.

and narrow escape during the battle there have been handed down in a great Epic poem by the King's laureate, Pentaur. On many a temple wall was this Egyptian Iliad inscribed for our reading. The statue of the king was left carved in stone at the mouth of the Nahr-el-Kelb in Syria. Wars he waged against the Canaanites, Amorites and Syrians, and in the account of these the ancient records give us the political reason for his cruel treatment of the Hebrew tribes. Raids into the Soudan country were also made by his soldiers, who brought back thousands of slaves to work under the lash in the erection of great edifices. Temples to the gods did Rameses build at Memphis, Thebes and Abydos. Colossal statues of himself were set up everywhere in Egypt. Carved in the rock as the frontispiece to the great temple of Abou-Simbel, in Nubia, are four seated colossal images of the king, larger than all other statues in Egypt with the sole exception of the Sphinx. The silent figure of the proud-faced monarch, guarding the rock-hewn temple of the god, and with eyes fixed on the rising sun, is a personification of the religious civilization of the Nile, where the monarchs were goddess-born, and proudly claimed to be sons of the sun.

The successor of Rameses II. was Meneptah II.—the Pharaoh of the Exodus. At Thebes his tomb was found, but the body was not within. In great strife and turmoil his reign probably ended. He followed not the example of his boastful predecessors by emblazoning his victories on stone. He gained no victories to record. The monuments are silent concerning his closing years, nor do they mention the Hebrews at all. This is entirely in accord with the custom of the Egyptians. The destruction of the royal army at the Red Sea was a great disaster to the ruling house—and no disasters were ever recorded on the ancient monuments by those who suffered them.

The Sun-gods—Ra and Osiris.

The Nineteenth Dynasty represents the period of greatest interest in the history of Egypt. From that time onward the rivalry with Assyria and Babylon was developed until the Twenty-Sixth Dynasty fell beneath the blows of Nebuchadnezzar and Cambyses. But during the reign of Rameses II. the religion of the Egyptians reached a point in its development which offers an excellent vantage-ground whence we may observe the growth of the entire system

Mr. Renouf has examined all the inscriptions in which is used the Egyptian word for "god"—*nutar*, and he claims that the primary meaning thereof is *power*.* This is the meaning of the Hebrew El, and the Egyptian term *nutar nutra* indicates the Almighty Power in heaven, just as El Shaddai—God Almighty—was the name of God known to Abraham and Isaac.† But the Egyptian *nutar* referred not to a person, but to the general force in nature, while the Hebrew El was the name of the God who was seen and heard by the patriarchs. In its earliest form, then, the Egyptian religion marks a step downward from the knowledge of God as He was known in Noah's day, while the Hebrew religion of the time of Abraham marks a step upward. God revealed Himself to Abraham again and again, but the dweller by the Nile forgot all about the God of the deluge, except that in the unseen world there lives a great power.

The next step in the Egyptian creed was the addition of personifications of that power. His home and his surroundings soon furnished the dweller on the Nile with imaginary beings to represent the unseen power. The powers of nature were one by one clothed in the garb of deity.

Egypt was only a narrow strip of land shut in between rocks and boundless wastes of sand. The sky was always blue; was rarely obscured by clouds; from year to year the Egyptian could watch the daily progress of the sun from the moment when his first beams came shooting across the eastern hills until they were swallowed up in the western desert. When those bright rays were thus smothered in the unexplored solitudes of sand, the Egyptian saw that his valley-home was given over to the control of dense darkness. But out of that prison of apparent death the sun always escaped and came in triumph to begin his morning course once more. All these changes in nature were as a parable to the Egyptian, telling him of life and death and the resurrection from the dead.

There were other changes wrought out before his eye that taught the same parable with additional force. Within the

---
* Renouf: The Religion of Anc. Egypt, p. 102.   † Exodus 6: 3.

limits of the cliffs that walled in his home, all was life and growth. Plants and animals teemed in that fertile strip of soil. But at the edge of the desert the touch of death seemed to rule. Silence and barrenness had their home in that waste into which the sun sank from sight. This waste itself seemed a symbol of the eternity in which dwelt the sun and where he regained his life and strength.

A third parable was added to the other two. The river Nile was the source of a hidden power that lay at the origin of all plant life. Wherever the waters of that one river came in their overflow, there the soil gave forth rich harvests. But the power of the sun worked in harmony with the power of the river. When the midday beams of light and heat came down upon the alluvial deposit left by the receding water, then it seemed but an instant until a rich carpet of verdure was stretched along the banks. The sun himself must be the power whom they called their god and the Nile must be like him in character. Thus did they pass from the idea of an unseen power to the worship of the sun as the greatest of the powers of nature.*

Now let us see how much of this progression of ideas had taken place in the time of the kings of Memphis. The seven chief gods in the pantheon in that earliest capital were :†

1. Ptah, the Architect of the Universe . . . . Hephaistos.
2. Ra, Son of Ptah, the Sun . . . . Sol.
3. Shu, Ra's Son, the Air . . . . Agathodaemon.
4. Seb, Shu's Son, the Earth . . . . Saturn.
5. Osiris, Seb's Son, the Sun (after his setting) . . . .
6. Set, Seb's Son, Darkness . . . .
7. Horus, Son of Osiris, Light . . . . Hermes (?)

It will appear from this that at Memphis the chief god was still the hidden power, dwelling in eternity as the architect of the universe and worshipped under the name of Ptah. But the sun and other nature-powers were also worshipped as the sons and representatives of Ptah. The Sphinx was dedicated to Horus, the morning sun. According to our first knowledge of this Egyptian religion, it was a system embracing many gods, with the sun making a good start to attain the first position. There is no evidence to support the theory that the Egyptian religion was monotheistic.

---
*Keary's Dawn of History, pp. 178-181.   †Brugsch, p. 12.   Cf. Renouf.

When first we catch a glimpse of it on the Memphian* monuments it is already polytheistic, and any theoretical monotheism that may have existed is cast away and forgotten in practice.

When we reach the Twelfth Dynasty at Thebes, we find that Ptah has lost his place as the chief god and Ammon-Ra is the head of the pantheon. Ammon was the patron deity of the city of Thebes and had erected in his honor the greatest temple in all Egypt. The name Ammon means "the hidden," and since he was identified with Ra, the noonday sun, it would seem that Ammon referred to the sun after his setting. In this deity—Ammon-Ra—whom they called "the king of the gods," their Zeus, the Egyptians at last worshiped the sun as the real power whom they had revered from the first. Ptah was still worshipped, but even to the latest times was known as "the Memphite Ptah." †

The multitude of Egyptian gods may be arranged in two clans, that of Ra and that of Osiris. Ra was the ordinary Egyptian word for the sun, and as a religious term meant the sun-god. Unlike the sun in the Greek myth, who went across the sky in a chariot, Ra was borne across the sky in a boat. The name given the sky was Nu, and the Nile was its earthly representative. Since Nu, as the home of Ra, was called "the father of the gods," the Nile received the same title. Shu, the air, was the son of Ra.

The myth of Osiris has the same meaning, although it presents a more elaborate story of the sun's course through the sky and his disappearance in the shades of night. Osiris sprang from Seb and Nut, Earth and Heaven. His sister was Isis, the Dawn. From the union of Osiris with Isis sprang Horus, the Morning Sun. Osiris engaged in deadly conflict with Set, Darkness, but was liberated by Horus. Through many other details the legend went on to tell of the great struggle between Light and Darkness, between Life and Death. This was the great contrast stamped on physical nature in Egypt, and the sun, as the chief actor in that routine of change, was made the chief god. On earth the King was the sun's representative. In the address of Rameses II. to the dead Seti I. he said: "Thou

---

* Lenormant: Manuel d'Hist. Anc. 1: 522. † Brugsch, p. 235.

restest in the deep like Osiris, while I rule like Ra among men."

Into the details of domestic and public life this worship of the sun was carried. A minute symbolism was developed, and the life of the Egyptian soon became linked to his gods through the medium of animal worship. The origin of this form of religion is not certainly known. Mr. Lang thinks it was the result of the development of *totemism*, like the creed of some of the North American Indians.* Others affirm that it came from the practice of finding on earth types of the workings of the unseen power. A hawk was the usual symbol of Ra and of Horus. In the time of the later Persian conquest, animal worship had become the leading feature of the religion of the Nile.

One further step in this downward progress must be noted. This is the identification of the Pharaoh with the sun-god himself, a climax of vanity reached by the kings of the eighteenth and nineteenth dynasties. From the earliest times the kings claimed divine origin as "sons of the sun." But Rameses II. set himself forth as an object of worship, and in the inner shrine of his temple at Abou-Simbel placed his own image by the side of the figures of Ammon, Ptah and Horus!

Some modern scholars insist that the Hebrew religion was the result of a course of natural development. But Judaism was based upon a series of facts entirely different in their character from the foundations of the Egyptian religion. The latter was developed by the imagination of men. The Egyptians began with the knowledge of God as their ancestors turned away from the Ark of Noah and from Babel. They lost that knowledge, and more and more they deified the powers of external nature. The doctrine of a future life, of a resurrection from the dead, of a trial of the soul after death by Osiris, who weighed it in a balance, and if found wanting in goodness, sent the soul again into the bodies of various animals—all this teaching was likewise developed. An elaborate system of rules concerning right and wrong was set forth in "The Ritual of the Dead."† This moral code was, perhaps, superior to any other that has ever been developed among

---
*A. Lang's Myth, Ritual and Religion. †Bunsen.

men. It raised the Egyptians above the other heathen peoples of that time. God brought His own chosen into contact with that race as part of His course of training for them. Organized government was here at its best among the nations of the earth. What effect their sojourn here had upon the Hebrews, we shall see. But at this point we may ask wherein lay the permanent force in a religious creed like the Egyptian that was always developing *downwards?* What elements of it could be seized and placed in the divine faith that was meant to be eternal? Everything in the Egyptian code was transient and much of it degrading. Not much authority could be vested in teachings concerning the gods and their relations with men, where a despot like Rameses II. could be received as an actual god. This low point of degradation had been reached when Moses was preparing to lead the Hebrew children out of Egypt to Sinai.

CHAPTER III.

THE CIVILIZATION OF BABYLONIA.

The Land Between the Rivers.

IN the highlands of Armenia, the triangular plateau that lifts itself between the Black, the Caspian and the Mediterranean seas, two great rivers begin their course. The Tigris breaks from the hills and starts away toward the southeast; it flows along the base of the Zagros range of mountains and thus separates the Persian plateau from the plains of western Asia, and then pours its waters into the Euphrates just before the entrance of both into the Persian Gulf. The Euphrates flows westward at first from its sources in Armenia, but soon it turns southward from the Taurus mountains, and then southeastward through the Syrian Desert in a course nearly parallel with the Tigris until it finds an outlet in the Gulf more than 1,700 miles from its starting-point. At Bagdad, the seat of the old Caliphs, these two rivers are only twenty miles apart.

The narrow tongue of land between the Euphrates and the Tigris was the home of the earliest civilization in western Asia and was known as Mesopotamia, the midriver country. The people who lived here, and the State and church polity established were Semitic, the greatest and best known among the Semitic races apart from the Hebrews. The one governmental name applied more than any other to this district was Babylonia. The civilization was stamped with the seal of the great city, Babylon. And yet there were two great Semitic empires and one Cushite that rose and fell in this land of Babylonia. These were the Accadian, which was Cushite in its beginnings, the Assyrian and the Babylonian, and the three capitals were Ur, Nineveh and Babylon.

This long district is divided near the thirty-fourth parallel of latitude into two distinct regions—Upper Mesopotamia and Lower Mesopotamia. The former is made up of mountain slopes and rolling hills—the great pasture ground of the time of Jacob and Laban; the latter is the great alluvial plain formed by the deposit from the two rivers. This flat river-plain is about 100 miles in width and 400 in length, and on the west it touches the sands of Arabia; on the east it extends beyond the Tigris to the foothills of Susiana. This plain encroaches constantly upon the Gulf that marks its southern boundary. At the rate of one mile in a period of seventy years the alluvial deposits force the plain upon the sea. The capital of the region of Upper Mesopotamia was Nineveh, on the Tigris; the capitals of Lower Mesopotamia were Babylon, on the Euphrates, and Ur, on the Persian Gulf, for at that time the waters of the sea had not been pushed southward by the alluvial soil.

The Accadians.

Down the long, narrow region of Upper Mesopotamia flocked the descendants of Noah as they turned from Ararat, the mountain that towers up near the sources of the Euphrates and Tigris. In the northern edge of the alluvial plain, on the bank of the Euphrates, they upreared the great brick Tower of Babel. When they at last turned away on account of diversity of speech, they left the tower standing to mark the site of the future city of Babylon. The Semitic races scattered themselves over the neighboring hills and plains to watch their flocks, while the Hamitic peoples started westward across the desert to build the first empire of the earth, on the banks of the Nile, or to plant themselves among the rocks of Ethiopia and Southern Arabia. This same energetic race was to send a detachment eastward again to found the first kingdom in Lower Mesopotamia at the head of the Persian Gulf. Nimrod, of the Cushite race, closely related to the people of Egypt, erected in the "land of Shinar," or Southern Babylonia, as the foundation of a kingdom, four capitals—Babel, Erech, Accad and Calneh.* This kingdom has been handed down by inscriptions as divided into two regions—Sumir and Accad —and the ruling race called themselves Accadians.

The language and the religion and the physical characteristics of the Accadians were non-Semitic. The exact classi-

---
* Gen. 10: 8, 10.

fication of the language itself is the puzzle of modern philology. From its agglutinative character and general resemblance to the Finnish tongue, some scholars would call this a Turanian language, connected with Northern Asia.* But from the testimony of Babylonian tradition, from Accadian words of Cushite origin, and from the general resemblance of the Accadian or cuneiform system of writing to the Egyptian hieroglyphic, other authorities hold that the Accadians came from the mountains of Arabia or Ethiopia—home of the Cushites.†

In this region near the sea, not far, perhaps, from the site of the Garden of Eden, the Accadians planted themselves in the rich soil. Sheltered by the multitude of palms they gathered crop after crop in the same season and established a commerce and developed a literature that lay at the basis of all later Babylonian civilization. They brought with them a system of pictorial hieroglyphics, which afterwards developed into the cuneiform, or wedge-shaped, style of writing. On papyrus and on clay they wrote treatises on religion, science, law and language. Their cities all contained libraries stocked with books. The Erech of Nimrod, the modern Warka, has been found as the sacred burial-place of this old race; Calneh is Niffer, not far from Babel or Babylon. And now Mr. Budge holds that the Accad of Nimrod was the ancient Ur of the Chaldees.‡ Modern discoveries thus declare that Ur was the capital and seaport of the great Accadian empire that grew rich from commerce before the Semitic tribes poured in to take possession. These Semitic people adopted the empire as their own, and the Accadian religion and literature was absorbed into the great system of civilization that now began its course as the Babylonian. This earliest Semitic kingdom was sometimes called Chaldea.

A cuneiform cylinder in the British museum suggests the date 3800 B. C. as the beginning of the reign at Agade or Accad of the earliest known Babylonian king—Sargon I. This date rests on the sole statement of Nabonidos, of Babylon, who lived 554 B. C.§ What means he had of calcu-

---
*Sayce: Anc. Empires of the East. † Rawlinson: Anc. Monarchies, and " Essay VI. to Herodotus." ‡ Babylonian Life and History, p. 23. § Babylonian Life and History, p. 38.

lating the date of Sargon are not known, and his statement may not be correct. After Sargon reigned Ur-Bagas, who built in the city of Larsa a temple to the sun-god, and in his own capital, Ur, he built a great temple to the moon-god. Thus began the old Babylonian kingdom in the capital of the Accadians, the Semitic people worshipping as their chief god the moon-god of the Accadians.

The size of this early Babylonian or Chaldean empire was not great. Perhaps one large Semitic clan established itself in Ur and ruled over Accadia. Other tribes afterwards became dominant and the centre of power gradually moved northwards. Larsa and then Babylon succeeded Ur as capitals of the whole country. About 2100 B. C. a Kassite monarch, Hammurabi, became ruler of all Babylonia.* Ur had then perhaps ceased to be the imperial centre. Not long after his reign, Abram departed from the city of the moon-god.

The people of Elam, the district east of Tigris, whose capital was the later Persian city Susa, next acquired control of Babylonia. Chedorlaomer, an Elamite king, extended the power of Babylonia as far west as the Jordan river, but was there defeated by the patriarch Abram. After the Elamite rule, various factions fought for the possession of Mesopotamia, and during this period of anarchy Thothmes I. and Thothmes III. of Egypt overran the country.

The Moon-god of Ur.

Six miles west of the river Euphrates, where it unites its waters with those of the Tigris, among the low sand-hills of the level plain, have been found the ruins of Abram's early home, Ur of the Chaldees. The oval heap of ruins, 1,000 yards long and 800 broad, is called now Mugheir, or "Asphalt-city." Upon the summit of the principal mound there stands a rectangular building, two stories in height, yet buried in its own *débris*. The lower story is built within of sun-dried bricks, laid in bitumen, but enclosed without by a wall of kiln-dried brick, red in color and ten feet thick. This wall is likewise laid in bitumen. The size of this first story is 198 by 133 feet. Outside stairways led up to the second story, which measured only 119 by 75 feet. Red

---

* Babylonian Life and History, p. 42.

brick is the material of the inner and of the outer walls. Less than half a century ago, according to local Arab tradition, a third story surmounted these two. In size this story was a mere chamber, and was probably the shrine of sin, the moon-god whose temple this structure was. Inscribed bricks found within it give the name of King Ur-Bagas as the builder. This town of asphalt is the oldest seat of civilization, after Babel, of course, yet discovered in the lower Euphrates region. Here was the earliest capital of the Cushite kingdom that sprang into being out of the fragments of Nimrod's empire, and also the first capital of the Babylonian kingdom. In this temple assembled the ancient Accado-Babylonians to worship at the altar of their chief god, the moon. Many other gods had the Accadians, all of them adopted by the Babylonians. The sun and the stars were revered as controllers of human destiny, but in the imperial city was kept the temple of the chief of all the gods. These early dwellers on plain and mountain-slope were a star-gazing people, making continual observations as they watched their flocks by night. Hence it was that the chief luminary of night was the first god in their pantheon. They did not, as we do, regard the moon as of the feminine gender. A masculine deity he was to them, and the father of the sun-god, and also the father of their line of kings.

The moon-worship of the Accadians, or Cushites, afterwards gave way to the sun-worship of the Semitic desert-dwellers. As these nomads coursed the burning sands, the eye of the sun came to signify the divine insight of the king of the gods into the affairs of men. Babylon and other cities became the great centres of sun-worship, but the moon always retained a high place in the Babylonian pantheon. We have an inscription telling how Nebuchadnezzar boasted of rebuilding the temple of sin, the moon-god.

Even in the time of Abram, about two thousand years B. C., Ur was a comparatively ancient city. Its commercial *prestige* still remained, for the alluvial deposit of the river had not yet pushed the Persian Gulf so far down toward the south as at present. But an air of antiquity lingered about this old capital of the Cushite founders and the worship of the moon was sacred even to Semitic hearts both on account of her benignant rays and of her long-established respectability. But the god, or spirit of the sky, who used the disk of the moon as his face-mask was not unconnected with other deities. He was the father of the sun-god and permitted a minor influence to the king of day. The early Babylonian legends named the goddess Istar as the daughter of the moon-god. Istar was the "spirit" of the planet Venus, and was the chief Accadian goddess. As the evening star she was known as Istar of Erech, as the morning star she was worshipped at Accad, or Ur. She was "the lady of battles" and the goddess of love, and often invoked as "the queen of heaven." At Erech was her chief temple in those old days, and the rites celebrated in her honor were a mass of unmitigated horrors. In later times she became the Ashtoreth or Astarté of the Canaanites and the Aphrodité of the Greeks. When Solomon set up the worship of "Ashtoreth the abomination of the Zidonians,"* which became a thing of horror unto all the prophets, he was simply instituting those superstitious orgies that blotted the land whence God called Abram. Degrading to the body and damning to the soul was this worship of the heavenly bodies whose centre was at Ur. The waxing and the waning of the chief luminary of night and the kindly influence of her rays was the nearest approach to *personality* in the nature of the spirits of the unseen world, according to the conception of these heathen countrymen and kinsmen of the father of the chosen race.

Assyrian and Babylonian Kings.

Asshur, son of Shem, built the city of Asshur on the right bank of the Tigris, and hence came the name Assyria as applied to the northern part of Mesopotamia. The marginal rendering of Gen. 10: 11, indicates that Nimrod went into Assyria and founded Nineveh; this accords with the tradition handed down by Herodotus (1: 7) that Ninus, son of Belus, founder of Babylon, was the builder of Nineveh. As in the case of Ur, the Semites soon rushed in to possess and absorb the Cushite Kingdom.

The inscriptions are minute in giving details of certain periods of the story of Assyria and later Babylonia. Hero-

---
* II Kings, 23.

dotus gives only scant notices. Ctesias of Cnidos has recorded many myths and legends. Berosus, priest of Bel at Babylon, in the time of Alexander the Great, arranged the kings of all Babylonia in dynasties, like the historical work of Manetho of Egypt. But in 1862, Sir Henry Rawlinson discovered fragments of tablets showing the royal dynasties of Assyria, called "the eponym canon" of Assyria.* This canon establishes a definite chronology for this country from 1330 B. C. to 620 B. C. In 1330 B. C. Assyria was a strong and mighty empire under Rimmon-Nirari I. This king has left an inscription telling of his conquests in Mesopotamia. In his time, or a little later, Assyria conquered Babylonia and became the centre of power in Western Asia. This was about the period of the Hebrew exodus from Egypt.

The Babylonian empire that began its course upon the ruins of Accadia at Ur was not powerful in arms until after the destruction of Nineveh. But from the first, the Babylonians were a nation of scholars and agriculturists. They made constant use of the Accadian cuneiform style of writing. They developed an extensive religious and scientific literature. A complete system of civilization grew up on the banks of the Euphrates and Tigris, elaborated in codes and creeds. About the year 1450 B. C., while Israel was in Egypt, the King of Babylon and the King of Assyria entered into covenant with each other concerning the boundaries of their kingdoms. This contract was written on a tablet in the Babylonian dialect and remains to this day.

The Assyrians were a nation of warriors. More ferocious were they than any other Eastern people of that period. Their art and their literature and their religion were borrowed from the Babylonians. Nineveh was only another capital of Babylonia itself—the great military centre of the empire—as Ur was the first and Babylon the last literary and religious centre. It was during the time of Assyria's growing ascendancy over this Semitic empire, about 1600 B. C., that Thothmes III. overran Naharain, or Mesopotamia, and captured the city of Nineveh itself. He carried away to Egypt princes of Asshur, cattle, silver, gold, war-chariots, ivory

---

* Babylon, Life and History, pp. 35, 36.

and precious stones, costly inlaid work and fine cloth and armor. To such extent had Babylon developed long before the time of Moses.* As a representative of the magicians of Babylonia came Balaam westward to curse Israel, just about the time of Rimmon-Nirari I., 1330 B. C. From a tablet inscribed by this king we copy a curse pronounced against his enemy, similar to the curses that gave Balaam his fame:

> " The great gods, the spirit of heaven,
> And the spirit of earth in their ministry,
> Mightily may they injure him, and
> With a grievous curse, quickly
> May they curse him; his name,
> His seed, his forces, and his family in the land
> May they destroy:
> The glory of his country, the duration of his people
> And his landmarks."†

These glimpses reveal some of the cultivation and some of the power that belonged to the Babylonians prior to the era of Moses. With their subsequent history we are not here concerned, except to give a passing view of the collection of inscriptions that were buried in the ruins of Ur, of Nineveh, and of Babylon. Already have we learned of the zeal of the early Accadian and Babylonian kings in leaving records of their deeds in the first imperial city—Ur. Now, let us search out the story of Nineveh's scholar-tyrant—Asshur-bani-pal, and of Babylon's builder, historian and King —Nebuchadnezzar.

Asshur-bani-pal.

Assyria, as left by Rimmon-Nirari I., might have advanced into Palestine to destroy the tribes of Israel just then entering their promised home. But for several generations civil war raged in Babylonia. The princes of Babylon made continual assaults against the kings of Nineveh. The chosen nation under Joshua and the Judges was given time to grow. Two centuries after they had crossed the Jordan, Nineveh began again to extend her power under Tiglath-Pileser I. He carried the arms of Assyria as far west as Cilicia; he defeated the Hittites on the upper Euphrates; he made rebellious Babylon to feel the strength of his despotism. He might then have made Israel subject to himself, but in 1100

---

* Brugsch, p. 163-5.   † Babylonian Life and History, p. 48.

B. C., five years before the accession of King Saul, death carried Tiglath-Pileser away. After him at Nineveh ruled a line of weak-minded Kings; Babylon again fought for independence, and thus was opportunity given for the extension of the Hebrew Kingdom under David and Solomon. By the time that Assyria again grasped her sword for conquest westward of the Euphrates, the Hebrew tribes had been trained to trust in the arm of Jehovah. Shalmaneser II. (858–823 B. C.) kept Babylon quiet by means of a treaty while he overcame the neighboring kings, one of whom was Jehu, King of Israel, who forgot to ask aid from the God of Israel. A century later Sargon, of Assyria, captured Samaria and carried captive the Ten Tribes of Israel; he also defeated Merodach-Baladan and captured Babylon and established there an Assyrian viceroy; likewise did he defeat the army of the ruling Pharaoh and collect tribute from Egypt. Sargon's son, Sennacherib, waged long wars against Babylon, yet struggling for independence; and it was Sennacherib's host that felt the destroying power of Jehovah's angel in the time of King Hezekiah. Sargon, haughty and cruel, wreaked stern vengeance upon Babylon. All her ancient temples, her towers and walls, were torn down and cast into the river; Babylon's great libraries, filled with the accumulated learning of the past from the time of the Accadians, were all pillaged. The wonderful palace built by Sargon at Khorsabad, ten miles from Nineveh, was not sufficient expiation for the ruin wrought among the artistic and literary treasures at Babylon. Sargon's great-grandson, Asshur-bani-pal, was the last great King of Assyria, and his chief work was to restore the libraries of Babylonia from the fragments left by Sargon's cruel vandalism. This king was the Louis XIV. of Assyria, and was known to the Greeks in the legend of Sardanapalus. He was a great conqueror—and kept his lieutenants busy in holding in subjection the provinces of his empire. Egypt became rebellious and was invaded twice— the second time by the King in person. He captured Memphis and Thebes, and destroyed the walls of the latter city, tore down her temples and carried away the palace-gates as trophies to Nineveh. The voice of the prophet Nahum greeted him on his return with the prophecy that his own

Nineveh—"city of bloods!"—should suffer the same ruin inflicted upon Thebes.

While Asshur-bani-pal was thus holding his empire together he was completing a greater work. His palaces excelled in splendor those of any other Assyrian monarch. But his patronage of learning was his leading passion. He seems to have gloried in the fact that he had been crowned at Babylon as the successor of the old Accadian kings. He sent his scribes to all the ancient cities and libraries of Babylonia. Accadian and Babylonian inscriptions were copied, and a great library at Nineveh was filled with the clay tablets. The fragments left by Sargon were collected. When he had completed this collection of national records the empire was already slipping from his grasp. Babylon had gained vigor from her long struggles and was soon to be triumphant. Asshur-bani-pal closed the door upon his treasury of inscriptions just in time for it to be buried beneath the ruins of Nineveh, there to wait until the spade of the excavator of our own century should call forth this witness of the past.

Nebuchadnezzar.

Nebuchadnezzar was the leader of the Medo-Babylonian army that destroyed Nineveh. When he came to the throne, in 604 B. C., he began to rebuild the city which Sargon had shattered. In addition to his conquests, Nebuchadnezzar was the author of all of Babylon's magnificence. The great mass of brick found in the ruins of the city to-day have his name stamped upon them. As corroboration of the King's boast, recorded in Daniel 4 : 30, this inscription, bearing his name, has been found : "I say it, I have built the great house which is the centre of Babylon for the seat of my rule in Babylon."*

Two cylinders brought to the British Museum in 1878 contain an outline of his works at Babylon, recorded by his own command. First among these was the temple to Merodach, chief god of the Babylonians, built with four great gates. Next in order he constructed a double wall around the city. A great canal was dug connecting the Euphrates and Tigris ; extensive quays were made along the river's

---

* Buddensieg : Die Assyrischen Ausgrabungen u. d. A. T.

edge. A vast reservoir was constructed to furnish a supply of water for irrigating the level plain ; the hanging gardens were made on terraced mounds. In other cities of Babylonia he erected great numbers of temples, walls and public buildings. For he proceeds to say :

" The temple of the Sun, the temple of the Sun-god of Sippara ;

The temple of the eyes of the god Anu, the temple of the god Dar of the city of the planet Venus ;
The temple of heaven, the temple of Istar of Erech ;
The temple of the Sun, the temple of the Sun-god of Larsa ;
The temple of Kis-kur-gal, the temple of the Moon-god of Ur,
These temples of the great gods,
I rebuilt, and I caused their beautiful adornments to be completed."*

In this same inscription occurs this statement :

"The temple, the foundation of heaven and earth, *the tower of Babel*, I built anew."†

Eight or nine miles westward from the site of ancient Babylon, a huge mound like an oblique pyramid lifts itself 153 feet above the plain. A large mass of brickwork is on the top. The structure was originally built in seven stages; the first three stages, each 26 feet in height, the last four only 15 feet each in height. The lower stage is 272 feet square; each succeeding stage is square but smaller, the last one having dimensions of only 20 feet. Each of these stages was given a distinct color by means of glazed brick. The upper was silver-colored and was dedicated to the moon; the sixth was dark-blue, dedicated to Mercury; the fifth was pale yellow, sacred to Venus; the fourth, bright yellow, sacred to the Sun; the third, bright red, was consecrated to Mars; the second, of orange color, was allotted to Jupiter, and the first was clad in black in honor of Saturn. This was the Temple of the Seven Spheres. It is now supposed to have been the same as the temple of Bel-Merodach, the great sun-god of Babylon. It is possible that Nebuchadnezzar built this temple upon the ruins of the Tower of Babel.

The last great king of Babylonia was Nebuchadnezzar. This ancient civilization had now run its course. In her religion we find many of the elements of the Greek mythology. These elements had been already transmitted to the western nations by the Hittites and Phœnicians. Nebu-

---

*Budge, p. 23.   †Budge, p. 21.

chadnezzar lived long enough to stamp the character of his nation upon the brick tablets for our instruction. In the visions which Daniel interpreted, the king foresaw the doom which came upon Babylon in the next generation at the hand of Cyrus, the Persian.

Merodach, the Sun-god of Babylon.

In the story of his public improvements at Babylon, Nebuchadnezzar tells us that he was incited thereto by his "lord and judge" Marduk, or Merodach. This chief of all the gods is further described as "Merodach, king of heaven and earth."* This latest head of the Babylonian Pantheon is named among the earliest known Accadian inscriptions as Merodach, "mighty to save."† Merodach's promotion from a minor position in the early family of gods presided over by the Accadian moon-god to the place of supremacy at Babylon is connected with the absorption of the Accadian creed by the Babylonians.

The religion of the Accadians was intimately connected, like that of the Egyptians, with the surrounding forms of external nature. Living in a vast plain, they supposed the earth to be flat, roofed in by the arching sky and surrounded by the ocean stream. This cosmogony was adopted by the Greeks in Homer's time. These parts of nature were deified and worshipped; the sky was called Anu, the earth was named Mul-ge, and the ocean was known as Ea or Hea. These gods were parallel to the ideas of the Greeks concerning Zeus and Hephaistos. The Babylonians substituted the name Bel for Mul-ge. From the three nature-gods, Anu, Ea and Bel, sprang all the rest. The idea of a process of *emanation* whereby the powers of nature sent forth these various deities was passed onward to the Greeks and became the first principle of the philosophy of Thales and, perhaps, the basis of the modern theory of evolution.

As a result of this *emanation*, Merodach sprang from Ea, god of the ocean or "abyss." The name Merodach, in Accadian, meant "the radiance of the sun," and he was designated as the "lord of life and light," and "mighty to save." Merodach thus meant the morning-sun, rising out of the "abyss" of night, like the Egyptian Horus.

---

* Budge, pp. 20–25. † Idem, p. 127.

In addition to the worship of the sun as Merodach, the early Babylonians also worshiped this luminary as Samas, the sun-god proper. Samas was the son of Ea and was known as the "King of Judgment." Therefore it is probable that Samas was the noon-day sun, darting down fierce beams. When the Babylonians received the Accadian creed they gave the moon-god a subordinate position and elevated Merodach to first rank which he retained to the end. He was the patron deity of Babylon, and was also known as Bel "lord," the Baal of the Canaanites, and represented the sun in all his aspects. The worship of Merodach began with the recognition of the triumph of light over darkness in the rising of the sun, but finally degenerated into a gross idolatry paid to the disk of the sun himself.

In connection with this downward growth, there was the parallel development of a debased system of idol-worship. The basis of the practical forms of the Accadian religion was the recognition of a "spirit" in every part and element of nature. Most of these "spirits" were evil and must be placated. A hierarchy of sorcerers was selected, who made use of charms and incantations to ward off the baneful power of the desert-winds and other unpropitious powers of the earth and sky. Merodach was first among the beneficent powers invoked to deliver men from disease, witches and other evils sent by some of the gods. Out of these priestly incantations grew the system practised by Balaam and by the magicians and sorcerers of Babylon in the time of Daniel. From very early times these priests used idols and offered their prayers to wood and stone. In Daniel's time the Babylonians "praised the gods of gold and of silver, of brass, of iron, of wood, and of stone." * Chief among these images was the idol of the sun-god, for Jeremiah cried, "Bel is confounded, Merodach is broken in pieces," † using the name of the sun-god to designate Babylon herself, so widespread had become this worship.

Those who claim that Judaism was the result of a long course of natural development and came not by revelation, may place it for comparison beside the Babylonian creed.

---

* Dan. 5: 4. † Jer. 50: 2.

The latter system of religion began its course before the time of Abraham; it grew and grew until its gods were beyond number and its devotees the type of human debasement and ignorance. This was a religion that attained its final form through a process of natural development. Like the creed of the Egyptians, the religion of the Babylonians was marked by a downward progress, and the last state of both was worse than the first.

CHAPTER IV.

DISCOVERY AND INTERPRETATION OF THE ANCIENT INSCRIPTIONS.

The Library of Asshur-bani-pal.

THE records upon the obelisks and temple walls and tombs of Egypt have never been hidden from the sight of men, but their meaning became a mystery not long after Rome gained possession of the land of the Nile. The secret of the interpretation of the hieroglyphic language was buried with the Egyptian kingdom itself and was not brought to the light until the present century.

In Babylonia, the inscriptions themselves were hidden beneath the débris of abandoned cities. The sun-dried brick used in constructing the great buildings and city-walls in Mesopotamia all crumbled to dust, and a harvest of grass and weeds sprang up from the ruins. Heaps of crumbling clay and grass-covered mounds, scattered along the banks of the Euphrates and Tigris, were for centuries the only witnesses of Babylonia's past glory. The silent witnesses beneath were awaiting the resurrection that came but a few years ago.

Under the touch of the Turkish government, the prosperity of Mesopotamia has withered away. The glory of the capital of the Caliphs, Bagdad, has faded into a dream. Mosul has been a minor centre of trade and the residence of a Turkish pasha. The Arabs built the latter city on the right bank of the Tigris, just opposite the burial-place of Nineveh. "Jonah's Mound" was the name given by the Arabs to one of the two heaps of ruins that stood on the site of the capital of Assyria. From these two mounds and from others not far away on the same river-plain the spade of the explorer exhumed the State records of Assyria and Babylonia.

The year 1820 marked the beginning of discovery. But the results of Mr. Rich's excavations were small. In 1842

Mr. Botta, French Consul at Mosul, began to dig into the larger of the two mounds opposite the town. Koyunjik is the name given this heap of ruins by the modern Arabs. Not far distant another mound, Khorsabad, was partially explored by this French *savant*. But chief of all the Assyrian explorers stands Sir Austen Layard, who began his excavations in the year 1845, at the mound called Nimrud, lying farther than the others down the Tigris. In 1848 a second expedition was undertaken by Layard, and the mounds of ancient Nineveh ere long were all made to give up their treasures.

Buried beneath the Nimrud mound the palace of King Asshur-nazir-pal was discovered. From its relative location Layard called this building "The North-west Palace." Khorsabad gave up King Sargon's palace with five immense halls. But Koyunjik, opposite Mosul, was found to be the veritable site of ancient Nineveh. Beneath this heap of earth that rose to the height of 95 feet above the Tigris at its base, and covered a space equal to one hundred acres—beneath this the explorer's spade found the greatest treasures ever yet brought to the light—the palace of Sennacherib, of stupendous extent, and the Library of Asshur-bani-pal. Two chambers of Asshur-bani-pal's royal residence contained naught but piles of clay tablets. Broken were some of them, but others, piled in regular order, gave the appearance of shelved volumes, and the contents themselves confirmed the supposition that this was the King's library. Linked with Layard's name is that of George Smith, the decipherer of these Assyrian texts. As he arranged them in systematic order for the shelves of the British Museum, the desire to read the tablets was aroused within him. His triumphs as an Assyrian scholar have linked his name with those of Rawlinson and Oppert, while his zeal as an explorer places him by the side of Layard. He, too, searched in the palaces at Koyunjik and added to the storehouse of ancient records until he was called upon to pay the price of martyrdom to the cause of science. The Syrian fever carried him off in 1876.

The labor and inspired zeal of such men as Layard, Rawlinson and Smith have made sacred the volumes of this royal library of Nineveh, were they not already the sacred messengers of God bearing the truth from the past to the present. Ten thousand volumes have been found on Assurbani-pal's shelves. One of these bears the following: "Palace of Asshur-bani-pal, King of the World, King of Assyria, to whom the god Nebo and the goddess Tasmit (the goddess of knowledge) have given the ears to hear and have opened the eyes to see what is the true foundation of government. They revealed to the Kings, my predecessors, this cuneiform writing, the manifestation of the god Nebo, the god of supreme intelligence: I wrote it upon tablets, I signed and arranged them, and I placed them in my palace for the instruction of my subjects."

Concerning the books of clay stored in this library, Layard says this: "These documents appear to be of various kinds. Many are historical records of wars and distant expeditions undertaken by the Assyrians; some seem to be royal decrees and are stamped with the name of a king, the son of Esar-haddon [Asshur-bani-pal]; others, again, divided into parallel columns by horizontal lines, contain lists of the gods and probably a registering of offerings made in their temples."* Catalogues of these books inscribed on clay tablets indicate more clearly still the character of Assyrian literature. (1) Grammars and Lexicons of the Chaldean and Assyrian languages are found on the same shelves with comparative dictionaries of the cuneiform and hieroglyphic modes of writing. (2) The history and chronology of the Mesopotamian kingdoms are preserved in many fragments. Lists of the kings, with the date of their respective reigns, are found side by side with great stores of governmental *statistics*. (3) Mathematics and astronomy are represented by the largest part of the inscriptions. The kindred branches of astrology, magic and divination, are elaborately illustrated in these clay folios. (4) Religion is minutely set forth in the myths and hymns to the gods. The entire life of these Semitic tribes of Western Asia has in very truth been laid bare by these state archives. The manners and customs of the people, their knowledge and their beliefs, their kings, priests and gods, are made known in systematic order. The treasure-house of many generations the library of Asshur-bani-pal has proved to be. The records

---

* Layard: Nineveh and Babylon, p. 296.

of Babylonia were brought to Nineveh by this scholar-prince. These Babylonian documents, in their turn, embodied the story of the Accadian kingdom, whose foundations were laid by the mighty hunter-king, Nimrod. Therefore, as we turn the pages of this Assyrian collection of books, we are enabled to look backward along the history of those sons of Shem, who were closely akin to God's chosen people.

The Rosetta Stone.

In the month of August, 1799, Bouchard, a French officer of artillery, attached to Napoleon's Egyptian expedition, was superintending the establishment of a redoubt on the ruins of Fort Julien. As the spade worked its way downward into the sand on that western bank of the Rosetta branch of the Nile and near the river's mouth, a large slab of black marble was brought to view. Various signs were written on the surface of the slab, a part of these being an inscription in the Greek tongue. This Greek writing was found to assert that the remaining characters on the slab were two translations of the same royal decree, the one in hieroglyphic, or sacred writing, the other in demotic, or the popular language of the Egyptians. The decree, thus set forth in three languages, related to the coronation of Ptolemy Epiphanes, 195 B. C.

This slab of marble was given to the British Museum, and an engraved copy of the inscriptions sent to all the learned men of Europe. Here at last was the solution of the problem wrapped up in the strange language of the Egyptians. A specimen of their ancient speech, in its two forms, had come forth accompanied by a literal translation in the Greek. Dr. Young, an English scholar, first pointed out on the Rosetta stone the name of Ptolemy in the hieroglyphic part of the inscription. He also discovered the fact that the demotic, or popular, form of speech inscribed on the slab was merely a "running form" of the hieroglyphic. These results were reached in the year 1814. But the glory of completely probing the mystery of these ancient symbols was reserved for a French scholar, Jean François Champollion. After some years of patient labor, Champollion showed that the hieroglyphic writing was *phonetic* as well as *symbolic*— that is, that the signs or images cut on the stone, represented *ideas*, and thus formed a system of picture-writing, and in addition to this each picture was used to represent a *sound*. He was at length enabled to compile an alphabet of the hieroglyphic writing, which he gave to the world in the year 1824. The ancient records of the land of sphinxes and pyramids were thus made to yield up their secrets. The expedition of Napoleon into Egypt was made the means, under the Providence of God, of reading the strange characters in which the Pharaohs of the oppression and of the exodus told the story of their deeds. The wrath of man was truly made to praise God.

Clearly to comprehend the import of Champollion's discovery, let us glance briefly at the story of Egyptian writing; how the strange symbols on the monuments mocked the efforts of men to interpret them until God inspired the scholars of the nineteenth century. Already have we seen how God's witnesses were buried in the dust of crumbling empires, but now further do we find that the tongues of His witnesses were fast closed by the intricacies of a language that soon passed away from the knowledge of men. The classic writers of Greece and Rome might have learned the form of speech in which the priests of Egypt and Babylonia inscribed the story of past eras; but national pride was the bar that held them back from such knowledge. The second book of the historian Herodotus is concerned with what he heard and saw in Egypt. But this old writer of gossip and folk-lore did not take the trouble to learn the language of the Egyptian priest-historians.

About 180 B. C., in the time of Ptolemy Philadelphus, lived and wrote Manetho, a priest of Sebennytus. He wrote the three volumes of his history of the dynasties of ancient Egypt in the Greek language, but professed to draw his material from Egyptian documents and inscriptions. The original work of Manetho is lost, and we know him only through the quotations made in the writings of Josephus and Eusebius. Many facts did these historians transcribe from the pages of Manetho, but the secret of the Egyptian language was left in its old mystery. As late as the middle of the third century of the Christian era, while Decius sat on the imperial throne at Rome, the priestly symbols were still used in writing by the Egyptians. Even in Babylonia the wedge-shaped or cuneiform characters of the language of the Euphrates region were used in the end of the first Christian century; that is, during the reign of Domitian. But the interpretation of the speech of these ancient peoples remained unknown. The only link of knowledge that connected the Christian world with the mysteries locked up in the images of birds, beasts, reptiles, and men carved on Egyptian monuments, was the Word of God translated into a kindred speech. The Coptic tongue is the lineal descendant of the ancient Egyptian, and *seven* of the characters in the Coptic alphabet were drawn from the *demotic* form of Egyptian. Nearly the whole of the Scriptures with Greek and Arabic translations have come down to us in the Coptic language as a great storehouse for minute comparison in searching the ancient Egyptian letters and parts of speech. The only thing needful to make this linguistic treasure available was the key to the hieroglyphic language which God brought to light when He led the scholars of this century to see the meaning of the Rosetta stone. Not merely did God store up his treasures of testimony in the olden days, when His servants wrote and the kings of the earth inscribed their deeds on stone and clay, but He preserved the secret of the interpretation of those records through many ages and at length brought forth the key in the very day and hour wherein the truth of His own word might be most triumphantly vindicated by the inscriptions of heathen kings and heathen priests.

The Behistun Inscription.

The second stage in the progress of the art of writing is represented by the characters or signs in use among the people of the land between the rivers Euphrates and Tigris. The objects, or images, employed in *picture*-writing, the hieroglyphics of the Egyptians, were represented in the language of the Babylonians and Assyrians by "conventional groups of straight lines." These lines were made by stamping soft clay with the end of a pointed instrument. The impression left upon the clay was a simple straight line with one end enlarged; hence this method of written speech was termed *cuneiform*, or wedge-shaped writing. An abbreviated type of the *cuneiform* writing was used by the Persians whom we have already seen established at Babylon under Cyrus. The story of the decipherment of these wedge-shaped characters and of the interpretation of the languages they recorded is closely connected with the history of the Persian kings who came after Cyrus.

The royal decrees issued by these Persian kings who ruled over Babylonia were written in the three prominent dialects spoken by their subjects, after the manner of Pilate's inscription fastened upon the Saviour's cross in the three languages—Hebrew and Greek and Latin. Upon the ruins of the Persian capital, Persepolis, and upon those left at Ecbatana, these inscriptions continued to speak long after the downfall of the Persian empire at the touch of the Macedonian sceptre.

In the same year that saw the Rosetta stone borne from the Nile to the British Museum, the German scholar Grotefend began the work of unravelling the mystery of the three-tongued cuneiform characters. A more difficult task than that of Young and Champollion confronted Grotefend. One of the three languages inscribed upon the Rosetta stone was Greek, furnishing a well-known key to the other two. But the three forms of speech in the wedge-shaped characters were all unknown. By comparison with the Sanskrit Grotefend was enabled, in 1815, to make an approximate translation of the Old Persian dialect, which always occurred first in these inscriptions. The mystery was virtually unlocked. But the translation of the Behistun inscription in 1846, by Sir Henry Rawlinson, laid bare the last secrets of these strange forms of speech.

High up on the smooth surface of a cliff at Behistun, on the western frontier of Persia, there had long been noticed pictorial representations and line upon line in the cuneiform writing. Here by the side of the public highway that crosses the Zagros mountains from Babylonia to the highlands of Persia, some one of the Aryan kings had evidently left his royal edict, or perhaps the record of his own deeds. The difficulty of ascending the smooth surface of the tall rock prevented a close examination of the inscription until the daring and skill of Henry Rawlinson brought away a partial copy of the record in the year 1835. The year 1844 saw the young scholar again at his dangerous task, and this effort was rewarded with an accurate transcription of the entire stone-document. Two years later he published a translation of the Old Persian part of the inscription, which proved to be an account of the chief events in the reign of Darius Hystaspes, inscribed by his own order. The Persian dialect now being known, it was used as a key to solve the difficulties of the remaining two dialects of the cuneiform inscriptions. One of these was a form of speech once used by the common people of the Aryan plateau, not unlike the language now in use among the Turks. The third was found to be similar to Old Testament Hebrew. It was evidently a Semitic dialect, and was most probably the medium used by Darius in making known his deeds to his subjects in Babylonia.

As the genius of Rawlinson was thus making this ancient form of speech begin to tell the secret of its structure, the spade of Austen Layard was laying bare on the site of the Assyrian capital, Nineveh, the library of King Asshur-banipal. Layard's work was just fairly begun that summer of wonderful revelations—the summer of 1846. The inscriptions upon the monuments and the clay tablets stored up beneath the ruins of Nineveh were brought forth from their hiding place in quantities vast and various, and all of them were found to be recorded in the same dialect that formed the third part of the Behistun inscription. God had wrought a wonder—for this coincidence was surely of His divine ordering. The ancient Assyrian and Babylonian tongue was made to give up the secret of its character from the record of the Behistun rock, just when the spade of the explorer was making God's witnesses to rise up and speak—those witnesses of Assyrian and Babylonian speech whom He had buried centuries before.

The Behistun inscription contains the name and records the deeds of Darius, son of Hystaspes, whose reign began in the year 521 B. C. The king's chief boast in the inscription concerns his restoration of the religion of Zoroaster. The greatest of his acts he did not record. No mention was made of the decree permitting the continuance of the building of the temple at Jerusalem. Yet, at the very time when the iron pen was making its proud boast on the rock, the Jews were rejoicing over their completed sanctuary.

Sir Henry Rawlinson has conjectured from the character of the record itself that the Behistun inscription was made in the year that saw the temple rebuilded, 516 B. C. It was perhaps a policy of conciliation that led Cyrus and Darius to restore the Jewish state and church—a policy that became the instrument of God in the furtherance of His plans. But in the philosophy of these kings it was never dreamed that in the far-off centuries, God would use an inscription made by Darius in the solid rock, not to glorify Zoroaster as Darius planned, but to unlock the secrets of the ancient monuments and make them stand forth as living witnesses to the truth of His Word.

PART II.

THE BEGINNINGS OF DIVINE REVELATION CONTRASTED WITH HEATHEN FOLK-LORE.

[*Genesis 1–11.*]

CHAPTER V.

THE CREATION.

The Chaldean Story of Creation.

OUT of the royal library of Asshur-bani-pal at Koyunjik, the zeal of Mr. George Smith and Sir H. Rassam has brought the fragments of an early Babylonian epic. So far as it has been possible to arrange these broken-up tablets in proper order, they make up a heroic story in twelve parts. The central figure of the epic is Gizdhubar, the fire-god of the Accadians, and the sun-god of the later Babylonians. Gizdhubar was probably the prototype of the Greek Hercules and the twelve labors of that national hero were perhaps foreshadowed by the twelve exploits of Gizdhubar. The most plausible explanation yet given of this Babylonian or Chaldean epic is that it celebrates the passage of the sun through the twelve signs of the Zodiac. An astronomical poem this interpretation would make it— the collected traditions of a sun and moon-worshiping people.

The broken tablets discovered in the library at Koyunjik are all written in the Semitic Babylonian dialect, and were inscribed by Asshur-bani-pal's copyists from Babylonian texts. The inscriptions now in the possession of the British Museum date, therefore, only from the time of Asshur-bani-pal, the seventh century before Christ. But they are transcriptions of legends that run far back into Babylonian history, and it is not improbable that in these tablets we have the survival of ancient Accadian folk-lore. We know that Asshur-bani-pal enriched his shelves with the literary treasures of all the great Babylonian cities, notably those of Babylon, Borsippa, Cutha, Erech, Nipur, Ur and Larsa. In addition to the Gizdhubar epic the king brought from these ancient places to Nineveh "a series of mythological tablets of various sorts, varying from legends of the gods, psalms, songs, prayers and hymns down to mere allusions and lists of names. Many of these texts take the form of charms to be used in sickness and for the expulsion of evil spirits; some of them are of great antiquity, being older than the Gizdhubar legends. One fine series deals with remedies against witchcraft and the assaults of evil spirits."*

Most important of all Mr. Smith's discoveries, perhaps, was the series of tablets containing the Babylonian or Chaldean account of the creation of the world. Fragment by fragment this series came to light, while he was still in search of the pieces of the Gizdhubar tablets. Thus has Asshur-bani-pal's library furnished us with the collected folk-lore of the Southern Babylonians running back to a period long before the time of Abraham and Moses. An outline of this literature of ancient Semitic legend may here be transcribed from Mr. Smith's "Chaldean Account of Genesis," pp. 10–11:

(1) An account of the creation of the world in six days, parallel to that in the first chapter of Genesis, and probably in its present form not older than the seventh century B. C.

(2) A second account of the creation, derived from the library of Cuthah, and belonging to the oldest period of Babylonian literature.

(3) A history of the conflict between Merodach, the champion of the gods, and Tiamat, "the Deep," the representative of chaos and evil. To this we may add the bilingual legend of the seven evil spirits and their fight against the moon.

(4) The story of the descent of the goddess Istar, or Venus into Hades, and her return.

(5) The legend of the sin of the god Zu, punished by Bel, the father of the gods.

(6) A collection of five tablets, giving the exploits of Dibbara, the god of the pestilence.

(7) The story of the wise man who put forth a riddle to the gods.

(8) The legend of the good man Atarpi, and the wickedness of the world.

(9) The legend of the Tower of Babel, and dispersion.

(10) The story of the Eagle and Etana.

(11) The story of the ox and the horse.

---

*Smith's Chaldean Genesis, p. 28.

THE CHALDEAN STORY OF CREATION. 73

(12) The story of the fox.
(13) The legend of Sinuri.
(14) The Gizdhubar legends: twelve tablets with the history of Gizdhubar and an account of the flood.
(15) The story of the destruction of Sodom and Gomorrah. Besides these there are fragments of other legends, which show that there was a considerable collection of such primitive stories still quite unknown to us.

As we read this catalogue of cuneiform books we may easily imagine that it represents the early form of the cycle of Greek legends. "The sin of the god Zu" suggests the Greek story of Prometheus, and so does the fact appear when the legend is examined. Gizdhubar came through Phœnician lore into Greece to play his part there as Hercules. In short, the mixture of fact and fable in this summary of primitive religion—Babel and Sodom placed on the same book-shelves with the stories of talking horses and foxes—seems only a crude edition of the volume of Greek mythology. We are turning the leaves of heathen folk-lore wherein the vain imaginings of men sought to make gods out of stars and brutes.

Several copies of the Chaldean account of creation were made by Asshur-bani-pal's scribes. Fragments of these different editions have been carefully arranged and the original story approximately reproduced. Fearfully mutilated as the tablets are, the leading facts of the myth have been drawn from them. Since the texts themselves assert that they are only copies of Babylonian originals, scholars have coupled this with other kindred circumstances as evidence that this creation myth was first written down about 2000 B. C. If this supposition is in accordance with the fact, the Chaldean myth took a literary form among the kinsmen of Abram in Babylonia when the patriarch himself was a young man. Now since ten generations are named in Shem's family line, from Shem to Abram, it may be supposed that this tradition ran back through the course of these ten generations for many a decade, and possibly came down to Shem himself from his fathers before the flood. At least we may suppose that upon these tablets we have recorded the earliest workings of the Semitic and Cushite imagination—the very body of the religious faith of the descendants and successors of Nimrod and his Semitic cousins of the lower Euphrates.

Seven tablets make up the series that relate the story of creation. Let us examine the text itself and catch the spirit of the narrative. The first tablet gives us these fragmentary sentences:

1. At that time above the heaven was unnamed.
2. Below the earth by name was unrecorded.
3. The boundless deep also (was) their generator.
4. The chaos of the sea was she who bore the whole of them.
5. Their waters were collected together in one place, and
6. The flowering reed was not gathered, the marsh-plant was not grown.
7. At that time the gods had not been produced, any one of them;
8. By name they had not been called, destiny was not fixed.
9. Were made also the (great) gods,
10. The gods Lakhmu and Lakhamu were produced (the first), and
11. To growth they
12. The gods Sar and Kisar were made next.
13. The days were long, a long (time passed), (and)
14. The gods Anu (Bel and Hea were born of)
15. The gods Sar (and Kisar).*

These broken lines of the first tablet suggest the opening words of Genesis: "In the beginning God created the heavens and the earth. And the earth was waste and void." A hopeless confusion, however, is stamped upon the Babylonian narrative. The universe and the gods themselves are said to have sprung out of chaos. We seem to be standing in later times at the very beginning of Greek philosophy, itself a blind groping after something better and more reasonable than Greek mythology. The philosopher Thales seems to be speaking in the words of this cuneiform tablet and telling us about the emanation of all things, gods and beasts and men, from water! The inconsistency of this Babylonian myth will appear when we remember that "the chaos of the sea," "the boundless deep," here spoken of as

---

* Smith's Chaldean, Genesis, pp. 57-58.

the generator of all things, was afterwards deified and named the goddess Tiamat! An evil demon she became, making war upon the gods and tempting men. And yet this goddess was the mother of divinities and other entities before a god or goddess had materialized from the primitive confusion!

Again, in tracing the origin of the gods, the Sky, Anu, is said to be the offspring of Sar and Kisar, the upper and lower *firmaments*. Bel and Hea, or Ea, are placed, likewise, in the same family—that is, the sun-god and the god of the "great deep," or ocean-stream, are descended from the *firmament*. The fact that the later Babylonians changed the name of Bel to Merodach and tampered with his genealogy so far as to make him the son of Hea, the lord of the "great deep," does not change the great truth taught in this inscription that the untutored imagination of these primitive tribes simply made gods out of the elements, the sky, the sun and the darkness of the underworld.

The next coherent statements in this Chaldean narrative appear on the *fifth* tablet:

1. Anu made suitable the mansions of the seven great gods.
2. The stars he placed in them; the *lumasi* he fixed.
3. He arranged the year according to the bounds that he defined.
4. For each day of the twelve months three stars he fixed.
5. From the day when the year issues forth unto the close,
6. He established the mansion of the god Nibiru, that they might know their laws.
7. That they might not err nor deflect at all,
8. The mansion of Bel and Hea he established along with himself.
9. He opened, also, the great gates in the sides of the world;
10. The bolts he strengthened on the left hand and on the right.
11. In its centre, also, he made a staircase.
12. The moon-god he caused to beautify the thick night.*

---
*Smith's Chaldean Genesis, pp. 64-65.

Through twenty-four lines this tablet continues to describe the ordering of the heavenly host in a manner that suggests the story of the fourth day of creation in the first chapter of Genesis. Two facts, however, are written prominently on the face of this record. The establisher of heavenly mansions for the various star-gods is Anu, the sky. A part of the created universe itself is exalted to the majesty and power of deity. We are taken back to the original form of Babylonian mythology or folk-lore. The sky sits on the throne which is afterwards to be occupied by the chief sky-dweller, Bel, the sun.

Again, we notice that this account gives priority to the moon-god over the sun-god. Conclusive evidence is this that the ancient Accadian myth in circulation long before the time of Abram is inscribed on these creation tablets. The moon-god, who held the first place in the pantheon of Nimrod's age, still holds sway in these inscriptions.

The entire record reveals a condition of religious thought upon the same level with the beginnings of Greek mythology. The Zeus of Mount Olympus was the Dyaus, or clear sky, of their Aryan forefathers. Similarly, these Cushite and Semitic dwellers on the plains bordering the Euphrates looked up into the vault of heaven and ascribed personality and deity to the blue expanse. Their chief god, Anu, thus soon became known as the father of the star deities—the moon, the sun and the planets.

A fragment of the seventh and last tablet in the series refers to the work of creation which the book of Genesis places on the sixth day:

1. At that time the gods in their assembly created . . .
2. They made suitable the strong monsters. . . .
3. They caused to come living creatures . . .
4. Cattle of the field, beasts of the field and creeping things of the field. . . .
5. They fixed for the living creatures . . .
6. . . . cattle and creeping things of the city they fixed . . .
7. . . . the assembly of the creeping things, the whole which were created . . .
8. . . . which in the assembly of my family . . .
9. . . . and the god Nin-Siku joined the two together . . .

10. . . . to the assembly of the creepings things I gave life . . .
11. . . . the seed of Lakhamu I destroyed.*

So ends this story of creation without mention of the greatest of created beings, man. Out of the obscurity of the closing lines just quoted, some scholars attempt to draw references to the creation of human life by the god Hea, who appears on this tablet under one of his names, Nin-Siku. Other inscriptions seem to refer to Hea under the title, "the Lord of Mankind," as the creator of the human race. A very long hymn to the creator Hea, on a tablet apart from the creation series, refers to this god under a multitude of names: "The god of life"; of "good winds"; of hearing and obedience"; giver of "life to the dead"; "establisher of fertility." On the obverse side of various tablets, however, the statement is made that these diverse titles all refer to one and the same god. We are told that the Creator has *fifty* names. The interpretation of these statements does not warrant the supposition that these people believed in one, true God. The contrary belief in many gods is, the rather, demonstrated. In the ancient city of Eridu, the chief god was called Hea. When the citizens of this place repeated the creed which ascribed creation to Hea, they meant nothing more than the simple assertion that all created beings came up out of the sea. When the burgesses of Nipur called the creator Anu, they believed that the source of all existence is the sky. And the people of Babylon regarded the sunbeams as authors of all things when they called the sun by the names Bel or Merodach, "the lord." We find in early Babylonia the same crudeness and the same diversity of belief that occurs in the folk-lore of the people of Greece, who in one section declared that men sprang from the earth, or, in another, that the goddess Aphrodite was born of the sea-foam.

The Story of Creation in the Book of Genesis.

The first two chapters of the book of Genesis contain what the Pentateuch has to say concerning the beginning of the universe and of man. Placed by the side of Chaldean folklore, this narrative in Genesis is as much superior to the

---
* Smith, p. 71.

cuneiform account as divinity is above humanity. In two respects, viz., in regard to the facts dealt with and in regard to the purpose held in view by the narrator of those facts, the Chaldean account of Genesis is clearly upon the plane of human imagination, while the record of the Pentateuch is just as clearly upon the plane of divine revelation. That this may appear, let us trace the chief points in the Pentateuchal narrative. The facts given in these two chapters deal with the character of the Creator and the character of things created. An examination of the facts concerning created things themselves may very properly be made first.

(1) "In the beginning God [Elohim] created the heavens and the earth. And the earth was waste and void; and darkness was upon the face of the deep, and the Spirit of God [Elohim] was brooding upon the face of the waters."* "The deep" and "the chaos," which are made the same in the Chaldean Genesis,† and denominated the mother of both heaven and earth, are here the first among things created by the power of Elohim. After their creation these are still held under absolute control by the creator through the agency of His spirit, who broods upon them. Yet these first formless results of the creative will of Elohim were called deity by the Babylonians under the name Tiamat. Thus, in its opening sentence, the Pentateuch carries us back to the beginning of all things, and declares the god of creation in the Babylonian catalogue to be simply a form of things created. In the highest reach of their imagination, these people attained only to a knowledge of the creature rather than of the Creator.

(2) Origin of Inorganic Life.

The arranging power of Elohim, foreshadowed in the brooding of His spirit, is outlined in the work of the first four days of creation.‡ This work deals with the universe of matter already called into existence by the divine fiat. The forms of matter are due to the same power that gave origin to matter. As the various phases of inorganic life take their place in the line of God's creative acts we see the gods of the Babylonians twinkle into sight like stars in the eve-

---
*Genesis 1: 1-2.   †Vid., p. 116.   ‡Genesis 1: 3-19.

ning sky. As the work of the second day of creation, "God made the firmament," and gave it the name "Heaven." Lo! here is the chief deity in the great Babylonian triad of gods, Anu, the sky. In the narrative of the third day's work we are told that "the gathering-place of the waters called He seas," and we recognize the god Hea, the source of all things according to the Chaldean myth. On the fourth day God "made" and "placed in the firmament" the sun, the moon and the stars. These creatures of His power are not even dignified by a personal name, but are called simply light-bearers, stationed in their proper order and rank to do His service. Yet the Babylonians made out of these material things gods and kings, and invested them with all power and majesty. God created the sun, but Cushite and Semitic imagery led him forth in the garb of divinity. As Bel and Merodach, he ruled the superstitious minds, who at the same time looked up with reverence to the moon as Sin and to Venus as Istar. We need only to trace more minutely the details of God's formation of inorganic life to find the entire catalogue of Babylonian gods.

(3) ORIGIN OF ORGANIC LIFE.

Self-moving existence, the animated part of creation, was brought into being on the fifth and sixth days.* As the "swarm of living souls" come from the Creator's hand we remember the animal worship of the people of Egypt. The narrative in Genesis tells us of the creation of all the gods of the Nile.

But we notice here a great contrast in the histories of creation. Man is the climax in the list of "living souls." Not only does he come last and noblest from the hand of the Creator, but he bears the Creator's image and the breath of His life. This best product of God's creative power stands supreme in character above the most eminent of the heathen gods. The highest flights of the heathen imagination never dreamed of an origin so exalted for man himself. Debased by fear and superstition, they looked up to the forms of inorganic life—sun, moon and stars—as the highest types of existence. All these did God create, and among

---

* Genesis 1: 20-2: 3.

them he made man the chief. Then He ceased from the work of creation, and looked upon it all as holy and good. The heathen conception of matter as essentially evil finds no support in the scriptural declaration that all matter, in itself, is absolutely good.

(4) THE IMAGE OF GOD.*

The character of the created universe has not been sufficiently stated in the first chapter of Genesis. The revelation concerning the mutual relation of all the parts thereof has not been finished. The divine author of all existence continues to reveal to the writer of Genesis what is meant by the image of God and breath of His life and the double sex of the human race. Is man simply the climax in a self-developed process of creation ? Is the image of God simply the seal set upon the last coin of a self-operating mint ? Not so. Of a higher order than all the rest of created beings is man, and so was he made according to the deliberate purpose of His Creator.†

In behalf of man, the Lord God (Jehovah Elohim) controlled and directed all the forces of created nature. The formation of the human race was contemplated even while God was creating the forms of inorganic life; for the story of man's creation is linked to that period in the six days when "no plant of the field was yet upon the earth, and no herb of the field had as yet sprung up ; for the Lord God had not yet caused it to rain upon the earth, and men there were not to till the ground."‡ Then the Lord God sent up the mist from the earth and sent down the rain from heaven and thus caused the whole face of the ground to become the home of plant-life and a suitable mansion for man. Then " the Lord God formed man out of the dust of the ground."§

A certain form of the Babylonian story of creation has been transmitted through Berosus, a Babylonian priest-historian. In this form of the myth it is asserted that the god Bel was decapitated and the blood that dropped down was mingled with the earth, and so was man formed. Even to this fable does the record in Genesis present a striking contrast. Not only did the Lord God use His infinite power

---

*Genesis 2 : 4-24. †Genesis 1: 26, 27. ‡Genesis 2: 5. §Genesis 2: 7.

to make the body of man from the dust of the earth, but He gave to him a spiritual nature, a fact far beyond the conception of heathen imagination. "He breathed into his nostrils breath of life; and so man became a living soul."* The first explanation has now been made concerning the character of man as made in the image of God. Not only a material body is he, but also a living soul. Two natures have been moulded together in him—the nature of flesh and the nature of spirit.

But the relationship between man and God means yet more than this. The impress of the divine image implies that man is endowed with reason and with knowledge. Not merely the capacity to know, doth he possess, but many of the *facts* concerning the relationship between the parts of creation are known to him. He is invested with authority after the manner of the Creator's authority. The plants in the Garden of Eden are caused to spring up for his benefit and pleasure. In four directions flow the streams through this garden, and man is made the master of it all. He possesses faculties that enable him to dress and keep the plants of the garden and to give names to all the beasts of the field. He has a personal history which begins its course on these flowery banks, and which is made up of actions prompted by his own reason and linked with creature and creator.

Moreover, the possession of the image of God implied a *moral* nature in man. Means were offered him for the development of that moral nature, just as food and power were bestowed for the strengthening of his body and his reason. By *abstaining* from the fruit of the tree in the midst of the garden, the man's character with reference to right and wrong was to be built up in *goodness*, just as *partaking* of other fruit was to build up his body. The penalty for voluntary disobedience made its appeal to the man's moral nature. It indicated that he possessed knowledge and righteousness. Conformity to God's standard was one of his characteristics and the stability of his moral nature was to keep him in that state of righteousness.

Holiness, likewise, was a result of the possession of God's image. Not merely because God's own nature, the source of man's nature, appears in the narrative as holy, but man

---

* Gen.: 2-7.

himself as a part of creation was pronounced to be "good," and that goodness was left dependent upon his own obedience. All of creation was good, but man's goodness had its seat in his rational, moral nature, and he might change it if he chose. Such a future choice of evil rather than of good is pointed out as the cause of deterioration in character. "In the day that thou eatest .... thou shalt surely die."

The highest condition of rational and spiritual life is meant by the possession of God's image. Final emphasis is laid upon this truth when we are told that none of the animals were of such a nature as to share the responsibility of man's position. In body and in spirit they were not fit helpers and companions for his exalted calling. Flesh of his flesh was woman formed, to be the very counterpart of himself—physically, intellectually and spiritually—to help him carry out the duties of his calling as the bearer of the divine image.

Jehovah is God.

Another series of facts in these two chapters remains for our examination. These facts relate to the Creator Himself.

The unity of the godhead is clearly stated in the midst of a diversity of creative acts. Thirty-five times is Elohim named as the creator of both inorganic and organic life.* The same unity is declared in connection with God's revelation of Himself. The Elohim who stamped His image upon man is the same as Jehovah Elohim who laid responsibility upon Adam, making him the image of the divine power and authority. As our God, who created man and began immediately to make Himself known to His creatures, does He appear in these two chapters. The name Elohim describes Him as a being of infinite power and majesty. The name Jehovah means simply that He is The Eternal One. Where the second chapter continues the story of creation by using the title Jehovah Elohim, we have simply the statement that Elohim, who existed already in the beginning before His first creative act, still continues the same God in His establishment of a vital relationship between Himself and man.

---
* Gen. 1: 1—2: 3.

The continuity of these facts in the two chapters appears still more clearly when we are told that the Elohim who existed as a rational Being in the beginning and caused things to exist outside of Himself by the mere power of His will; the Elohim, whose spirit was present as the agent of His will in controlling and ordering created things; the Elohim who pronounced His own work good and made the seventh day holy by stamping His own nature upon it, making it the type of Himself; the Elohim who created man, male and female in his own likeness; that this creator and revealer through His works is also the creator and revealer through His word. Jehovah, the ever-living, is the same with Elohim, the all-powerful. Elohim, the God of eternal power and personality, is also Jehovah Elohim, the God who communes with the creatures of His handiwork. These facts are entirely beyond the range of the folk-lore we have just examined. A personal God endowed with all reasonable and moral and spirital faculties as the back-ground of His power and of His self-revelation unto man, was unknown to Babylonian mythology.

The Purpose of the Narrative.

The purpose underlying the recital of all these facts is not of human but of divine origin. That purpose belongs to both chapters as a unit, and may be thus expressed: *The making of man as the best part of the work of creation.* The relationship between God and things created is set forth finally in the declaration that the highest result of the creative agency bears God's image. The establishment of this relationship is the single purpose kept in view from the beginning to the end of Gen. 1–2. That this may appear more clearly, let us recall certain facts:

(1) In the end of the sixth day God created man in His image, male and female, and said unto them, have dominion over every living thing. (Gen. 1: 28.) The end of the sixth day must, therefore, have been the time when Adam and Eve stood together as lords of the garden of Eden. (Gen. 2: 25.)

(2) The seventh day whereon God rested from all His work was the day following the close of active creation, described in Gen. 1: 1—2: 3, and also the day following the

close of active creation, described in Gen. 2: 4–25. The day of God's cessation from creative agency was the day when Adam and Eve were not ashamed before Him and entered upon their stewardship in Paradise.

(3) The establishment of the Sabbath is *implied* at the close of 2: 4–25, as it is stated at the close of 1: 1–2: 3. In both cases the Sabbath is the symbol of the relationship between God and man. At the close of 1: 1–2: 3 the Sabbath is the sign of the fact that man bears God's image; at the close of 2: 4–25, the Sabbath symbolizes the beginning of that kind of life devolved upon him by the possession of his maker's image.

(4) It is very clear that Gen. 1: 1–2: 3 and Gen. 2: 4–25, both carry the story of creation from the beginning through six active days as far as the opening of the seventh day. They both set forth, the one directly, the other by implication, the Sabbath-day as a symbol of what God has accomplished. They both declare that creation has culminated in Adam and Eve, stamped with the image of Jehovah, who is God. The first part of the entire narrative tells how they came to possess that image, and the second part tells how they began to exercise the rights and privileges implied in its possession.

(5) The revelation of this one chief purpose of creation is the single purpose that underlies the narrative in Gen. 1–2.

Further than this, it is very clear that this purpose is imbedded in the facts themselves. The facts were revealed by God Himself; the *purpose* is God's. This establishes the strong presumption that all of the facts in Gen. 1–2 were made known to a single writer at one time, since all of these facts are necessary to the statement of a single purpose.

The attempt to find two purposes in these two chapters is a vain search.* The institution of the Sabbath is not the primary purpose of Gen. 1: 1–2: 3. Nor is it the primary purpose of Gen. 2: 4–25, in itself, to furnish a prelude to the fall. This latter part is not a beginning but a climax, and that climax is the same with the climax of the story of creation in the first part, and the double culmination is symbolized in the Sabbath.

---

* Dr. Harper in Biblical World, Jan. and Feb., '94.

The assertion that this story of creation is nothing more than a piece of Semitic legend* is confuted by the Babylonian myths. These facts in Genesis are beyond the reach of human imagination. From God's own lips were they spoken, and by an inspired scribe were they set at the foundation of that great structure of Revelation afterwards to be completed by the words spoken to Isaiah and to Paul and to John. As revealed facts, the discussion of their *form*, apart from the underlying substance of truth, may not be permitted. Herein is found the weak point in the armor of the new school of criticism. The leaders of this school claim to deal only with the *form* of the Biblical narratives, but not to assault the *fact* of Revelation.† Vain claim! The form and the fact are bound in unbreakable bonds. To say that the form of this creation story places it upon the same plane with the creation myths of Babylon and Greece is, in effect, to affirm that the same human causes underlie both forms. This is, in effect, to deny that the Genesis history is divine revelation.

But we have later scriptural authority that the story of creation in Genesis i.–ii. is divine revelation. "The first man, Adam, was made a living soul ; the last Adam a quickening spirit."‡ The representative head of the race was that first man. His acts were binding on all his progeny. This truth could not be dreamed by men. It was revealed by God, and its authoritative statement for all time was made in the story of creation. To set forth that headship of the race and supremacy over all created things is the one purpose of the narrative in the first two chapters of Genesis.

Genesis and Science.

The teachings of the modern science of geology have been urged as indications that the Genesis story of creation does not reveal the true history of the development of the earth out of a chaotic mass. Up to a very recent date it has been regarded as a sufficient answer to say that the creation day in Genesis i. was not a day of twenty-four hours, but a long geologic period.§ But now it is held by certain scholars that

---
*Briggs: The Higher Criticism of the Hexateuch. Ryle: The Early Narratives of Genesis. † Driver's Int. to Lit. of Old Test., p. xi. ‡ I. Cor., 15–45. § Delitzsch on Genesis 1.

the period indicated by the writer of the history in Genesis can be only the ordinary day of twenty-four hours.* Along with this contention we have the statement that "there is no question that the order of creation indicated in the story is in general that which science teaches." However near this may approach the exact truth, let us remember that the writer of Genesis does not mean to give a treatise on science. He is revealing the result of God's creative fiat in the ascending scale of importance until the climax of humanity is reached. Science has not yet established the fact that error exists in the statements of the divine record. While the case stands thus, the presumption remains unshaken that the narrative in Genesis is in all respects absolutely true.

---

* Drs. Harper and Dods, Vid. Biblical World, pp. 6-16, January, 1894.

CHAPTER VI.

THE ORIGIN AND PROGRESS OF EVIL.

[*Genesis 3–5.*]

The Sacred Tree of Eridu.

CARVED upon Babylonian and Assyrian bas-reliefs, there often appears a tree, or plant, guarded on each side by a winged figure, who bears sometimes the head of a man, sometimes of an eagle. The tree is usually represented as a "plant of medium height, inclining to a pyramidal shape, having a trunk furnished with numerous branches, and at its base a bunch of broad leaves.* Since it generally bears fircones upon its branches, this tree is most probably referred to in the following inscription:

1. In Eridu a dark pine grew; in an illustrious place it was planted.
2. Its root was of white crystal, which spread towards the deep.
3. The (shrine?) of Hea was its pasturage in Eridu, a canal of water.
4. Its seat was the central place of this earth.
5. Its shrine was the couch of Mother Zicum, the mother of gods and men.
6. The roof of its illustrious temple, like a forest, spread its shade; there was none who within entered.
7. It was the seat of the mighty Mother Zicum, the begetter of Anu.†

The city of Eridu was the chief centre of the worship of the god Hea, and since this deity was sometimes called "the Lord of Life," scholars like Lenormant and Smith affirm that this sculptured plant is the "Tree of Life" mentioned in Genesis. As further confirmation of this view, reference is made to a Babylonian seal now in the British Museum. Upon this seal is carved a tree "with a human figure seated on either side of it, with the hands stretched out towards

---

* Lenormant's The Beginnings of History. p. 86. † Smith's Chaldean Genesis, pp. 85–86.

the fruit, and a serpent standing erect behind one of them. . . . . . It must be admitted, however, that the two figures seem both to be males."*

No evidence has yet come to the light to show that these figures symbolize the fall of our first parents through the temptation of the serpent. There are, however, certain facts in the Babylonian folk-lore that seem to fit in with these figured symbols to make a complete story. The sun-god, Merodach, is represented in the legends as contending with Tiamat, the "chaos of the sea" or the "serpent of darkness." Tiamat is also called the "monster of seven heads, like the huge serpent of seven heads," who lashes the sea into waves. Against this deity of the power of darkness comes the power of the light, Merodach. A flaming sword he bears:

"The sun of fifty faces, the lofty weapon of my divinity, I bear.
The hero that striketh the mountains, the propitious sun of the morning, that is mine, I bear.
My mighty weapon which, like an orb, smites in a circle the corpses of the fighters, I bear."†

The lightning is evidently this sword of the sun-god, with which he hews his way to victory through opposing darkness. Merodach's conquest of the serpent-headed deity of darkness, "the dragon of the deep," may be an obscure reference to the expulsion of the serpent-seduced Adam and Eve from Eden, and Merodach's sword may be a suggestion of the flaming sword that guarded the way to the tree of life. But more probably this story is only a form of the ever-recurring myth of the struggle between light and darkness. A certain moral significance gradually attached itself to this legend. For the seven heads of the god of darkness came to represent seven evil spirits. In many incantations the gods are called upon to ward off the power of these demons:

"Seven are they, seven are they!
In the abyss of the deep, seven are they.
In the brightness of heaven, seven are they.
. . . .
Law and order know they not.
Prayer and supplication hear they not.
Among the thorns of the mountains was their growth,
To Hea are they hostile.
The thronebearers of the gods are they,
Disturbers in the . . . . . are they set.
Evil are they, baleful are they." ‡

---
* Smith's Chald. Genesis, p. 89.   † Smith's Chald. Genesis. p. 86.   ‡ Budge's Babylonian Life and History, p. 137.

As the hidden source of diseases and bodily evils, these spirits are thus personified. Thus did the myth of Merodach and Tiamat lift its dark front into the domestic life of the Babylonians as the basis of foul superstitions and sorceries. The storm-clouds were the seven evil spirits who oppressed the life of men. The spirit of the southwest wind was the king of terrors among these evil demons. With glaring eyeballs was he pictured in little clay images; amulets were worn to ward off this bringer of death. With fear of their gods and demons were these ancient people ever weighed down. Even their prayers, as found in the cuneiform inscriptions, are mere grovellings and supplications before some atmospheric monster :

"O my goddess that knowest that I knew not, my transgression is great,
   many are my sins.
The sin that I committed I knew not.
The sin that I sinned I knew not.
The forbidden things did I eat.
The . . . . did I trample upon.
My lord in the wrath of his heart has punished me.
God in the strength of his heart has overpowed me.
I lay on the ground and no man extended the hand.
In tears I dissolved myself and none my palms took.
I cried aloud; there was none that would hear me.
The feet of my goddess I embraced."*

Babylonians Held Physical Origin of Evil.

As this old heathen creed thus passes in review before us we see that, with them, evil had a physical origin. It had its seat in the devastating power of the storm-cloud or in the deadly fury of the malarial winds that swept over the plains. The pantheon of great gods had no power to give complete protection, and hence did they build about themselves a fortress of sorceries and magical rites. Gross superstition bound them fast to the earth. No mercy dwelt in the heart of the cloud-monsters. There was no hope in such a creed. Downward into "the land of no return" were they driven by these fear-inspiring gods. Even the "prayer" just quoted is merely a cry of anguish against the cruelty of the god. There nowhere exists in the Babylonian religion the idea of holiness as an attribute of the gods. The sin which is so often confessed is not a violation of the righteous standard of the gods—for they have no such standard.

---

*Budge, p. 146.

The god is capricious and cruel, and the fear of punishment is the nearest approach this prayer makes to an expression of penitence. Not the horror of sin as an evil thing, but the horror of punishment as a cruel thing, is the leading sentiment of the suppliant's cry.

The Fall of Man and His Expulsion from Eden.

Perhaps the most striking fact that appears in the beginning of the third chapter of Genesis is the *continuity* of the narrative. The same joyous paradise offers its fruits to the man and woman as lords of the forest and the field. The same exaltation over the brute creation stamps these parents of the human race. The same exalted relationship with the Creator is still the privilege of the first pair, created, as they were, in the image of God. To outline the continuance of that relationship, with a view to a clearer manifestation of God, is the evident aim of this sacred narrative. The communion between the Creator and His creature is most intimate. Their relationship is set forth on an exalted plane of life. The image-relationship is followed by the obedience-relationship. God institutes His moral government over His creatures. His character as a moral being comes into touch with them, and they are trained to act from the prompting of moral and spiritual motives. God walks and talks with His creatures, and unto them makes revelations through the medium of their intelligence.

Voluntarily these creatures violate God's command. Willingly they obey the suggestion of the serpent and eat the forbidden fruit. The serpent is only the instrument of Satan, the spiritual adversary, the prince of the power of evil, for immediately after their disobedience Adam and Eve are made to see the evil which they have chosen and the holiness which they have rejected. Spiritual truths are revealed to man under symbolic forms that are unmistakable. All these truths belong to the realm of the reason and the soul, and they centre about the free exercise of choice in the mind of the man himself.

(1) The act of disobedience wrought its first result upon their own minds. The eyes of Adam and Eve were opened to see the ruin that had seized upon their own characters. The shame which caused them to flee behind garments of

fig-leaves was only a mute expression of the trembling fear that hurried them from God's presence. The outward manifestation of this inward sentiment was the revelation of their own fall in spiritual character. They were lower in the scale of being than they had been, and they knew it, and their degradation centred around that voluntary act committed against their better knowledge. The eating of the fruit was the expression of a change that took place in the innermost shrine of their spiritual being, and upon that spiritual part of the human temple did the penalty now fasten itself. Man deliberately and voluntarily flung away that attribute of his soul which made him find congenial companionship in the presence of his Creator. He saw the full meaning of holiness only when he had lost it.

(2) God's curse upon the serpent was the severest part of the result of disobedience. By placing the serpent above every beast of the field in the scale of His displeasure, God made it clear that the crawling animal was only the representative of some spirtual power. The serpent was the mouthpiece of those spiritual whisperings that suggested man's disobedience—and those whisperings had their source in a personal evil being who was to carry on a warfare against the coming generations of the human race. The friendship of the serpent was only a victory of this spiritual enemy over Adam and Eve, and he was ready to strive for similar victories until the seed of the woman should crush him forever. Thus does God declare that evil, or unholiness, is represented in the spiritual world by a personal head who can use all the weapons of reason and language, and by a principle which may take up its dwelling in the human soul in the form of a fixed resolve. In such a connection does the Lord reveal the elements of man's relationship with Himself and at the same time foretell the Saviour, "the seed of the woman" who will crush the head of the prince of evil and give to every man a new principle as the foundation of moral character.

(3) The ideas of holiness and mercy which God makes known to man as the stones that rest by the side of His absolute sovereignty over man and beast in the foundations of His moral government—these ideas are still more clearly brought out in the spiritual character of the penalty al-

lotted to Adam and Eve. The death foretold as the result of eating the forbidden fruit is now specially pointed out as belonging to the realm of spirit. "I will greatly multiply *thy sorrow*" is the form in which God expresses to the woman the fact that her disobedience has sent an arrow into her own soul. The anguish of spirit that seizes upon a woman in travail is a symbol of that trembling unto death that has entered into every soul. "Cursed is the ground for thy sake" is the sentence of death upon the man. With reference to himself, the power of death has touched the earth and made it the producer of much sorrow and soul-trouble. In sorrow and in labor must he draw his sustenance from the earth, and after the pangs of dissolution must he become dust again.

Thus, as a climax in this revelation of His own holiness, God drives the human pair from His presence. Unholiness has set her seal upon them and they must take up their abode in the fields of the earth, which is cursed for their sake. The cherubim and the flaming sword guard the way to the Tree of Life. This food of holiness and immortality must be regained through spiritual warfare.

Thus does the narrative in Genesis start the human race upon its journey in an obedience-relationship with God. Backward upon a period of physical and spiritual prosperity do they look as they think of the Garden of Eden. Winged figures, representing the race of all animated creation serving the Creator as the attendants of His presence, and the flame of fire made the instrument of His power, continue to call after the departing man and woman the lessons of His authority and His love. Not merely penalty but likewise promise do they symbolize. They are the servants of a holy God—all creation renders obedient service to Him. Only in the soul of man has disobedience been found. There has evil found its first resting-place on the earth. The source of all the evils that rest upon him is in the heart of the man himself. In that same spiritual kingdom must the battle be fought for the conquest of the prince of evil and the regaining of holiness and the joy of God's presence.

It is this idea of holiness as an actual attribute of God and as a possible attribute of man that marks the narrative in Genesis as divine and not human. The vague pencilings of the figure of the sacred tree of Eridu and the myth of the struggle between light and darkness in the persons of Merodach and Tiamat are but imaginative mists in the presence of this clear revelation from God himself. The bare facts themselves and also the form of presentation must have been suggested by the divine voice unto the scribe who wrote them down.

The Cainites and the Sethites.

In the fourth and fifth chapters of Genesis, the divine record continues to speak concerning holiness and evil. Each of these principles is subject to growth. Each of them makes progress upon the plane of the obedience-relationship with God. Obedience tends to the growth of holiness, and this means a nearer approach into His presence. Disobedience fosters the progress of evil in the heart—and this means a further flight from His presence.

In the offerings of Cain and Abel we have the practical workings of the obedience-relationship after the expulsion from Eden. God required of men an offering—an expression of gratitude from the creature to the Creator. The worship of Himself was to be the central element in human life. This worship was to be the expression of love and not of terror. It was to be based upon the intelligent reception of God's revelations. For Abel's sacrifice of the firstlings of his flock and the fat thereof was a more acceptable offering to God than Cain's fruit of the ground, because of Abel's disposition of mind. His faith* was made manifest in the offering, while Cain only showed his insolence. The relationship between God and his creatures still inhered in the realm of reason and spirit. For Abel's faith evidently rested upon his clearer knowledge of the Lord's revelations. The sacrifice of blood had clearly been commanded by the Lord as a symbol of the obedience-relationship. All the facts hitherto made known in the narrative show that this relationship is in the inner life of the spirit. Evidently, then, the Lord had said that the formal intercourse of this rela-

---

* Hebrews 11 : 4.

tionship should be typified only by blood. Abel understood and obeyed—Cain did neither, because he had not the desire.

The Lord punishes evil. So runs the narrative. Spiritual anguish, an unbearable burden of it, came upon Cain for his persistence in the course of sin. Hatred and murder have made him unfit for the presence of God and even for the presence of good men. Off into the land of "banishment" (Nod) was he driven, and there his generations continued in the pursuit of evil. Cain built the first city; Lamech established polygamy; Jabal introduced the nomadic form of life; Jubal first contrived instruments of music; Tubal-Cain was the first artificer in brass and iron; Lamech's song of the sword is written in the stately language of poetry. A high cultivation of the arts and a successful seeking after the luxuries of life was the result of the efforts of the Cainites. But they were a sensual, disobedient and lawless race. In Lamech the generations of Cain reached a climax of outlawry:

> "For I slay a man if he woundeth me,
> Even a young man if he hurteth me,
> Lo! Cain would be avenged seven-fold,
> But Lamech seventy-and-seven fold."*

These words of insolent defiance imply that the line of disobedient men has resulted in an outlaw who takes vengeance into his own hands.

Contrasted with these evil-doers is the line of Seth. They come nearer and nearer into touch with the Lord because they start out by calling on the name of Jehovah. The God who reveals Himself is besought to make still further known all His plans for the life of men. The Sethites are the successors of Abel in their cultivation of knowledge and faith. Two great landmarks stand out in this faithful generation. Enoch walks with God and is translated without suffering the pangs of death. Noah marks the climax in this contrast between the two races. The restlessness of the Cainites is opposed to the "comfort" which Lamech predicts for the sons of Seth through the character and work of Noah. A confidence and trust in God's mercy and in His willingness to make further revelation of Himself is stamped upon these men who aspire after holiness.

* Genesis 4: 23.

The Documentary Theory.

The supposition that two ancient documents have been pieced together to form the narrative of the two human types is controverted by the facts. The two genealogies are given to illustrate God's holiness and His hatred of sin, and how these facts constitute the central factors in the life of men. The idea of holiness as a mark of human character springing from God's holiness was absolutely unknown to heathen mythology. Men never dreamed of such a relationship. God had to reveal it. In making the revelation He must needs dictate the form of the narrative. Human actions were woven into a narrative to express the divine message. God directed the writer in choosing the character of that narrative. A complete unity of thought and purpose stamps the history in Genesis, thus far examined, as the message delivered to one inspired writer.

CHAPTER VII.
THE DELUGE.

The Babylonian Legend.

IN the twelve tablets, or cantos, of the epic of Gizdhubar is incorporated the largest known cycle of Babylonian folk-lore. Three cuneiform copies of this mythological work were found in the royal library of Asshur-bani-pal, and a fourth edition has been handed down through the copy made by Berosus, the priest. Mr. George Smith who unearthed the three editions of the clay tablets was of the opinion that Gizdhubar was the Nimrod of the Book of Genesis. But no adequate evidence in support of this conjecture has yet come to the light. The course of this epic narrative points very clearly to the fact that Gizdhubar was only the fire-god of the ancient Accadians who became the sun-god of the later Babylonians and the Hercules of the Greeks. The twelve tablets of the epic correspond with the twelve signs of the Zodiac, the path of the sun in his yearly flight. The second tablet tells of Gizdhubar's meeting with a great bull-shaped monster who answers to Taurus of the Zodiac. The fifth tablet records the prowess of Gizdhubar in slaying the lion, the counterpart of the sign of Leo in the Zodiac. The virgo of the Zodiac is paralleled by Istar who vainly pays court to the hero in the sixth tablet. "And just as Aquarius is in the eleventh Zodiacal sign, so the history of the deluge is embodied in the eleventh tablet."*

A still more striking resemblance exists between the Gizdhubar epic and the Greek legends concerning Hercules. This hero was brought into Greece from Phoenicia where he had played his part as sun-god, Baal-Melkarth. His twelve labors were the twelve legends concerning the Babylonian solar hero, Gizdhubar. The bull-shaped monster Hea-bani reappears in Cheiron, the centaur. The lion victim of Gizdhubar's strength is the human lion slain by Hercules;

---
*Sayce's Assyria, p. 110.

"the winged bull made by Anu is the famous bull of Crete; the tyrant Khum-baba is the tyrant Geryon; the gems borne by the trees of the forest beyond the gateway of the sun are the apples of the Hesperides; and the deadly sickness of Gizdhubar himself is but the fever of Hercules caused by the poisoned tunic of Nessus."*

The only part which Gizdhubar plays in the story of the flood, recorded on the eleventh tablet of the epic, is to listen to the recital thereof by the hero Xisuthrus. This patriarch is saved from the deluge and carried by the gods to a far-off paradise, and thither Gizdhubar follows him to ask healing balm for his sickness. He entreats Xisuthrus to reveal the circumstances that have brought the privilege of immortality, and in reply Xisuthrus relates the story of the flood from which he has been rescued. The artificial links that bind together all the parts of this epic appear here in the introductory part of the Babylonian account of the deluge. The chief elements of the legend may be learned from a few quotations:

1. Xisuthrus to himself also speaks, even to Gizdhubar.
2. Let me reveal to thee the story of my preservation.
3. And the judgment of the gods let me relate to thee.
4. The city Surippak, the city which thou knowest on the Euphrates is placed.
5. That city is ancient, and the gods are within it.
6. To make a deluge the great gods have brought their heart;
7. Even he their father, Anu,
8. Their king, the warrior, Bel,
9. Their throne-bearer, Ninip;
10. Their minister, the lord of Hades, Nin-si-kha, wife of Hea, with them sat, and
11. Their will he (Hea) repeated; to his minister, the minister of the city of Kis, he declared what he had in mind.
12. His minister heard and proclaimed attentively:
13. Man of Surippak, son of Ubara-tutu,
14. Build a house, make a 'ship to preserve the sleep of plants and living beings;
15. Store the seed and vivify life;

---
*Smith's Chald. Genesis, p. 177.

16. Cause, also, the seed of life of every kind to go up into the midst of the ship.
17. The ship which thou shalt make—
18. Six hundred cubits shall be its measure in length;
19. Sixty cubits the amount of its breadth and its height.*

Those who are to be preserved in the ship are thus enumerated:

Into the midst of it, thy grain, thy furniture, thy goods;

Thy wealth, thy woman slaves, thy handmaids, and the sons of the host;

The beasts of the field, the wild animals of the field, as many as I would protect,

I will send to thee, and thy door shall guard them. †

Now came the flood of waters at the command of Shamash, the sun. "The water of Twilight at the dawn of day rose up from the foundations of the sky in a black cloud; Ramman thundered in the midst of this cloud. . . . . The archangels of the abyss brought destruction; in their terrors, they shook the earth. The inundation of Ramman swelled up to heaven, and the earth, having lost its brightness, was changed into a desert." ‡

Death came upon the living creatures of the earth, and "in heaven the gods became afraid of the waterspout and sought a refuge; they ascended even to the heaven of Anu. The gods were stretched motionless, pressed close against each other, like dogs. . . . . The gods on their chairs were seated in tears, and they kept their lips closed." §

Seven days the storm continued. Xisuthrus looked forth upon the corpses of men that "floated like seaweed," and at the sight he "sat down and wept." Thus for seven days the ship rested on "the mountain of Nizir," and at the end of that time Xisuthrus sent forth a dove, a swallow and a raven. The two former returned to the ship, but the raven remained without, and then came forth all the dwellers within the ship. Then did Xisuthrus offer a sacrifice to placate the angry Bel, who had sent the flood. Xisuthrus and his wife were then led far away and their dwelling fixed "in a distant place at the mouth of the rivers," where they were to "live like gods."‖

---

*Smith's Chald. Genesis, pp. 279–89. †Smith's Chald. Genesis, p. 281. ‡Lenormant, p. 396. §Lenormant, pp. 396–7. ‖Lenormant, pp. 398–403.

In this cuneiform record we have folk-lore in its unadulterated form. The sky-gods enter into conspiracy, with the sun as leader in the plot, and pour down rain for seven days. The gods are frightened at their deeds and hide their faces behind the storm-clouds. Xisuthrus is a king with many servants and cattle, and these are saved in a large ship.

The Greek Legend.

Lay this cuneiform account of the deluge alongside the Thessalian legend of Deucalion. The Greek imagination in this bit of local fiction set forth the god Zeus as the author of a flood that swept away all the people of the bronze age except Deucalion and his wife Pyrrha. The crimes of the race had stirred up the anger of Zeus. But Prometheus forewarned Deucalion and the latter built a floating chest and took refuge therein with his wife. The waters upon the earth increased to a great flood, and for nine days and nights did they toss the chest about on their waves. Then was it left on the summit of Parnassus, and Deucalion and Pyrrha came forth to offer sacrifice unto Zeus and to fill the earth again with people by flinging stones behind them, which the god forthwith changed to men. Other traditions besides had the Greeks concerning a deluge, but in general form and outline each story resembles all the rest. All the Aryan nations, in fact, have incorporated in their primitive lore one or more versions of a national deluge. Concerning these legends, Lenormant follows Knobel in asserting that "the ancient tradition of the cataclysm by which all mankind were destroyed and which was common to all the Aryan nations, is confused . . . . . with the more or less distinct recollections of local catastrophes occasioned by extraordinary overflowings of the banks of lakes or rivers by the rupture of the natural embankments of certain lakes, by the depression of portions of the sea-coast, by tidal waves following upon earthquakes or upon partial upheavals of the ocean bed."* Without entering into details, we may further quote this distinguished scholar to the effect that "the account of the deluge is an universal tradition" in "the three great civilized races of the ancient world," viz., the Semites, the Aryans and the Cushites, and that this

---
* Lenormant's The Beginnings of History, p. 436.

deluge occurred "before the ancestors of these three races were as yet separated, and . . . . . in that Asiatic country which they inhabited conjointly."* If these assertions be correct, this universal tradition is strong collateral evidence to the truth of the story of the flood in the Book of Genesis. But there is no testimony in this similarity of national traditions to show that the Babylonian legend was used by the author of Genesis. On the contrary, Lenormant's investigations have served to demonstrate this fact: that the Babylonian account of the deluge belongs exclusively to the category of heathen folk-lore. Even if it does concern the deluge of Noah's time, the form which it has finally taken in the cuneiform inscriptions is due to Babylonian imagination. Local events have been given a place in the story, and the heathen creed of this sun-worshiping people has been glorified in this particular canto as in all the remaining parts of the great epic. Folk-lore it is, with the usual foundation of superstition and all the details of a debased heathen mythology.

The Story of the Flood in Genesis—Genesis 6-9.

Let us preface our examination of the biblical account of Noah and the flood by repeating an argument already made by Bickell, a German, and by the Abbé Vigouroux, a French scholar. They insisted † that the repetitions occurring in the story of the flood in Genesis are found also in the cuneiform account, and hence they asserted that these repetitions in Genesis do not indicate two different sources for the biblical narrative. If this Babylonian inscription be received as a consecutive history of the flood, yet containing repetitions, then the presence of repetitions in the story in Genesis cannot prove that it is non-consecutive. Such was the position taken by these writers. Now, Lenormant denies the fact of the repetitions in the cuneiform account, but asserts a repetition in Genesis. He affirms that the supposition of the above-named scholars was based upon imperfect translations by George Smith in his Chaldean Genesis. "None of the repetitions of the final text of Genesis can be found in the Chaldean poem."‡ In this manner has Le-

---
* Lenormant, pp. 486-88. † Vigouroux: La Bible et les découvertes modernes. Bickell: Zeitscrift für Katholische Theologie, 1877. ‡ Lenormant, pp. 404-5.

normant met the argument. In opposition to him stands Dr. Sayce in his revised edition of Smith's Chaldean Genesis, whom we find declaring in regard to the Babylonian story: "The compiler of the epic seems to have used for this purpose two independent poems relating to the event; at least it is otherwise difficult to account for *the repetitions observable in certain lines.*" These repetitions are specified thus: "According to 1: 13, the deluge was caused by "all the great gods"; according to 2: 30, by Samas only; according to 4: 4, 5, by Bel." * This takes away the ground from beneath Lenormant's feet, for he quotes the above lines as his reason for dividing the biblical narrative into two documents, because he there finds Elohim and Jehovah both named as the active agents in bringing on the deluge!

Dr. Sayce would break the force of the argument of Bickell and Vigouroux by saying that both the epic and the biblical account are compilations—that neither is an original, consecutive narrative. But we notice that this is entirely a conjecture on the part of Dr. Sayce. He furnishes little evidence, or none, to show that the epic itself is a compilation, and we begin to suspect that his assertions concerning different sources for Genesis rest upon the same foundation of conjecture. It seems more probable that the repetitions in the epic are nothing more than the confusion of ideas that marks all heathen mythology.

When our eye falls upon the narrative concerning the flood, at its beginning in Genesis vi., 1, we recognize the continuance of the same divine record already examined up to this point. The outline of the generations of the two diverging classes of men is naturally followed by a narrative based upon that period of time "when men began to multiply on the face of the earth and daughters were born unto them."† Then catching up the spirit of the preceding history, a climax in the moral condition of the race is set forth by the biblical record when it declares that "the sons of God saw the daughters of men, that they were fair ; and they took wives of all which they chose."‡ Those who are here termed "the sons of God" were evidently the descendants of Seth, that line of Adam's sons who "called upon the name of the Lord." The children of God were they—

---

*Smith's Chald. Genesis, p. 301.   †Gen. 6: 1.   ‡Gen. 6: 2.

a little church in the midst of the worldliness and wickedness of the sons of Cain. And now had the power of evil become so great that it found a welcome even in the midst of the hitherto faithful Sethites. Some of them contracted marriages with the daughters of the heathen families about them. The salt lost its savor. The little church itself became corrupt, and only Noah and his family were at last left as the true "sons of God," the real heirs of the faith of Seth. All but these were totally corrupt. Enemies to the mercies of Jehovah and ready to contend against the workings of His Spirit were these multiplied generations. Wherefore "Jehovah said, My Spirit shall not always strive with man, for that he also is flesh."* But when the Spirit of the living God withdrew from dwelling with men, because of continued repulses, then great was the wickedness of man as it stood revealed to heaven and to earth. "And the Lord saw that the wickedness of man was great in the earth, and that every imagination of the thoughts of his heart was only evil continually. And it repented the Lord that he had made man on the earth, and it grieved Him at His heart. And the Lord said, I will destroy man whom I have created from the face of the ground; both man and beast and creeping thing and fowl of the air; for it repenteth me that I have made them. But Noah found grace in the eyes of the Lord."† In these statements we find something entirely foreign to the spirit of the cuneiform narrative. Here we have a distinct revelation of the secrets that belong to Jehovah. Before the story of the flood is set forth, the *moral cause* thereof is plainly declared. Through many generations that cause has been growing up into strength in the human heart. The seed of evil that found a place in the heart of Adam and in the heart of Cain has grown up into a tree that has driven all goodness from the souls of these later generations. Even the Spirit of God has been repulsed and the Lord himself set at defiance by the race of giants whose hearts are fixed in the love for things of the flesh. The only hope of saving the earth as the abode of righteous men is to destroy this rampant corruption. The iniquity of men cries to heaven until Jehovah declares that He must vindicate His righteousness and His holiness. He

---

*Gen. 6: 3.   †Genesis 6: 5–8.

is still the same Jehovah of many mercies and continued revelations, who is ready to drive iniquity from His presence, as He sent forth Adam from the Garden of Eden. He is still ready to look with favor upon some, even as He received Abel and his offering.

The man who "found grace in the eyes of the Lord" must be clearly described. "Noah was a righteous man and perfect in his generations, and Noah walked with God."* The moral cause for judgment was not found in Noah's heart, and hence Noah received the message of divine mercy. Along with him his household received the same favor from Jehovah. Because that "all flesh had corrupted his way upon the earth," and the earth was "filled with violence through them," the Lord determined to "destroy them with the earth." This purpose was revealed to Noah, and the command was given this servant of righteousness to make "an ark of gopher wood."†

Two points of difference have thus far appeared between this biblical narrative and the cuneiform account of the flood. The first is, that we have revealed here in Genesis the *moral cause* of the divine judgment, viz., the vindication of God's holiness against the insolence of human iniquity, a characteristic which places this part of the divine narrative in consecutive connection with the early chapters of Genesis. Then, again, we find the biblical narrative dealing with a history of divine warning and exhortation that covers a period of one hundred and twenty years. At the beginning of this term of years, Jehovah announces His purpose to destroy corrupt humanity, and at the same time makes known the way of escape to Noah. A part of this long period is spent by Noah in the construction of the vessel. Steadily before the eyes of the iniquitous race is the divine purpose kept in view by the work and teachings of Noah. Jehovah's mercy cries out to them from every piece of timber added to the ark. The entire transaction is wrought out upon a scale entirely beyond the conception of merely human imagination. Not the sudden, capricious anger ascribed to the heathen gods, but the slowly wrought vindication of the holiness of Jehovah is narrated in the Book of Genesis. A merciful governor of the universe

---

*Gen. 6: 9.   †Gen. 6: 9-14.

sends a flood as a step in the divine administration. The destiny of a world is in the balance. How very different is the cause assigned for the flood in the cuneiform story. The caprice of the elements, the sky and the sun! In only one place is there an intimation of a *moral* cause. In 'lines iv., 15, 16 occur these words:

> "The doer of sin bore his sin, the blasphemer bore his blasphemy, Never may the just prince be cut off, never may the faithful be destroyed." *

But this is a remonstrance addressed by one of the gods, Hea, to the sun-god, Bel, *after* the deluge. The narrative describes Bel as still enraged and unwilling to permit Xisuthrus to come forth from his ship. The fate of his victims is held up as a reason why he should be appeased and cease his capricious enmity—

> "As thou didst not consider, a deluge thou madest." †

cries Hea to the sun. Then, after the protests of Hea are uttered,

> "Again also Bel considers, he approaches the midst of the ship,"

and delivers Xisuthrus. The wild rage of the sun-god is quieted and the hero of the deluge escapes his further fury. Thus does it appear, that the connection in which the terms "sin" and "blasphemy" occur rather precludes the idea that they are stated to be the moral cause of the deluge. They are stated in that part of the narrative concerned with appeasing the *inconsiderate* wrath of the god who sent the flood. The ideas here are not in the high moral plane with those in the Genesis history of the deluge where Jehovah's divine character of goodness and of justice is established in the presence of the whole world; for we must follow the story beyond the catastrophe that befell the earth in order to learn Jehovah's final purpose. "With thee will I establish my covenant," said the Lord unto Noah. With Noah in this covenant were numbered his wife and his children and also a representative pair "of every living thing of all flesh." ‡ The ultimate design of God in sending the flood is here declared, viz., the establishment of a *covenant*-relationship between Himself and His creatures.

---

* Smith's Chal. Gen., p. 288.   † Smith's Ch. Gen. p. 288.   ‡ Gen. 6: 18, 19.

The Covenant with Noah.

Let us pause here to impress upon our memory the plan of this sacred narrative in the Book of Genesis. It bears the stamp of a divine origin. We have seen how the story begins with the revelation of the *image*-relationship between God and man. In direct continuation, the record deals with the story of our race under the aspect of the subsequent *obedience*-relationship. Now are we led through the history of a great judgment, long delayed and often spoken of, to the climax of God's early training of His creatures, to the *covenant*-relationship. Here the Lord lifts the human race up to the plane of free, rational, self-controlling action. He treats Noah as a being worthy to enter into contract with Himself. He accepts Noah's oath as binding the whole category of living things. He has wonderfully exalted the human race and out of the midst of the destruction of iniquity has He brought men into closer fellowship with Himself.

In perfect obedience to the command of Jehovah did Noah move in and out, until the great transaction was completed. Minute directions for the construction of the ark—explicit orders how to people it with human kind, and "every creeping thing of the earth after his kind"—these came directly from the mouth of Jehovah unto Noah. After all this, "the Lord shut him in."* It was a divine work. The salvation of these representatives of the living creatures upon the earth was worthy of the care and close watchfulness of God Himself. Then came the working of His might in the terrors of judgment. The waters below seemed to leap up to meet the great flood that poured down upon the earth. "The same day were all the fountains of the great deep broken up, and the windows of heaven were opened, and the rain was upon the earth forty days and forty nights." †

Over all the inhabited earth did the waters establish themselves, until the mountains were covered and "every living substance was destroyed which was upon the face of the ground, both man and cattle, and the creeping things and the fowl of the heaven; and they were destroyed from

---
*Gen. 7: 16.   †Gen. 7: 11, 12.

the earth; and Noah only remained alive and they that were with him in the ark."*

Not for seven days did the flood continue, as the cuneiform record states, but during *ten days and one year* was Noah shut up within the ark. Then the word of Jehovah called forth the creatures, man and beast, and as the smoke of Noah's sacrifice ascended unto Him the great covenant was consummated. As a new creation did these ark-dwellers now go forth to possess the earth. God's blessing rested upon them. God's covenant-promise was whispered in their ears, and betokened by the bow in the cloud that destruction by flood should never again visit the whole earth. In subordination to man was placed the animal creation. "Every moving thing that liveth shall be meat for you." So ran the divine decree with reference to the new exaltation given to the animal who possesses the faculty of reason. Side by side with this enactment was set another that declared the sacredness of human life and the sacredness of animal life. Wanton destruction must not be visited upon either member of that vast body of creature life with whom He entered into solemn covenant. "And God spake unto Noah, and to his sons with him, saying, 'And I, behold, I establish my covenant with you and with your seed after you, and with every living creature that is with you.'" †

The Destiny of the Families of Men.

The relationship between God and His creatures was fixed upon the lofty plane of moral government. In telling the story of the consummation of this covenant-relationship, the sacred narrative goes farther to point out the destiny of the races that sprang from Noah. Under the freedom of choice left to men by the terms of this covenant, God foretold through Noah that Japheth should come into possession of the largest portion of the earth as his inheritance; that the offspring of Shem should be Jehovah's own peculiar people; that Canaan, representing the sons of Ham, should be brought down to a condition of servitude.‡ The movements and characteristics of generations yet unborn were prophesied in this narrative. Divine wisdom gave the seal of foreknowledge to this record of the deluge, which bears

---
*Gen. 7: 23.   †Gen. 9: 9. 10.   ‡Gen. 9: 25-27.

throughout the marks of divine revelation. Conscious of heavenly foresight is the Genesis narrative of the flood from beginning to ending. The coming of a flood of waters after a period of one hundred and twenty years—the career of the races of men until the end of time—these are seen with equal clearness by the author of this sacred history. When were the cuneiform records ever conscious of the future!

CHAPTER VIII.

ONE GOD AND ONE RACE OF MEN.

[*Genesis 10–11.*]

Heathen Views of the Origin of Man.

WHEN we knock at the door of the ancient heathen oracles to inquire after the character of the divine being and the origin of human creatures, we are answered by a chorus of traditions that point to the heavenly luminaries as gods and tell us to ask the earth or the sea or the sky concerning the birth of man. The people of the Nile country affirmed that men are emanations from the eye of the sun-god Ra, and the dwellers along the Euphrates and Lower Tigris had to suppose a convocation of many gods and the decapitation of one god in solving the problem of the beginning of animate life upon the earth.

These myths or legends we have chosen to classify as part of the folk-lore of the Egyptians and Babylonians. The term folk-lore, as here used, represents the mass of racial traditions. Whatever view be taken concerning the origin of folk-lore—whether that of Müller, that it has sprung from the variation in the meaning of words, or that of Andrew Lang, that it is the survival of beliefs current among the people of a race during a primitive, savage condition*—the general consensus of scientists as to the essential character of these tribal legends seems to be in accord with St. Paul's view, that men "became vain in their imaginations and their foolish heart was darkened. . . . Wherefore God also gave them up to uncleanness through the lusts of their own hearts." †

"The emptiness of human imagination" is the legend written on the fabric of these heathen creeds. Indefinite dreams woven out of dense ignorance make up the genealogy of gods and of men.

---
† Lang's Myth, Ritual and Religion.   ‡ Romans 1: 21–24.

The Dispersion from Babel.

In clear contrast with the teaching of these heathen myths we have the revelations made in the book of Genesis. The same eternal God, who has preserved the race of men intact from Adam to Noah, is declared to be the one Lord of all the earth. His blessing goes out into all the districts of the earth then known and inhabited, along with the sons of the man preserved from the deluge. As colonies scatter abroad from the original seat of human life, the same Lord superintends the migrations and keeps the families and the tribes together. Once or twice in the narrative we see the name of an individual standing forth into prominence at the separating point between families of the same tribe or clan. "Nimrod, the mighty hunter," appears here as one of God's creatures—the son of Cush, who was the son of Ham. Now, some scholars have supposed that Nimrod is to be identified with the Babylonian god Belus, or Bel.* The heathen imagination seized upon the prowess of this empire-founder and transferred his personal attributes to the sun-god, and thus transformed the chief luminary of day into a hero king! This may be so. But the Scripture record holds the great race heroes, like Nimrod and Asshur and Abram, down to the plane of ordinary humanity—all mere stems from the great parent stock created by the eternal God Himself. High above all the migrations of men and the variations that come into their forms of government and forms of speech, towers the Jehovah of the past, the present and the future, "the same yesterday, to-day and forever."

Unity of the Race.

Further than this, the sacred narrative speaks clearly concerning the origin of man. The tenth chapter of Genesis is an authoritative declaration concerning the unity of the human race. The various tribes and families then scattered upon the face of the earth are traced back through Noah to the first pair of human beings placed in Eden by the Lord God. Modern physiological science now rises up to say that the author of this table of the nations spoke the truth in affirming the original unity of the human species. "The isles of the Gentiles" are only peopled by the various

---
* Speaker's Commentary on Genesis, ch. 10.

"tongues and families and nations" that have sprung in the third generation from the loins of Japheth the son of Noah. Likewise are other "lands" passed in review as the abode of the "tongues and families and nations" that have descended from Ham and from Shem. The seventy families are pointed out as representatives of the people of the whole earth, and all these are the descendants of Noah. Unity of stock is the lesson that these seventy branches speak.

Unity of Human Speech.

Again, the eleventh chapter of Genesis asserts the original unity of human speech. Modern philology, from merely scientific grounds, has now reached the conclusion set forth in the sacred record, that all the varieties of human language have sprung from one original form of speech.* "And the Lord came down to see the city and the tower which the children of men builded. And the Lord said, *Behold, the people is one, and they have all one language.* . . . Go to, let us go down and there confound their language, that they may not understand one another's speech. So the Lord scattered them abroad from thence upon the face of all the earth." †

Thus does the early part of the Scripture narrative draw to a close. The branches of the family of Shem are catalogued at the end of this eleventh chapter, and we see the name of Abram appear, surrounded by all his kindred. But beyond these circumstances, the truth of great importance is made luminous, that the chosen instrument of revelation, Abram, "the mighty father," is of the same blood and the same original speech with all the tribes of the earth. The diversity that stamps the families of men is the work of the same God who created them and the man now chosen to receive special blessings is the brother of all the rest of mankind. The "confusion" of speech has been sent upon men to check the working of their own evil schemes. The variety of soil and climate has been assigned them in order that Caucasian frosts and Arabian sands and Nile inundations may bring out the peculiar strength and individuality of each tribe and teach unto all their common dependence upon the great Creator and moral Governor of the universe.

---

* Cabell's Unity of Mankind.   † Gen. 11: 5-8.

Origin of the Early Genesis Narrative.

Certain conclusions concerning the origin of the narrative in the first eleven chapters of Genesis may now be set forth.

(1) Most assuredly this story of the antediluvian race is not an old Semitic epic stripped of its pagan deformities by later Hebrew saints and prophets.* The distinct marks of revelation are stamped upon the history in Genesis. This history forms the authentic beginning, acknowledged by the Hebrew prophets and Christian apostles, of the long series of self-manifestations of God that fill up the sacred scriptures. In its essential teachings there is no connection with the series of Babylonian myths.

(2) The narrative is not a compilation from different documents. The claim that there are two creation stories, two stories of the descendants of Adam, two stories of the deluge and two stories of the dispersion of the race from Babel,† is based upon alleged variations in language and style. In so far as these variations exist, they are the natural variety in the usages of human speech in dealing with a variety of subjects. Dr. Driver admits that variation in subject-matter does result in variation in language.‡ Against the general claim, however, we urge the positive evidence for the essential unity of the entire history. So comprehensive in outline, so clear in important details, this brief history of a long period of time excels in compactness and unity any merely human narrative of similar length ever written.

(3) This early narrative as it came down to the Hebrews of the time of Abraham and Moses was most probably a divinely corrected tradition. God Himself appeared from time to time to impart new messages and to give correct views of those preceding. He told Adam the story of creation (Gen. 1: 28, 29; 2: 15). He appeared unto Noah and repeated to him the same story (Gen. 6: 7), even as He told Noah's father, Lamech, about Adam's expulsion from Eden and the curse upon the ground (Gen. 5: 29). To Noah likewise He probably told the story of the offerings of Cain and Abel (Gen. 8: 20, 21, and 9: 5), and of the establishment of the Sab-

---
*Ryle: Early Narratives of Genesis, p. 13.   † Biblical World, Jan., '94.   ‡ Int. to O. T. Literature, p. 110.

bath as the sign of a covenant between himself and Adam (Gen. 9: 6, 9, 15). The story of creation and of the covenant with Noah was very probably recited to Abraham by Jehovah (Gen. 12: 7; 14: 22; 15: 5, 18; 17: 10). Although Abraham knew all this past history from tradition, just as Melchizedek knew it (Gen. 14: 18, 20), Jacob heard a divine message rectifying his knowledge of the past (Gen. 28: 13, 14). As the necessary preparation for his mission, Moses was minutely instructed in the past history of God's revelations and his view of the traditions of his race thoroughly rectified (Exodus 4 and 6) by Jehovah Himself.

This view of a corrected tradition thus seems amply sustained by the facts of the scriptural narrative. It is not at all the Romish view of an infallible tradition in the church. Nay, for in the case of the Genesis narrative, the repeated revelations from God were made in completeness at each time, including those already given from the very beginning.

It would follow from this that the Babylonian myths are *uncorrected* traditions. They are departures from the original revelations delivered before the flood. Until that time, all men alike knew the story of the past. All of Noah's sons knew it. But from that time divergence arose. The old tradition was corrected only in the line of Abraham. The other tribes of men "changed the truth of God into a lie."* Here and there an individual like Melchizedek held on for the space of a few generations to the essential facts of revelation, but afterwards all those beyond the pale of Abraham's house were "given over to a mind void of judgment." †

(4) This period of deterioration is marked in the cuneiform records. These heathen myths required time for downward development. Therefore, the Babylonian stories are conclusive evidence that the revelations of these eleven chapters of Genesis were made at a very early period: in short, they argue the clearest revelations to Adam and to Noah.

(5) But the corrected tradition forming the substance of this narrative was probably not written down until the period of the Hebrew Exodus from Egypt. When Jehovah,

---

*Romans 1: 25. †Romans 1: 28.

God of the fathers of the Hebrew race, appeared unto Moses, He declared that by the name Jehovah was He not known unto those patriarchs.* But in the history of that patriarchal period the name Jehovah does appear as synonymous with the name Elohim. The conclusion is thus forced upon us, that the corrected tradition of the Hebrews was first written after the divine rectification of the history made unto Moses.

* Exodus 6: 3.

PART III.

DIVINE REVELATION CONTINUED IN OPPOSITION TO HEATHEN NATURE-WORSHIP.

[*Genesis 12–50.*]

CHAPTER IX.

ABRAM CALLED OUT FROM THE LAND OF THE MOON-WORSHIPPERS.

THE lesson taught by the flood soon spent its force upon the hearts of the tribes who turned away in disappointment from the tower of Babel. As a tradition in many dialects the story of Noah still lingered down through the years, but it gradually lost its essential character as a narrative of God's judgment visited upon the sins of the race. In many parts of the earth, around new centres did the descendants of Noah now congregate, and very soon there sprang up in their minds visions of other gods. The flesh and the heart of men became divorced from Jehovah and were wedded in iniquity unto the soil of the ground. The beneficent powers of earth, air and sky in the form of water, wind and light engaged the chief interest of superstitious minds and received worship as personal beings of supernatural character. Widespread systems of such nature-worship went on increasing in influence until monarchies and empires were founded upon the supposed dignity and supremacy of the sun and the moon and the stars among the orders of spiritual existence. Iniquity was thus again lifting its unholy power against the government of Jehovah and His previous revelations were now opposed by the active teaching of vast numbers of priests, the sworn votaries of debasing forms of belief and worship. Now, therefore, did Jehovah, as it were, accept the challenge of opposition and declare Himself in the very midst of the most iron-handed despotism that superstition had as yet established. Amidst the orgies of moon-worship on the banks of the lower Euphrates in the imperial city of the early Babylonians was heard his voice. A single family was called out from ancient Ur and led away to be Jehovah's pupils in learning His covenant mercies. Not apart from heathenism, but in presence of its greatest earthly power and stoutest *opposition* were these lessons in tribal and personal religion to be given. Abram and his sons were to be kept in close contact with heathen men in order the more clearly to learn their need of dependence upon God.

Ur of the Chaldees.

It was the grandson of Ham, Nimrod the "mighty hunter," who established the first organized government in the country watered by the Euphrates and Tigris. With a band of his Cushite brethren this mighty leader had, perhaps, forced his way eastward across the desert from the Nile country, and had builded four cities—Babel, Erech, Accad and Calneh—on the banks of the Euphrates as the four corner-stones of his kingdom. Into this Cushite kingdom came strong bands of the sons of Shem to take possession of the land and to impress their race characteristics upon its social and political organization. These Semites learned to inscribe their own history in the cuneiform language. They made the arts of the early Accadians their own; but they made the sun chief of the gods instead of the moon, and thus instituted that form of sun-worship afterwards practiced by the Semitic kingdoms of Babylonia and Assyria. One Semitic family took up its abode within or near the capital city, Ur, and so brought themselves beneath the very shadow of moon-worship. Through Arphaxad, the son of Shem, there arose the family of Eber, called from him, Hebrews. These people moved southwards from the borders of Armenia until they found a home in Ur. In the tenth generation from Noah, the head of this line was Terah, to whom were born three sons. The youngest of these was Abram, to whom Jehovah had allotted the right of spiritual primogeniture over all the races of the earth. The age of Terah at the time of Abram's birth was one hundred and thirty years, and all these years had been spent in worshipping idols. Not Jehovah, but "other gods"* did Terah and his family reverence, and long afterwards his descendant, Laban, gave evidence of his heritage of idolatry by giving the name of gods to the little images concealed by Rachel.† Abram's early years were spent beneath the shadow of that temple whose ruins still stand on the central

---

*Joshua 24:2.   †Gen. 31.

platform of the city of Ur. His eyes and his ears were besieged by the sights and the sounds peculiar to the ritual of the chief luminary of night.

The native Accadians were a cultivated people. The sciences of astronomy and astrology were developed at a very early date among them, and before the coming of the rude Semitic shepherds of the upper plains they had a prayer-book filled with exorcisms and magical incantations. Sargon, the Semitic king of Ur, imitated his Hamitic brethren in his patronage of learning, in his legislation and in his conquests. He brought his countrymen into close contact with the peoples of Syria and Palestine. He started Semitic civilization upon that career of development which wrought out afterwards the splendor of Babylon and Nineveh.

The first form of the Accadian religion was pure sorcery. Popular imagination peopled every object in nature with a good or an evil spirit. These spirits brought health or disease, woe or blessing, and were to be dealt with through charms or the magic of the sorcerer-priest. The character of the latter was about the same as that of the medicine-man of the North American Indians. After a time the Accadians began to deify these forces of nature, and at the head of their hierarchy of gods they placed the moon. The sun held the second place of honor as a god, and temples were erected to him at Erech and Larsa. When the Semites gained control of the country they adopted the entire religious creed of the Accadians and made it a part of their own. Now was the sun given the precedence over the moon, but the queen of night was left in sole possession of the ancient centre of empire, the city of Ur. The Babylonian creed seems to have been a strange mixture, with its Accadian basis of sorcery and the Semitic reverence for the sun, moon and stars. A vast number of hymns were written in honor of these deities of the sky, and the chanting of them was mingled with the wild incantations of the sorcerer-priest.

Among these Accadians and Semites of Ur, real advances in knowledge were gained. The Accadians invented the calendar and the signs of the Zodiac. The art of writing was developed and large works on astronomy and astrology were written at the same time with vast numbers of addresses to the gods. But it cannot be said that there was an upward movement in religious ideas. The last state of these people was worse than the first. A continual terror of evil spirits and demons rested upon the soul of every man. Each hour of the day was filled with a hideous ritual that sought to quiet men's slavish fears by the use of charms and images, or kept them crouching in abject trembling before the shrine of the sun or the moon.

Abram's First Call.

Suddenly there came into this land of spiritual darkness the clear shining of the light. Jehovah broke the silence that had lasted since the days wherein He spake to Noah. After centuries—we know not how many—the thread of divine revelation was again taken up and the man who had the spiritual capacity to see and hear was Abram. The prominence of this new servant of God is attested by contract-tablets lately dug up near his old home bearing the name Abu-ramu (Abram), "the exalted father." His influence was sufficient to remove a great tribe from the metropolis of moon-worship to a home on the frontier of the empire—from Ur to Haran. The Book of Genesis speaks of the exodus as a tribal migration. "And Terah took Abram, his son, and Lot, the son of Haran, his son's son, and Sarai, his daughter-in-law, his son Abram's wife; and they went forth with them from Ur of the Chaldees, to go into the land of Canaan; and they came unto Haran and dwelt there."* The personal names borne by this moving tribe are all Semitic: Sarai is the Assyrian *sarrat*, "queen." Milcah, daughter of Haran, and wife of Nahor, who tarried behind, is the Assyrian *milcat*, "princess."† But the name Haran as the objective point of this journey is a word meaning "the road." This linguistic guide-post, then, reveals the route of this Semitic family. From the southern to the northern limit of the old empire, up the level valley-plain between the Euphrates and Tigris, they took their way. Leaving Babylon on the left and the rising Nineveh on the right, they pushed on to the frontier district of northern Mesopotamia, in which Haran was the chief city. Through it ran the great "road" from the Euphrates region to Syria

---

*Gen. 11: 31. †Sayce: Fresh Light from the Anc. Mon., p. 44.

and Palestine in the west. This city—Haran—was dedicated to the worship of the moon-god. The conical stone with star above it, which was the emblem of this deity, has been found to confirm the other evidence in favor of this view. Through this city some centuries before had Sargon, of Accad, marched across the fords of the Euphrates to the Mediterranean coast. The land of Canaan was, therefore, not unknown in Babylonia. But the first stage in the journey of Terah and Abram left them still beneath the shadow of moon-worship. And beneath its shadow did Terah die. Whatever the impulse that moved the elder chief of this tribe, he never shook himself free from the sight of the idolatrous worship paid the moon. If it was only the roving disposition of Terah that led him away from Ur to Haran, it was the voice of God that moved Abram. "*The God of glory* appeared unto our father Abraham, when he was in Mesopotamia, before he dwelt in Charran, and said unto him, 'Get thee out of thy country and from thy kindred and come into the land which I shall shew thee.'"* We know not what was the manner of God's appearing unto Abram. The sacred narrative simply takes up the thread of divine revelation as made to the descendants of Shem, whom the Lord blessed in Noah's presence. No open vision from the Lord had been granted since He stood among men as the "God of blessing"† and the God of the covenant with Noah. Neither His form nor His face were seen there, nor do these appear in the interview with Abram at Ur. Perhaps the tradition of the rainbow covenant was fresh in Abram's memory, and most probably the Lord gave adequate proof of His divine character in the method of His revelation. At all events the command was understood and acted upon. It touched the main point in the matter of beginning a life of supernatural faith, and it touched no more. Absolute divorce from country and kindred devoted to moon-worship was naturally the first step in such a new life. The objective point of the journey could be left to Him who first of all commanded Abram to *set forth*. Whether he set fire to the temple of the moon-god and thus caused the death of his brother, Haran, who sought to rescue his beloved idols,‡ we know not, but it is cer-

---

* Acts 7: 2, 3.   † Gen. 9: 1.   ‡ Book of Jubilees, ch. 12.

tain that he was not disobedient unto the heavenly vision and "*went out,* not knowing whither he went."* Perhaps the Lord interfered with miraculous power to redeem Abram from perils threatened by the rulers,† as Jewish and Mahometan legends affirm. Perhaps his faith was strengthened by guidance furnished him during the long journey of three hundred miles from Ur to Haran. There at last, however, he established himself and there he dwelt for some years—fifteen or twenty. There was he joined by his brother, Nahor, who was to remain as the head of a rich clan. In future years the descendants of Abram were to return to Haran to seek wives among the posterity of Nahor. At length Terah, the father, was gathered unto his fathers, and lo! the voice of God immediately spake a second time to Abram.

The Second Call.

The second call was more definite than the first, and moreover there was added a threefold promise: "Get thee out of thy country and from thy kindred *and from thy father's house,* unto the land that I will shew thee; and I will make of thee a great nation, and I will bless thee and make thy name great; and be thou a blessing; and I will bless them that bless thee, and him that curseth thee will I curse; and in thee shall all families of the earth be blessed."‡

This second step in Abram's new life was a divorce from the idol worshippers of his own *family.* His *country* and his *clan* were left at Ur, and now at Haran were left the devotees of moon-worship who belonged to his *father's house.* Abram was called to be the head of a new tribe unto which the promise was made of a permanent *home;* in that home the tribe should be made a great *nation,* and, as such, the *source of blessing* to all families of the earth. "So Abram departed as the Lord had spoken unto him; and Lot went with him: and Abram was seventy and five years old when he departed out of Haran."§

The Vision at Sichem.

Across the Euphrates and thence southward through the desert came the new tribal leader. Perhaps he looked upon Damascus as he journeyed onward "unto the oak of Moreh."

---

*Heb. 11: 8. †Isa. 29: 22. ‡Gen. 12: 1, 2, 3. §Gen. 12: 4.

Beneath the spreading branches at Sichem, in the most fertile and most beautiful valley in all Palestine, the patriarch pitched his tent and gathered about him all the souls that had journeyed with him. "The Canaanite was then in the land," but ere Abram came into contact with their religion the Lord appeared unto him.* While Abram was still wondering, perhaps, whether his pleasant abode was beyond the power of the moon-worshippers, he saw and heard the Lord. It is a significant fact that the first *visible* appearance of the Lord was granted to a man just fresh from the sights of moon-worship. It is true, the appearances of the Lord in Ur and in Haran may have been in visible form. But Adam simply heard His voice, and unto Noah he spake, but now unto Abram did he "appear" and speak. The three distinct messages received by Abram in this first stage of his life of faith reached a climax in this vision at the oak of Moreh. The covenant-relationship established with Noah and his sons was now taken as the basis of further revelations. In sharp opposition to the debased teachings of the Chaldean priests, the Lord of Heaven appeared to Abram and made definite promises on condition of obedience. Trusting himself absolutely to the guidance of the divine voice, Abram was led by degrees entirely beyond the bounds of the religion of his fathers. And now appeared unto him the Heavenly Governor to specify in distinct terms the *home* which constituted the first part of the promise. "Unto thy seed will I give *this land.*" The gods and the home of his fathers had he surrendered, but he had gained instead a home and a God of his own, with greater things yet to come. Thereupon, even as Noah had done before him, Abram "builded an altar unto the Lord" and worshipped before Him. As he journeyed southward seeking pasture for his herds, he continued to erect the altar and to "call on the name of Jehovah."† Abram's "faith" was, in fact, the new life opened up to him. He had obeyed the heavenly voice; he had followed its guidance, and now he offered praise and honor to the Lord who appeared to him and made good His promise. Abram had been translated from the kingdom of human superstition to the kingdom of divine revelation,

---

*Gen. 12: 7.   †Gen. 12: 8, 9.

and just at the moment of complete entrance he was granted a vision of his Master.

What was the form of the Lord's appearing we do not know. Since "no man hath seen God at any time," some scholars have supposed that the Son of God appeared here to Abram, as He afterwards did appear as the "Angel of the Covenant" unto patriarchs and prophets. It would be fitting that not the Father but the Son should manifest Himself in indicating the *home* promised Abram, since the Son must be the medium through whom have since been fully accomplished all the promises of power and of blessing accorded unto this father of them that believe.

CHAPTER X.

ABRAM TEMPTED BY THE SUN-WORSHIPPERS.

The Famine in Palestine.

MOVED by the impulse of new and wider hopes, Abram proclaimed the name of Jehovah from every green hilltop between Sichem and the "south country" beyond the slopes of Judah.* But his faith must needs be tried, as silver is tried in the furnace. His experience of Jehovah's power and sovereign love was as yet limited to a narrow range of events. Weakness and error still lingered in Abram's soul, and these must be driven out as by fire. Notwithstanding all this, still was he Jehovah's servant and ever ready to learn Jehovah's will. His faith was real, but it must enter into struggles great and prolonged along the line of deeper and clearer knowledge of the God of revelation.

The tenderest and strongest hope in his new life was the first to feel the touch of the fire. The very basis of all the divine promises was a permanent home for himself and for his seed after him. This rich territory which he explored with increasing delight had been named as his heritage. Even now, as his herds grew in numbers and in value in this land of fruitfulness, Abram felt the joy of increasing ownership. He saw in anticipation his flocks and his tribes spreading over every valley and hill and worshipping under every towering tree. But suddenly the finger of blight was laid upon this fair vineyard, and famine brought grief to the heart of man and beast. The failure of crops and herbage at intervals of various length is a phenomenon peculiar to the land of Palestine. Just now did God so dispose the coming of winds and rains that the resulting desolation served as an instrument for testing Abram's faith.

Another vision now appeared to the Hebrew chief—an earthly vision—the fruitfulness of the land of the sun-wor-

---
*Gen. 12: 8, 9.

shippers on the river Nile. The abundance of food crops that sprang up in the track of that great stream's annual overflow seemed to challenge the vines and the verdure of Abram's rolling land, for these had to await their supply of moisture from the clouds of the sky. At once Abram set out on a journey of exploration. "He went down into Egypt to sojourn there."* There was no surrender of his own land of promise and no surrender of his own God. He did not give up the faith which he had, but he was soon to learn that he needed more than he had. He continued to call on the name of the Lord as he pushed across the wilderness of Shur. No doubt he did this, and no doubt he fully meant to proclaim the name of Jehovah in the fields of Egyptian plenty, but he was also to learn more of the character of Jehovah, whose name he sought to honor. In Egypt he probably found a king of the Hyksos dynasty on the throne.

Abram before the Pharaoh.

The Hyksos power was concentrated at Zoan or Tanis, near the Mediterranean. There the kings assumed the Egyptian title, Pharoah, and surrounded themselves with Egyptian gods. The hearts of shepherds of the desert were beating under Egyptian garments at the court of Tanis, when the shepherd chief, Abram, approached the land of Egypt. But these hearts, though hospitable, as desert-dwellers are, were corrupt after the manner of Egyptian corruptness. The long-drawn-out myths of the sun-worshippers, and their low system of morals, had found welcome at the imperial court of the rude shepherds. They imitated the culture of the more polished children of Ham. They kept scribes in order that they might keep pace with the literary works of the Egyptians, and they have left a papyrus on the subject of geometry to show how far they cultivated the science which was invented by the early dwellers on the Nile. They went so far as to keep standing armies in two fortresses which they built on the frontier of their royal domain. But the canker of Egyptian vice had eaten its way into the souls of these nomadic tribes, and Abram knew it, or guessed it. Therefore did he prepare a

* Gen. 12: 10.

scheme of deception to meet the violence which probably awaited him in the land of Egypt.

The immortality of the soul was the one idea which the Hamitic imagination brought forth on the banks of the Nile, and that idea links pyramid, sphinx and mummy into one long system of theoretical purity and practical abomination. The elaborate myths of Osiris and Ra were merely epic fragments in which the sun-god played a heroic part against the power of darkness. But the refrain of low morality which ran through these myths shows their origin. The sun is at times only an animal of the ground, playing his part in the sky, but never losing his bestial character. The priests chanted sun-worship, but the people practiced the morals of the field and the forest. Such were the possessors of Egypt when Abram drew near from famine-stricken Palestine.

Abram's Falsehood.

So far as the regard for truthfulness was concerned, Abram was not much above the Egyptians. He practiced falsehood in order to escape their enmity and to preserve the honor of his wife, Sarai. Certain writings on papyrus have come down from about the time of Abram[*] and others from the time of Rameses II.,[†] which deal with the social customs of that time. In one of these we are told that the wife and children of a foreigner were seized and made the property of the king, and in the other we are informed of a military expedition sent by the Pharaoh to bring to his harem a beautiful woman and to dispose of her husband by slaughtering him. Now Abram sought to contend against such practices in his case by pure deception. He passed off Sarai as his sister—but that which he had feared befell them. Sarah was taken by the officers of Pharaoh—and then Jehovah intervened to save Sarai, to deliver Abram and to give him a lesson in divine providence. The plague fell immediately and a great awe rested upon the souls of the Egyptians. When Pharaoh learned the truth he dismissed Abram and his people in peace. They went away "rich in cattle, in silver and in gold,"[‡] and richer still in the divine lessons they had learned.

---
[*] Chabas: Les papyrus hiératiques de Berlin. [†] Story of the Two Brothers, Papyrus d'Orbiney. British Museum. [‡] Gen. 13: 1, 2.

The Altar at Bethel.

On the mountain-top at Bethel, by the side of his old altar, as he again offered sacrifice and called on the name of Jehovah,* Abram was a stronger and a wiser man. The God who had kept His word by showing him his future home, had taught Abram that he also must keep his word and speak the truth. Jehovah had manifested His power against the sun-god even as before against the moon-god. Thus did Abram return to his pasture-lands with the new knowledge that not Palestine nor even the valley of the Nile supply temporal needs but Jehovah Himself. He had given this increase of wealth to His servant. He had interfered with miraculous power to teach Abram that not his own shrewdness, not his human schemes could avert danger, but that Jehovah's love watched over him day and night to keep him in all his ways. Therefore did Abram entrust himself to the Lord's keeping and allow the Lord to choose for him when the hour came to separate himself from Lot. The occasion of their separation was the wealth acquired in Egypt. For "the land was not able to bear them, that they might dwell together; for their substance was great."† In the walled towns dwelt the Canaanites, and along the fertile slopes in huts dwelt the rustic Perizzites. In seeking out the pasture-lands, the herdmen of Abram and the herdmen of Lot began to engage in strife. Then the lesson of the Egyptian experience wrought its good result in Abram. Worldliness had been crushed out of his heart and godliness had taken a stronger hold. Contention about cattle and lands could not be engaged in by a man who had so impressively learned that God disposes of both. Abram, therefore, gave Lot the choice of territory.

Abram's Separation from Lot.

Now Lot had not learned as Abram had. The Egyptian fever had seized him with fatal force. The cattle brought up from the Nile were now more to him than his uncle's friendship. They were of more value than Abram's God, of whom he had been told. Further than this, a great worldly vision was floating before his eye. "Lot lifted up his eyes and beheld all the plain of Jordan; that it was well

---

*Gen. 13: 3, 4.   † Gen. 13: 6.

watered everywhere before the Lord destroyed Sodom and Gomorrah, even as the garden of the Lord, *like the land of Egypt*, as thou comest unto Zoar." * Another Nile-region seemed the Jordan plain, irrigated by many waters and rejoicing in plenty, as it were, the very garden of Eden. The cattle of the Nile were already his, and now there seemed to be offered a Nile which he might make his own. The dangers which had beset the tribe in the land of Egypt were no longer in the mind of Lot. Even greater dangers to body and to soul lurked in those districts of the plain, for "the men of Sodom were wicked and sinners before the Lord exceedingly." † Thus had the contact with the sun-worshippers prepared Lot for a still lower grade of morality, and he hesitated not to pitch his tent among the Sodomites. But that same contact with the Egyptian religion had prepared Abram for a higher grade of morality and a clearer revelation from God Himself. As he dwelt still on the hill east of Bethel and watched the departure of Lot toward the plain, so easily seen from that high vantage-point, the Lord spake again in renewal of the former promise. "And the Lord said unto Abram, after that Lot was separated from him, 'Lift up now thine eyes, and look from the place where thou art, northward and southward, and eastward and westward: For all the land which thou seest, to thee will I give it, and to thy seed for ever. And I will make thy seed as the dust of the earth; so that if a man can number the dust of the earth, then shall thy seed also be numbered. Arise, walk through the land in the length of it and in the breadth of it; for I will give it unto thee.'"‡ What an expansion of the promises was here shown the man of growing faith. From his trial by means of Egyptian morality and wealth, Abram had been led up to Bethel to hear again the voice of Jehovah—to have his promised *home* measured off before his eyes, and to have more definite words concerning the second part of the great hope already set before him. The Lord had not forgotten any part of His previous pledges, and now was Abram ready to receive confirmation of this promise, that he should become a great *nation*. His own seed after him were to become "as the dust of the earth," and fill all these hills and valleys that lay be-

* Gen. 13: 10.   † Gen. 13: 13.   ‡ Gen. 13: 14-17.

fore his eyes.   Uplifted with joy and confidence, Abram removed his tent southward until he came to the Oaks of Mamre.

The Home in Hebron.

In Hebron he "built an altar unto the Lord."* There he found the third resting-place since entering Palestine. Sichem, Bethel and Hebron were three great stages in this life of faith. Rich and varied experiences were behind him as he reared the altar at Hebron, and the promises of Jehovah had been made more and more definite. Near Hebron, in the cave of Machpelah, were Abram and Sarai to sleep earth's last sleep. Abram's only personal possession of land in this promised territory was to be that burial-place, bought with silver from the Hittite. But he first came to Hebron, just after his acquisition of a great measure of personal faith in Jehovah, and as he dwelt there from year to year that faith grew to such magnitude that it could reach a hand through time to catch the joy of the perfect fulfillment of all God's promises in the day of Jesus Christ.

---

* Gen. 13: 18.

CHAPTER XI.

THE FAITH OF ABRAHAM CONFIRMED BY THE DIVINE COVENANTS.

FROM the period of Abram's first entrance into the rich valley of Hebron, until he died there, and was laid to rest in the cave of Machpelah by the side of his wife Sarah, the story of the Hebrew Patriarch is drawn out through nearly twelve chapters of the Book of Genesis.* This period covers about ninety years of his life, extending from the year prior to Ishmael's birth, when Abram was eighty-five, until the year of his death at the age of one hundred and seventy-five. This is a period of great development in God's revelations, and of consequent development in the faith of Abram. The twofold growth of knowledge and of Godlike character runs parallel with a line of heathen opposition. God trains the father of the faithful in the very presence of heathen power and heathen belief. The growth in the patriarch's spiritual character is symbolized in the change of his name from Abram, "the exalted father," to Abraham, "the father of a multitude." The progress in God's revelation of Himself and His purposes is symbolized in the covenants made with the chosen leader, wherein Jehovah swears by sacrificial emblems and by Himself that He will make good His promises. A corresponding climax in the patriarch's faith, which was counted to him for righteousness, is revealed in his independence of heathen friendship when he buys a burial-place from the Hittite possessors of his own promised home, and lies down in death with absolute confidence in the power and the truth of Jehovah.

There are other characters introduced into this long history. The weakness and the strength of Abram's wife seems an echo of his own character, and she also is given another name, Sarah, as a sign of the coming blessings. Isaac is already seventy-five years of age when his father

---
* Gen. 14-25: 10.

dies, and a part of Abram's life is taken up with the interests of his son. Esau and Jacob also engage his attention, for they are fifteen at his death. Abram's later years, too, are connected with another line of descendants from Keturah, a second link, as Hagar was the first, with the heathen nations. These minor events are merely echoes of the great conflict which runs through this period of Abram's life. When he turns aside to these important, but subordinate matters, it is only the busy work of the warrior rejoicing in his tent after a new victory. If we fix our attention upon the leading events of this time, we shall find Jehovah leading his soldier-patriarch up to greater strength and wisdom in the very face of the opposition made by the worshippers of Baal and Ashtoreth.

War with Babylonia—The Sacrificial Covenant.*

There were many tribal divisions of the Canaanites, who dwelt on the eastern and western banks of the Jordan river. They were all descendants of Ham, and possessed many elements of Hamitic civilization and religion, but they seem to have used the Semitic form of speech and to have practiced chiefly the forms of Semitic religion. In short, while their blood was Hamitic they were subject to the Babylonian government, language and religious faith. The late discoveries by Mr. Bliss at Tel-el-Hésy confirm this view of a Babylonian civilization among these Canaanite tribes in Palestine. The new period in the patriarch's life opened with a great revolt in the valley of the Salt Sea against the distant power of a new king of Babylonia. From Elam, a district east of the Tigris, a Semitic prince, Chedorlaomer, had issued forth and made himself master of Babylonia. From Shinar and Larsa, or Ellasar, places familiar to Abram's youth, came Amraphel and Arioch, the hereditary kings, to join the nomad tribes of Tidal and the imperial army of Chedorlaomer, monarch of all Babylonia. It was the power of the sun-worshipper and of the moon-worshipper combined that marched westward toward Palestine in battle array. From the valley of the Jordan and the Salt Sea there floated the sounds of battle across the hills to Abram at Hebron. The first battle was joined at Ashtoreth Karnaim,

---
*Gen. 14-15.

"Ashtoreth of the two horns," against the giant Rephaims. It was a battle of the heathen gods—the moon against Ishtar, goddess of the planet Venus. Her name was here called Ashtoreth, and later, among the Phoenicians, Astarte. Her image suggested the idea of a horned figure, and about some great shrine, therefore, was this first conflict. Thence southward did the Babylonian host march, gaining victory after victory, from "the plains of Kiriathaim" to the caves of Mt. Seir and the wilderness of Paran far south of Palestine. Thence northward turned the tide of battle as far as Kadesh and the palm groves of Engedi. Abram had listened to the sounds of war as they passed in a half-circle east and south of him, until now their trumpets were sounding along the cliffs west of the Salt Sea and not far away from Hebron. But the battles had been fought upon the hills and the slopes. In the central valley, about the mouth of the Jordan, there were still five kings unconquered. Sodom was the banner city, and Lot, Abram's kinsman, was allied with the cities of the plain. The veteran army was again victorious over depraved and enervated multitudes. The Babylonian army turned northward, bearing the prisoners and goods that had resulted from a brilliant campaign. The spirit of Abram was roused when the news was brought him of Lot's capture. A force of three hundred and eighteen armed men could he muster from his own tribal household, and besides these, the Hittite chiefs—Mamre, Aner and Eshcol—were willing to bear him company with their tribal contingents. A sudden attack in the far north, near Damascus, gave Abram the victory over his careless enemy, and he returned southward as the favored follower of God and a great hero in the eyes of the kings and tribal chiefs. "And the king of Sodom went out to meet him after his return from the slaughter of Chedorlaomer, and of the kings that were with him, at the valley of Shaveh, which is the king's dale." *

Probably the valley of the Kidron, near Jerusalem, was the "king's dale," whither the kings from the plains east of Jordan flocked to meet the conqueror. The King of Sodom desired to be generous of the spoil recaptured, but Abram refused to place himself under obligation to a king and peo-

* Gen. 14: 17.

ple who led such vicious lives. "And Abram said to the King of Sodom, I have lifted up mine hand unto the Lord, the most high God, the possessor of heaven and earth, that I will not take from a thread even to a shoe-lachet, and that I will not take anything that is thine lest thou shouldest say, I have made Abram rich."* The lesson of faith already learned in the land of the Pharaohs finds fitting illustration in this refusal of Abram to put confidence in earthly wealth and power. The divine assistance has enabled him to defeat Chedorlaomer and to reject the friendship of Sodom. He is the Lord's champion against the moon-god and against Baal and Ashtoreth. Therefore does he turn to render honor to God's priest, Melchizedek, the king of Salem, who likewise stands in the king's dale to do Abram honor. "Salem" was the name then given, it seems, to the fortress afterwards called Jerusalem. Melchizedek was the priest-king who ruled and worshipped there in accordance with God's primitive revelations. From Noah's days most probably the tradition of God's teachings had been handed down, and here in this mountain fortress was a sincere worshipper of the Most High God. The light of these early revelations shone forth for a moment amid the greater glory of the new teachings of Jehovah made known to Abram. As a type of the Son of God was he brought forward without announcement of his genealogy, nor was mention made of the beginning of his priesthood nor the ending of it.† He was God's king and God's priest kept pure and true in the midst of idolatrous nations in order that he might lay his hands in blessing upon Abram's head and so fulfill typically all the promises made to the receiver of new revelations. Melchizedek "brought forth bread and wine . . . and he blessed him, and said, Blessed be Abram of the Most High God, possessor of heaven and earth: and blessed be the Most High God which hath delivered thine enemies into thy hand."‡ Abram recognized the priest as God's representative, and gave to him a tenth part of all the spoil, as an offering due unto the divine giver of victory.

From the scene in the Kidron valley, where Abram had shown his independence of earthly princes and his strong trust in God, the patriarch was called immediately into the

---
*Gen. 14: 22, 23.   †Heb. 7: 1–4.   ‡Gen. 14: 18–20.

divine presence through the word of the Lord. In a "vision" the divine voice said, "Fear not, Abram: I am thy shield and thy exceeding great reward." *

The message was God's answer to His servant just fresh from the field of battle. A new danger had threatened his promised home. The power of the empire of the moon-god had sent its spears across the desert to invade the hills of Canaan. God's power had nerved Abram's arm and had given victory to his small army. But the fear of the Babylonian armies in the future may have crept into Abram's heart. The voice of Jehovah was intended to drive out such apprehension. The God of Abram declared Himself able and ready to make good His promises even on the battlefield. He affirmed that no array of heathen spears could pierce through the shield which His arm interposed between Abram and danger.

Then Abram asked for a sign concerning the promises already made, and Jehovah at once entered into the first solemn covenant with His servant. Beneath the sky, at eventide, the Lord brought Abram out into the plain. "He that shall come forth out of thine own bowels shall be thine heir." . . . . "Look now toward heaven and tell the stars if thou be able to number them; and He said unto him: 'So shall thy seed be.'"† As Abram looked at the stars he counted them not, but he counted the number of times the Lord had already kept His word of promise— he counted the great progress made in the revelation of God's love and wisdom. Therefore he surrendered at once his own human wisdom and accepted God's wisdom. "He believed in the Lord and He counted it to him for righteousness."‡ Abram's supreme confidence in the Lord became the motive-power of a new life, in which his will and choice were always made submissive to God's choice for him. It seems clear that "the Word of the Lord" that brought this vision and made the covenant with Abram was the Second Person of the Trinity—the Son of God Himself. Thus did Abram's faith rest upon the Person of Christ, and with Him was the covenant made. The only revealer of the divine will came in Person to say, "I am thy shield," and He also

---

* Gen. 15: 1.   † Gen. 15: 2–5.   ‡ Gen. 15: 6.

said, "I am the Lord that brought thee out of Ur of the Chaldees to give thee this land to inherit it."*

In the same day with these expanded promises, the Lord made a covenant with Abram, in accordance with the method of making covenants among the nations of that day. The Lord condescended to enter into an obligation after the manner of men, typical of His divine guidance in every detail of the life of His servants. "Take me an heifer of three years' old, and a she-goat of three years' old, and a ram of three years' old, and a turtle-dove and a young pigeon. And he took unto him all these and divided them in the midst, and laid each piece one against another; but the birds divided he not." † From Abram's staple of wealth were these animals selected as a sacrificial offering unto God. It is true they were not presented upon an altar, but the fundamental idea of sacrifice was carried out in the slaughter of the animals. To gain an accurate estimate of this transaction we must consult the cuneiform inscriptions of Babylonia.

As already stated, the name of Abram, Abu-ramu, has been found written on Babylonian "contract-tablets" of a very early date. In the British Museum there are large numbers of these tablets dating back as far as 2400 B. C.‡ They reveal a highly-developed system of law whose aim was the protection of property. The boundaries of property were marked off by *stelae;* deeds to land were formally drawn up, witnessed and sealed.§ On the one side of the contract-tablet are stated the terms of the contract and the names of the contracting parties; on the other side is given a list of the witnesses to the contract, also the date and the name of the king and his country. Sometimes the tablet bears the impression of the seals of the witnesses.‖ Concerning the character of these seals we have definite information from a contract-tablet of the seventeenth year of King Nabonidos, who began to rule in Babylon about 556 B. C. Of course this was long after the time of Abram, but the form of a legal document had probably not changed during all those centuries. On this tablet the seal of Zikir-ukin, the judge, is represented by "a priest standing before a large bird, over which is a star." The seal of Kiribtu is

---

*Gen. 15: 7. †Gen. 15: 9–10. ‡Budge: Babylonian Life, p. 114. §Sayce: Ancient Empires, p. 175. ‖Budge: Babylonian Life, p. 114.

represented by "a priest standing before an altar, over which, on the top of a pole, a cock is seated." The seal of Edir-Bel, the magistrate, is represented by "a priest standing before an animal seated on an altar, behind which two poles are standing."* Sometimes the later Babylonian documents were inscribed on large stones which were set up as boundary-marks. Dr. Oppert has translated one of these stones which contains a deed for a field near Bagdad. The land is described and measured off, assigned by Sirusur as a bridal gift to his daughter; then follow the names of twelve great gods, whose curses are invoked upon him "who will venture to take away the boundary-stone." † From these facts it seems clear that these ancient worshippers of the sun and the moon were accustomed to make contracts in the presence of their gods, and to invoke their aid by means of animal sacrifices. According to a human rite clearly understood by Abram, Jehovah entered into a contract with the patriarch. The favor granted was all on the divine side. Abram stood as the recipient of great gifts promised, but the Lord condescended to ratify Abram's title to the land by a formal contract. The boundaries of the future home were clearly specified. "Unto thy seed have I given this land, from the river of Egypt unto the great river, the river Euphrates:

The Kenites and the Kenizzites and the Kadmonites,
And the Hittites and the Perizzites and the Rephaims,
And the Amorites and the Canaanites and Girgashites and the Jebusites." ‡

So ran the terms of the agreement with reference to God's gift. To impress upon Abram the part which he must bear in this contract, just as the sun was going down upon the sacrifice which he had prepared and guarded from the attacks of the birds of prey, "a deep sleep fell upon Abram; and lo! an horror of great darkness fell upon him." § That faith which Abram had already manifested must remain steadfast through the darkness of coming trial. Not without suffering and struggling on the part of Abram and his seed were they to receive the promised inheritance. "And he said unto Abram, 'know of a surety that thy seed shall be a stran-

---

* Budge: Babylonian Life, pp. 120, 121.   † Budge: Babylonian Life, pp. 121, 122.   ‡ Gen. 15: 18-21.   § Gen. 15: 12.

ger in a land that is not theirs, and shall serve them; and they shall afflict them four hundred years; and also that nation whom they shall serve will I judge; and afterward shall they come out with great substance.'"* A definite reason for the postponement of the time of Abram's complete possession of the land is written down in the contract. Abram's seed must gain strength and substance by suffering. They are not yet ready to hold the land. Nor is the cup of Amorite iniquity yet full. The present holders of the land have not yet run that complete course of sin which shall forfeit their right to this territory. But when the time of the contract shall have been extended to the specified limit, then Abram shall have been "buried in a good old age," and "in the fourth generation" his greatly multiplied seed shall come hither and possess their estate."†

Then followed the ceremonial that completed the covenant and made it binding on both parties. On such occasions it was customary for the contracting parties to walk between the divided victims as a symbol that they were made one by the shed blood. Abram was then to walk between the parts of the sacrifice for himself, but Jehovah sent an emblem of His power and wisdom to represent His personal presence. "And it came to pass that when the sun went down and it was dark, behold a smoking furnace and a flaming torch that passed between these pieces."‡

In a manner sublime and terrible did Jehovah manifest His presence. It was an act of the deepest condescension that Jehovah should thus swear unto Abram by the blood of this sacrifice. It was a revelation of the love and mercy of an infinite Ruler who set up this memorial of Himself as an act of defiance to the heathen gods who claimed the land and the people thereof. It was the first link in that great chain of federal covenants with which He bound Abram unto Himself forever—covenants which He inaugurated by an oath upon the blood of these victims and which He completed when He swore by His own divine personality.§

The Egyptian Hagar—The Covenant of Circumcision.

Scarcely had the first covenant been ratified in the presence of the sacrificial victims when Abram and Sarai showed

---
*Gen. 15: 13-14.   †Gen. 15: 16.   ‡Gen. 15: 17.   §Gen. 15: 16.

their sympathy with the social standards of Egypt and Babylonia. Polygamy was a popular institution among the heathen of that day, as it is now. The custom of the people about her suggested to Sarai the expedient of giving her handmaid, Hagar, unto Abram to be his wife—the same custom suggested to Abram to follow Sarai's wishes. Both were prompted by the highest motive—both thought that they acted in accord with the letter and the spirit of the covenant already made with Jehovah. In that solemn agreement, an heir was promised Abram, but it was not specified that Sarai should be his mother. Sarai's advancing age and the custom of the people of the land suggested to her that the handmaid might legally become the mother of the promised heir. The impatience of both Abram and Sarai led them to adopt a scheme of their own devising in order to bring about the promises of Jehovah. Ten years had already passed since their first entrance into the land of Canaan, and now they determined to wait no longer for the fulfillment of the long-deferred promise. "And Sarai, Abram's wife, took Hagar her maid, the Egyptian, after Abram had dwelt ten years in the land of Canaan, and gave her to her husband, Abram, to be his wife."* This imperfect faith in yielding to heathen custom brought its results of strife and hatred between Sarai and Hagar. The maid no doubt thought herself the favored one of God, the future mother of the promised heir. The Lord saw and heard her affliction. He visited her in the desert of Shur and made promise of a seed that "shall not be numbered for multitude."† But her pride was rebuked by the further declarations of the Lord, which were not in accord with the promises covenanted with Abram. His seed should be a blessing—but Hagar's a curse. By that fountain of water in the wilderness where Hagar sat desolate and exiled, the angel of the Lord, who was the Son of God Himself, declared that this union of Abram with Hagar was outside of the terms of the covenant. Ishmael, her son, shall be a "wild ass among men; his hand will be against every man and every man's hand against him."‡ There was no warrant of blessing to all the families of the earth in such a prophecy as that. In quiet submission, Hagar returned to the patri-

---
*Gen. 16: 3.   †Gen. 16: 10.   ‡Gen. 16: 12.

arch's home, and there for thirteen years did Abram attempt to train the wayward Ishmael. Then came another vision, calling him into closer covenant with the Lord.

The meaning and purpose of this second agreement were indicated in God's declaration of Himself and His command to Abram, "I am the Almighty God; walk before me and be thou perfect."* All power was claimed by the Lord in the very title with which He announced himself to Abram. "The Almighty God" was not surely in need of the help of Abram in bringing the promises to pass. For thirteen years the character of Ishmael had been a burden on Abram's conscience. It had been, no doubt, for long, a thought in his mind, that the connection with the Egyptian had not tended to establish the reign of universal blessing foretold concerning his offspring. Now came a revelation, like a clap of thunder out of that dark cloud of anxiety, declaring the character of the Lord who had entered into covenant with him. God is able to make good all His promises; He is fully competent to devise means to further His own purposes. But on Abram there rests the responsibility of a perfect walk and conversation. The heathen-like act of taking Hagar as his concubine has not only been a willful distrust of God's power to keep His promise, but it has shown a defect in his moral character. Hitherto, the whole course of God's revelation has tended to draw Abram away from heathen gods unto Himself. Now has Abram taken a step contrary to the current of those revelations. He has shown a temporary weakness of faith, and has attempted to bring a heathen custom into the furtherance of God's plans. Now does God speak to draw Abram closer to Himself in a covenant, the ratifying bond thereof to be circumcision.

As Abram lies on his face and hears the voice of God, the terms of the second covenant are made known to him. The former promises are renewed, and Abram's name is changed to Abraham as a sign that he shall be made a father of many nations."† God declares that this covenant is made of His own free gift to Abram, and he repeats the promise that Abraham shall be a father of kings and a possessor forever of this land of Canaan. The terms of the cove-

---
*Gen. 17: 1.   †Gen. 17: 5.

nant thus outlined are exactly the same with the terms of the first covenant. But then, over the sacrifice the Lord condescended to swear to Abraham to keep the promises. Now is a solemn duty laid upon Abraham and his seed, and the bond is this time exacted from him. "And God said unto Abraham, Thou shalt keep my covenant, therefore, thou and thy seed after thee in their generations. This is my covenant, which ye shall keep between me and you, and thy seed after thee; every man-child among you shall be circumcised."*

The first covenant was a solemn contract, as it were, in which Jehovah bound Himself after a manner familiar to Abraham. This second covenant is a solemn contract in which Abraham is told that there are certain conditions to be made binding upon himself, to be symbolized by circumcision.

There is no adequate evidence to show that circumcision was practiced among the Babylonians or Egyptians before the time of Abraham. Herodotus and other Greek writers made affirmation that the Egyptian priests of their day made this ceremony a part of their ritual—and Herodotus further made some loose statements about the antiquity of the rite among the people of the Nile. Certain heiroglyphics on the pyramids are supposed by some to represent circumcision.† If this be the case, then Abraham may have seen the rite during his visit to Egypt, and, therefore, God simply gave a new meaning to an old ceremony, as in the days of Noah, He pointed to an existing phenomenon, the rainbow, as the sign of His new promise unto mankind. At all events, circumcision was a ceremonial part of that covenant-relationship which Jehovah was establishing between Himself and Abraham. It was intended as a token of Abraham's complete separation from the heathen nations about him. This separation must be both physical and moral—the body must be a living sacrifice unto God, and the soul must be perfect before Him. From the covenant terms we may easily draw the meaning of the rite: (1) Circumcision is the token of complete physical and spiritual consecration to the Almighty God; for unto Abram, just after seeking alliance with the Egyptian, Jehovah said, "I am the

---

* Gen. 17: 9, 10.   † Wilkinson: Rawlinson's Herodotus, p. 52.

Almighty God; walk *before me* and be thou perfect."* (2) This covenant is to be an everlasting covenant, binding both body and soul unto God." "I will establish my covenant . . . . to be a God unto thee and to thy seed after thee . . . . and my covenant shall be in your flesh for an everlasting covenant."† (3) Circumcision is to be the badge of a distinct society or nation of people, isolated from all others and devoted unto the Lord: "He that is born in thy house and he that is bought with thy money must needs be circumcised. . . . . And the uncircumcised man-child whose flesh of his foreskin is not circumcised, that soul shall be cut off from his people; he hath broken my covenant."‡

Not until this divine scheme had been unfolded to Abraham was he told that Sarai should be a party to the covenant, the mother of the promised heir. "And I will bless her and give thee a son also of her; and she shall be a mother of nations; kings of people shall be of her."§ In token of this future royal lineage, Sarai's name was changed to Sarah, from the Assyrian *sarrat*—"princess." At this disclosure, Abraham was carried beyond himself with astonishment, and "he fell upon his face and laughed and said in his heart, 'Shall a child be born unto him that is an hundred years old?'|| But his joyous wonder was changed in a moment to grief, for he cried aloud concerning the exclusion of his wayward boy, Ishmael, "O, that Ishmael might live before thee."¶ Then the Lord declared His gracious purpose to continue the covenant with his unborn son, Isaac, and with his seed after him. Nor did he forget the promise made to Hagar of a numerous offspring, for in answer to Abraham's cry, the Lord said, "As for Ishmael, I have heard thee; behold, I have blessed him and will make him fruitful and will multiply him exceedingly; twelve princes shall he beget, and I will make him a great nation."** Then Abraham arose and ratified this great covenant by the circumcision of himself and of every male among the men of his house. The ceremony was a solemn dedication of his household unto God; and very fitly was Ishmael included therein. Afterwards he cut himself off, keeping up the rite of circumcis-

---

* Gen. 17: 1. † Gen. 17: 7, 13. ‡ Gen. 17: 13, 14. § Gen. 17: 16. || Gen. 17: 17. ¶ Gen. 17: 18. ** Gen. 17: 20.

ion, but losing the spiritual meaning thereof, and thus casting away all his spiritual privileges as a member of Abraham's household. Henceforth, Abraham was committed to a divine policy in all things. His human method of bringing to pass God's promises had been discountenanced and miraculous means were foreshadowed. The laughing astonishment of Abraham when God announced so wonderful a fulfillment of promise, was referred to by our Lord Himself as the expression of wonder and joy: "Your father, Abraham, rejoiced to see my day, *and* he saw it and was glad."* The Apostle Paul lays special emphasis upon this great advance in Abraham's faith when he cut loose from things seen and cast himself completely upon the operation of things unseen: "Without being weakened in faith, he regarded not his own body now as good as dead (he being about a hundred years old), and the deadness of Sarah's womb; but looking at the promise of God, he wavered not through unbelief, but waxed strong through faith, giving glory to God, and being fully assured that what He had promised, He was able also to perform. *Therefore,* it was imputed to him for righteousness."†

Sodomites and Philistines—The Covenant of the Oath.
(*Genesis 18-22.*)

Abraham was now the sworn liege-man of Almighty God. The invisible King of Heaven had made use of visible signs in completing the covenant between Himself and His chosen creature. Now was Abraham plunged into the midst of a furnace of fire in order that his allegiance might be tried, even as the character of gold is tried. The fire which God used in testing the character of His servant was a heathen flame. Heathen customs and religious rites were burning at a fierce heat all about the home of Abraham. Into close contact with these was he brought, but he bore the test unscathed and proved himself the man of faith. Let us glance at the incidents connected with this fiery ordeal.

The tent of the patriarch was pitched in the midst of that same oak-grove of Mamre, where close communion with God had already taken place. Here was the scene of the clearest revelation of Himself thus far made by Jehovah unto Abraham. In visions had His word previously come to

---
* John 8: 56.   † Romans 4: 19-22.

Abraham. Now appeared an angelic-human Person who spoke with the authority of God Himself. From his tent-door in the heat of the day, Abraham lifted up his eyes and saw three men approaching. With eastern hospitality he offered them water and food. As they ate beneath the shade of the trees, one of these three men distinctly claimed to be Jehovah Himself, in asserting that Sarah should bear a son. Then departed the three men, but Abraham walked with them, until the fate of Sodom and Gomorrah was revealed to him by one of these men speaking as Jehovah. In the presence of Jehovah, manifested in this human form, Abraham stood and pleaded for Sodom. The promise of mercy was extended to Sodom on condition that ten righteous men be found therein. Meanwhile, as the patriarch interceded for the city and home of his nephew, Lot, *two angels* appeared at Sodom's gate at the evening hour and were entertained by Lot. These two angels were evidently two of the three men who had appeared unto Abraham at midday, and who left him in conversation with the Lord. The third *man* or *angel* who tarried behind on the hilltop overlooking the Jordan valley and made known Himself and His plans to Abraham was very probably Jehovah, the Son of God, the Revealer of the Godhead.

What an impressive object-lesson was spread out before the patriarch as he stood before the living God. The sentence of death passed upon Sodom and Gomorrah because their sin was grievous; a spiritual cause for temporal destruction; the visible and the invisible worlds governed by a divine being who can appear in visible form to speak the invisible will of heaven. Never in all his life was there a time when the meaning of *righteousness* could have been more effectually stamped upon Abraham's mind and heart.

The people of Sodom and Gomorrah were members of the Canaanite tribes then established in the land. Their chief deity seems to have been the Babylonian Istar. Reference has already been made to Chedorlaomer's first battle in the vale of Siddim at "Ashtoreth of the two horns." Around the temple of this goddess, represented by a horned figure, the profligate dwellers in the lower Jordan valley made a stand. The story of the destruction of the cities of the plain by fire from heaven, reveals the moral degradation of the devotees of the whole Babylonian creed—the leprosy of moral and spiritual iniquity that had eaten its way into the souls of an entire people, so that the only purification possible had to be effected by fire. This statement made to Abraham by the divine messenger was a volume of revelation in itself. Then the indignity offered to the angelic guests of Lot; the deterioration of character in Lot, and in his wife and daughters, were other flashes of light showing to Abraham the moral danger of heathenism. The subsequent development of this creed of Istar in the Phœnician orgies connected with the worship of Astarte was not seen by Abraham, but even these could scarcely have produced the shock upon the patriarch's feelings which he did experience at the incestuous origin of the Ammonites and Moabites. Most probably the cities of the plain were already worshipping the Babylonian Bel or Baal. Perhaps they were offering human sacrifices to this god, for he soon became the patron deity of the Ammonites under the name of Moloch, and of the Moabites and Midianites under the titles of Baal-Peor, and of Chemosh. The Moabite stone, inscribed by King Mesha about 900 B. C., claims Chemosh as the national deity of Moab. To Ashtar-Chemosh, King Mesha "devoted" the captured women of Nebo.* This was the same god to whom Mesha offered his own son in sacrifice. Perhaps the beginnings of this horrible ritual were to be seen in Sodom and Gomorrah. The moral revulsion that swept over the spirit of Abraham was exactly the impression which God's prophets sought later to convey when they spoke concerning heathen creeds. In the very beginning of his revelations to a chosen race, the clearest spiritual lesson was taught to Abraham by means of heathen immorality and heavenly fire.

In thoughtful mood, Abraham betook himself southward and pitched his tents among another tribe of Canaanites, the Philistines. Egyptian manners seem to have been in vogue in these grassy plains of the South, and the patriarch dropped into the sin which he had committed during his journey to the court of Pharaoh. The Lord intervened again with miraculous power to save Sarah from the Philis-

---
* Fresh Light, p. 74.

tine prince, Abimelech. As he turned away, laden with the gifts of the shepherd prince, Abraham must have felt the goodness of God in bringing happy results out of his mistakes. In this south country, when Abraham had reached the age of one hundred years, Isaac was born to Sarah. More than ever before Abraham seemed to recognize the bonds of his heavenly allegiance. At God's command he dismissed Hagar and Ishmael, and accepted Isaac as the covenant child. With the Egyptian woman went a goodly number of Abraham's mistaken views. He dwelt now in quietness at Beersheba, protected in his possession of the pasture lands and the well of water by the oath of Abimelech. In the shelter of a tamarisk tree of his own planting, he rested in the protecting power of "Jehovah, the God of eternity."* The covenant had brought him into close personal relationship with the Lord. Twice had he made intercession to save Sodom and to save Abimelech. God's justice and God's mercy were unfolded to him against the wide background of God's holiness. The faithfulness of God was likewise a growing truth as Abraham watched the increasing stature and intelligence of his son Isaac. In connection with this heir of the divine promises came the final test of Abraham's faith. "It came to pass after these things, God, testing Abraham, said unto him: Abraham! And he said, Behold, here I am. He said: Take thy son, thine only one whom thou lovest, Isaac, and go to the land of Moriah, and offer him there as a burnt-offering upon one of the mountains that I will tell thee."†

Perhaps the Canaanites had already begun to offer human sacrifices as they did afterwards to Ishtar-Chemosh and to Moloch. The altars in Sodom may have been disgraced even in Lot's day with the blood of human victims. Or, at least, the cruel orgies connected with the Babylonian creed as practiced by these Hamitic cities of the plain, may have presented a religious devotion which seemed stronger than Abraham's devotion to his God. The strength of the patriarch's devotion was to be tested. Abraham's obedience to Jehovah must be more implicit than the obedience of the idolater to the supposed wishes of his god. A command came to Abraham from God. The command itself was

---

*Gen. 21: 33.   † Gen. 22: 1, 2.

counter to his own wishes and counter to God's previous teaching that he must not imitate heathen morals and religious customs. But the speaker of the command was God, and obedience was his first duty. Abraham had accepted Jehovah as his absolute ruler, and hence Jehovah's command was the law of life to him. With unquestioning speed, the patriarch obeyed. Early the next morning he began his journey northward from Beersheba to Mount Moriah, on whose summit the Temple of Solomon was afterwards builded. The third day brought Abraham and his son near to the place of sacrifice. The attendants were dismissed, and father and son alone climbed upward to the hilltop. The love of the father was undiminished. "Then Isaac spake to Abraham, his father, and said: My father! and he said, Here am I, my son; and he said, Behold the fire and the wood; but where is the lamb for the burnt-offering? Abraham said, God will provide Himself the lamb for the burnt-offering, and they went both together."* Every step taken by the patriarch upon that upward journey was a step of victory. The darkest cloud that had yet appeared in his career now seemed to be settling down upon his beloved son and upon his hopes for the future. But behind the cloud was Jehovah, who said unto him, Go, and Abraham went. His faith was strong enough to change that which seemed darkness into light. There was absolute confidence in his heart where there might have been despair. "And they came to the place which God had told him, and Abraham built there the altar, and laid the wood in order, and bound Isaac, his son, and laid him on the altar upon the wood. And Abraham stretched out his hand and took the knife to slay his son."†

The man's uplifted arm was the sign that his faith had pressed forward to the last act of blind obedience. In Abraham's purpose the sacrifice was completed and his own human love and human hope were already offered up to the obedience which he owed to his God. "Then the angel of Jehovah called to him from heaven, and said: "Abraham, Abraham! And he said, Here am I. And he said, Stretch not out thy hand against the lad, and do nothing to him,

---

*Gen. 22: 7, 8.   †Gen. 22: 9, 10.

for now I know that thou fearest God and hast not withheld thy son, thy only one from me."

"And Abraham lifted up his eyes and saw, and behold a ram in the rear had entangled itself in the thicket with its horns; then Abraham went and took the ram and offered him as a burnt-offering in the place of his son."* Thus did Jehovah set the seal of his disapproval upon the practice of sacrificing human beings. Service and not the sacrifice of human life does He require. Moreover, the distinction of meaning between God the Creator and God the Redeemer was made in the names under which He appeared here to Abraham. *Elohim*, the Creator, tested him by giving the command to sacrifice his son; but *Jehovah*, the Revealer and Redeemer, caused him to stay the hand. These are names of one and the same godhead, but they disclose two parts of His divine character. It was Jehovah, the Redeemer, who now entered into the final act of the great covenant with His servant. "And the angel of Jehovah called to Abraham a second time from heaven, and said: *By myself have I sworn*, saith Jehovah, that because thou hast done this and not withheld thy son, thine only one—that I will bless, yea bless thee, and increase, yea increase thy posterity like the stars of heaven and like the sand which is on the seashore; and thy seed shall take possession of the gate of their enemies: and in thy seed shall all the nations of the earth be blessed, *because thou hast obeyed my voice.*"† Upon what a lofty plane was Abraham here elevated. The great promise which was at first declared to be God's gift was now declared to be the spoil won by Abraham's faith. The promises were doubly his. He stood here as the greatest victor of all time, with the single exception of our Lord Jesus Christ. Upon this mountain-top of faith which Abraham named, "Jehovah Sees," the patriarch first conquered himself in offering Isaac. Then he further won Isaac back again as the progenitor of an offspring countless as the stars of heaven, or as the sands upon the sea-shore. He won Isaac back as the father of a future race of victors, whose faith shall give them the gate of their enemies, and moreover bring a blessing upon all the nations of the earth. But beyond all these things, Abraham won the covenant of the

---

*Gen. 22: 11, 12, 13.   †Gen. 22: 15-18.

oath. Hitherto had God promised and had symbolized His truthfulness according to a human method, but now He swore by Himself. The covenant was complete and the promises were bound unto Abraham by the very nature of God Himself. As the writer of the Epistle to the Hebrews declares: "When God made promise to Abraham, because He could swear by no greater, He swore by Himself. . . . . For men verily swear by the greater: and an oath for confirmation is to them an end of all strife. Wherein God, willing more abundantly to show unto the heirs of promise the immutability of His counsel, confirmed it by an oath. That by two immutable things [His word and His oath] in which it was impossible for God to lie, we might have a strong consolation who have fled for refuge to lay hold upon the hope set before us."*

Human faith can be lifted to no higher pinnacle than that upon which Abraham stood. Out of the toils of hostile heathenism he was lifted up until he was face to face with Jehovah—until his obedience was reckoned as something divine. Unto such faith Jehovah was willing to bind His own nature by an oath. The divine Spirit had, in fact, passed into Abraham, and had enabled him to show a love for God greater than his love for himself. In the purpose which he had of offering his son, Abraham became a symbol of the Father himself, "who spared not His own son, but freely gave Him up for us all." † The son Isaac, whom he won, was the type of a victory in the interest of the whole human race. Isaac's sacrifice typified the death and resurrection of our Lord. As Paul said: "Now to Abraham and his seed were the promises made. He saith not, And to seed, as of many; but as of one, 'And to *thy seed*,' which is Christ." ‡ For himself and for all believers, in all time to come, had Abraham won heaven and God. Upon that mountain was the divine oath sealed to him, and the covenant was established forever. The author of the Book of Genesis has left us only one or two glimpses of the patriarch's life after that great transaction. In the retirement of Hebron, in the midst of his family and his flocks, we see him passing on down to his earthly limit of one hundred and seventy-five years. He bends in tender grief

---
* Heb. 6: 13, 16–18.   † Rom. 8: 32.   ‡ Gal. 3: 16.

over the tomb of Sarah. He buys the cave of Machpelah as the burial-place for all his dead. He perhaps makes a mistake in marrying Keturah, but at least her descendants are the sons of peace. He takes care about the marriage of his son Isaac, attends to the disposition of his property among his long line of heirs, and then lies down in peace to sleep with his fathers. But his work was finished on Mt. Moriah. As the friend of God he stood there, and will stand for all coming ages.

CHAPTER XII.

THE CHOSEN RACE KEPT PURE.

[*Genesis* 25: 11; 50: 26.]

WHEN Abraham gave up the ghost and was gathered to his fathers, Isaac was already seventy-five years of age. Since Esau and Jacob were born when Isaac was sixty, these two grandsons were fifteen when the patriarch passed away to receive the fulfillment of the promise in another world. Yet, ere he died, Abraham saw the character of Jacob unfolded along the line of his future career as the heir of the covenant. Let us recall Abraham's tender care in the selection of Isaac's wife Rebekah, and his probable part in making known to Rebekah the will of the Lord concerning her two sons.

The Marriage of Isaac.

After Jehovah had tested the faith of Abraham by the command to offer up Isaac as a burnt-offering, the young man had continued to dwell in his father's tent and among his father's flocks at Beersheba. Under the shelter of his father's stronger character, and in close contact with the imperious Sarah, his mother, did Isaac spend these years of early manhood. Of retiring, contemplative disposition, his grief was naturally keen when he lost his mother's wise care. From the age of thirty-seven until that of forty, Isaac was bereft of female companionship. Then Abraham bestirred himself to find for Isaac a wife of his own race. According to Eastern custom, he caused his servant, Eliezer, of Damascus, perhaps, to place his hand beneath his thigh and swear "by the Lord, the God of heaven and the God of the earth, that thou shalt not take a wife unto my son of the daughters of the Canaanites among whom I dwell. But thou shalt go unto my country and to my kindred and take a wife unto my son Isaac."* In addition to this oath that

---
* Gen. 24: 3, 4.

the wife of Isaac must be of Abraham's own house, he further made condition that Isaac himself should not return to Haran where his kindred dwelt. Out of the land of promise, Isaac must not depart. The servant was told that the angel of the Lord would go before to give success to the mission. As he drew near to the city of Nahor, in Mesopotamia, this servant appealed to Jehovah for assistance in the selection of Isaac's future wife. It was the Lord who prospered Eliezer's suit for the hand of Rebekah, the daughter of Bethuel and the granddaughter of Nahor. The latter was elder brother of Abraham, and hence the young people, Isaac and Rebekah, were first cousins once removed. The maiden seemed to recognize the will of God in the offer of marriage and willingly came to be the wife of Isaac. It was evening twilight at Hebron when Isaac saw Rebekah approaching. He led her to his mother's tent, and from that time was comforted from the grief occasioned by Sarah's death. Rebekah's active and ardent nature furnished a fitting supplement to the non-assertive character of Isaac. For many years they dwelt quietly in the south country by the well Lahai-roi.

The Birth of Esau and Jacob.

Few and unimportant were the events that made up the life of Isaac. In the land of the Philistines the experience of Abraham was repeated in his son's career. Divine power interfered to save Rebekah even as Sarah was formerly preserved. A quarrel arose about the self-same wells that Abraham had digged, and a new covenant was ratified between Isaac and Abimelech. But meanwhile the faith of Rebekah was put to the severest test. The barrenness of Sarah and her longing for a child were repeated in the life of Rebekah. For twenty years she waited, until both Isaac and Rebekah were led to see that the promised heir must be God's gift. Just as Jehovah interposed to give Isaac unto Sarah, so must He be the Giver of a son unto Rebekah. "Isaac intreated the Lord for his wife, because she was barren."* The Lord heard the prayer of Isaac, and also He revealed unto Rebekah that she should bear two sons and that "the elder shall serve the

---

* Gen. 25: 21.

younger."* How this communication was made to Rebekah we are not told. "She went to inquire of the Lord," † and it seems natural to suppose that she made this inquiry through Abraham, the priest of his own tribe. As in former days, the Lord may have appeared to the patriarch now to mark out the relative destiny of the two grandsons of Abraham and Sarah. Even before their birth, the Lord's will marked out the younger as the bearer of the sceptre over his elder brother. Abraham watched over their growing years and saw the character of Esau developing as a man of the field, skilled in hunting, while Jacob inherited the simple tastes of Abraham and Isaac, and remained steadfastly at home in the tents or near the flocks. The honor and prestige of his father's family were dear to Jacob. Therefore was he quick to offer the pottage to the weary and famished Esau on condition that the rights and privileges of the eldest-born son of the house should be transferred to him. Perhaps this trait of selfishness was apparent in the character of Jacob ere his grandfather died. Perhaps Abraham was told by Jehovah that this youth who set great value on the family history, who listened eagerly to the story of the divine promises, who watched over the increase of the family's herds and flocks while his brother amused himself in the chase—that this stripling should not only bear temporal rule over the elder brother, but should likewise hand down in his own line the promises already made unto Abraham's seed.

Jacob's Family Pride.

Pride of race was the basis of Jacob's natural character. As a controlling instinct, it blinded his early years to proper views of justice and truth. Sanctified by the power of God's Spirit, it rendered him in later years the exemplary tribal chieftain of the twelve divisions of God's chosen family. That elevation of spirit which Abraham naturally experienced in being made the instrument of divine revelation, now became in Jacob the leading characteristic. Hence was Jacob led to commit some of the mistakes that marked the life of Abraham and of Isaac. We have seen how these two patriarchs attempted to take into their own hands the

---

*Gen. 25: 23.   †Gen. 25: 22.

furthering of God's plans and how they were rebuked. Each of them used deception to save his wife from dishonor, and in each case God intervened to show that He was caring for the purity of these two mothers of the chosen race. In like manner did Jacob fall into the error of attempting to do God's work for Him.

Unto Rebekah the clear statement had been made by Jehovah that the younger of her two sons should rule the elder. Jacob was clearly the heir of the covenant according to this specific utterance of Jehovah's will. Perhaps the knowledge of this prophecy led Jacob to be a close dweller in the home-tent. By anticipation he felt the weight of the family name resting upon him. He therefore seized the first opportunity to extort from Esau a formal renunciation of all rights and privileges belonging to the first-born. They already belonged to Jacob by virtue of the revelation made to his mother—but this quiet yet enthusiastic guardian of the family hearth now showed a selfish spirit in demanding the rights of the first-born in exchange for a mess of pottage. His zeal for the family name led him into positive sin. The position of tribal chieftain—of patriarch of God's chosen family—which was intended for him as God's gift, to be bestowed in God's own way and in His own time, this was now eagerly snatched by Jacob from the dull and sensuous Esau as a mere matter of barter and sale. In the minds of both Jacob and Esau, the Jehovah of their fathers had yet a small place. Esau was indifferent to the birthright and Jacob was indifferent to the authority and power of Jehovah concerning this affair. Jacob had yet to learn that it was the headship of God's family to which he was called, and that he must act in strict submission to God's will.

It was this same family pride that led Jacob to use deceit and falsehood in obtaining Isaac's blessing. Whether consciously or unconsciously, Isaac was clearly in the wrong when he desired to give the benediction of tribal headship to Esau. He knew God's previous choice of Jacob for this position and all the attendant blessings. His haste and anxiety in the whole transaction is apparent. Did his conscience smite him? Perhaps it did. At any rate, the conscience of Jacob and of his mother, Rebekah, were not strong enough to prevent deception, nor was Jacob kept back from invoking the name of Jehovah upon his false oath. "And Jacob said unto his father, I am Esau thy first-born; I have done according as thou badest me: arise, I pray thee, sit and eat of my venison, that thy soul may bless me. And Isaac said unto his son, How is it that thou hast found it so quickly, my son? And he said, *Because the Lord thy God brought it to me.*"* How wonderful a change seemed to come over the parties engaged in this transaction when Jacob called upon the name of the God of his fathers. Absolutely erroneous were his views concerning Jehovah. Nevertheless, the divine touch seemed to open the eyes of Jacob and of Isaac. " And Isaac called Jacob and blessed him and charged him, and said unto him, *Thou shalt not take a wife of the daughters of Canaan.* Arise, go to Padan-aram, to the house of Bethuel, thy mother's father, and take thee a wife of the daughters of Laban, thy mother's brother. And God Almighty bless thee, and make thee fruitful and multiply thee, ... and give thee the blessing of Abraham, to thee and thy seed with thee; that thou mayest inherit the land wherein thou art a stranger, which God gave unto Abraham."† After receiving this blessing, Jacob hurried away. The anger of his brother Esau was threatening. Rebekah supposed that a few months would heal the quarrel and that Jacob might return with a wife from Padan-aram and at once be recognized as the successor of Abraham and of Isaac.

But Jehovah had a long course of training marked out for Jacob. As the young man lay down to rest from his journey at Bethel, he was inducted through the gateway of a dream into the presence of God Himself. In his dream, Jacob saw "a ladder set upon the earth, and the top of it reached to heaven; and behold the angels of God ascending and descending on it. And behold, the Lord stood above it and said, I am the Lord God of Abraham, thy father, and the God of Isaac; the land whereon thou liest, to thee will I give it and to thy seed; and thy seed shall be as the dust of the earth, ... and in thee and in thy seed shall all the families of the earth be blest. And, behold, I am with thee and will keep thee in all places whither thou goest."‡ After all his sharp practice, Jacob found that his title to the land rested not in Esau's surrender of his birthright

---

* Gen. 27: 19, 20.   † Gen. 28: 1–4.   ‡ Gen. 28: 12, 15.

nor even in Isaac's blessing, but in the deed of gift from Jehovah. He found further that the family at whose head he sought to place himself is God's family. The oil which Jacob poured upon his stone-pillow at Bethel, dedicating it as a symbol of God's house, was the first oil of consecration poured upon Jacob's own life. It was his first sight of things heavenly; his first glimpse of the God of his fathers. Instantly a new career seemed to open up before him. "And Jacob vowed a vow, saying, 'If God will be with me and will keep me in this way that I go, and will give me bread to eat and raiment to put on, so that I come again to my father's house in peace; *then shall the Lord be my God.*' " *

From that time forth Jacob's life was upon a higher plane. Chivalry and generosity began to find a place in his nature. Voluntarily did he make the proposition to Laban that he would serve him seven years for Rachel. These seven years seemed to him but a few days " for the love he had to her."† At the end of his term of service when Laban imposed Leah upon him instead of Rachel, even as Jacob himself had deceived his father, Isaac, there was no long complaining, for Jacob cheerfully served another seven years for the younger daughter. He found greater joy now in being the victim of treachery than he found in those earlier days in practicing deception.

Then spake the angel of God unto Jacob in a dream, commanding him to return to the land of Abraham and of Isaac. Another great crisis of his spiritual development was at hand. Forty years had passed since Jacob departed from Palestine. The anger of his brother Esau had not yet been appeased. But the goal of Jacob's ambition was virtually gained. He was the patriarch of an increasing family. He was rich in cattle. God had blessed him in giving him wives from his mother's kindred and in exalting himself and his tribe. His race-pride was increased, although he followed the guidance of Jehovah in most of the affairs of his life. Yet now did he fall into grievous error. His own shrewdness came to the front with a plan to appease Esau's wrath. It is true Jacob appealed to Jehovah for deliverance from the armed bands of his brother. But he seemed to trust to the siege-train of flocks and herds and camels which he sent

---

*Gen. 28: 20, 21.   †Gen. 29: 20.

in detachments to beleaguer the heart of his brother. A succession of gifts, he thought, would gain the day over the covetous nature of his brother sooner than any manifestation of God's power. In short, Jacob seemed to drop back to his earlier state of mind and heart, and to rest success upon a transaction of barter and sale with Esau rather than place implicit trust in Jehovah. As he tarried behind alone, by the brook Jabbok, anxious about the effect of his gifts, there wrestled a man with him until the breaking of the day. And when He saw that He prevailed not against him, He touched the hollow of his [Jacob's] thigh; and the hollow of Jacob's thigh was out of joint as He wrestled with him. And He said, "Let me go, for the day breaketh." And he [Jacob] said, "*I will not let thee go, except thou bless me.* . . . And he blessed him there, and Jacob called the name of the place Peniel ['the face of God'], for I have seen God face to face, and my life is preserved."* From this hour Jacob bore the new name given him by the divine wrestler, Israel, or God's Prince. His family pride had been sanctified. His ambition was attained through God's gift and not through his own craft. It was not Jacob, the supplanter, who entered into the land of promise, but it was Israel, God's patriarch. Therefore, the altar which he erected at Schechem, perhaps the Sichem of Abraham's time, was set up unto the God of his fathers, under the title, "God, the God of Israel."† Yet one more struggle remained ere Israel cut himself loose from heathen connections and heathen ideas and became in all things God's man. The fertility of the soil at Schechem attracted him, and he pitched his tents too near the tents of the Canaanites. The disgrace of his daughter Dinah, and the resulting slaughter of the Schechemites by Simeon and Levi, opened the patriarch's eyes to the danger of all heathen associations, and made him willing to hear God's command. Jacob had forgotten the vow made unto God so many years before at Bethel. Now he commanded his household, " Put away the strange gods that are among you, and be clean, and change your garments ; and let us arise and go up to Bethel, and I will make there an altar unto God, who answered me in the day of my distress, and was with me in

---

*Gen. 32: 24, 30.   †Gen. 33: 20.

the way which I went."* There by the stone of Bethel did Jehovah appear to Jacob and confirm unto him the name Israel; moreover, he repeated unto Jacob the promises made before to Abraham—that he should be a great nation under God's patriarchal control to scatter a blessing over all the earth.†

The Descent into Egypt.

When Jacob and Esau laid away the body of their father Isaac in the family burial-place in Hebron,‡ Joseph had spent already several years in the land of Egypt. From the most probable arrangement of the chronology of the life of Isaac and Jacob,§ we know that the seventeen-year-old Joseph was sold to the Midianite merchants about eight years before the death of Isaac. The grandfather mourned with the father Jacob over the disappearance of the favorite child, Rachel's first-born. Probably Isaac comforted Jacob by relating how Jehovah had ordained the headship of the tribe in a manner contrary to the first wishes of both Abraham and Isaac. Abraham loved Ishmael, and Isaac loved Esau, and Jacob loved Joseph, and now it perhaps occurred to Isaac that God was preparing to hand down the primacy according to his own plans. In very truth, ere Isaac died, the first movement had been made in furtherance of God's purpose announced to Abraham: "Thy seed shall be a stranger in a land that is not theirs, and shall serve them."‖

The narrative which relates the descent of the chosen family into Egypt¶ opens with a series of contrasts. The dukes of Esau's line with their heathen tribes and principalities are first named as representatives of a race-ideal which all of Jacob's sons might have followed but from which they were saved by the guiding power of Jehovah. Then follows a second contrast between Joseph, the inheritor of Jacob's race-pride, the dreamer of dreams, wherein he saw his own exaltation, and his brethren who were moved by malignant envy. Then again, the purity of Joseph's character and his implicit confidence in Jehovah far away in Potiphar's house and in the royal prison, are set in contrast with Judah's unholy alliance with Canaanitish women.**

---

* Gen. 35: 2, 3.   † Gen. 35: 9, 15.   ‡ Gen. 35: 29.   § Speaker's Com. I.: 178.   ‖ Gen. 15: 13.
¶ Gen. 36: 50.   ** Gen. 38 and 39.

Yet, ere this narrative closes, we are told that Judah's line shall hold the sceptre until the promised Saviour shall spring from the same source.* The meaning of it all must be that the power of God can mingle Canaanitish elements with the Abrahamic seed—that the offspring of the Babylonian votaess, Tamar, may be merged into the line of Isaac and Jacob—and His geople still be kept pure in the faith. What means, then, the Egyptian sceptre which Jehovah soon places in the hands of Joseph? It does not mean the establishment of Joseph's line as the direct heir of the promises, but it means the use of Joseph as an instrument for the education of the twelve tribes. As we read the record of Joseph's advancement at Pharaoh's court through his interpretation of dreams and through his practical administrative ability, we see the clear working of the power and wisdom of God Himself.

Joseph's Governorship.

About two full centuries elapsed from Abraham's visit to the Nile until Joseph was appointed to the office of Adon [President] "over all Egypt."† The entire life of Isaac, one hundred and eighty years, had passed away in this interval. The Hyksos kings were still holding court at Zoan, upon the Tanitic branch of the Nile. They made use of the Semitic tongue as an official language along with the Egyptian. The Pharaoh gave orders to proclaim in the Semitic language, an *abrek*, "bow the knee."‡ He gave to Joseph the title, *Zaphnatpa'neakh*, which means "Governor of the district of the place of life." Now the monuments have shown us that all the land of Egypt was divided into a number of *districts*, or nomes, for the convenience of civil administration. They have further revealed a special name given to Pithom, the capital of the Sethroite nome in the eastern delta region; this name was "The place of life." Therefore, the simple meaning of Joseph's official position was that he was made the governor of that province whose capital was Pithom. This district was made up chiefly of the pasture-lands of Succoth, and contained other fortresses and towns, as Etham and Migdol, connected with the later Exodus of the Hebrews. In this same district was On, the city of the

---
*Gen. 49: 10.   †Gen. 45, 9; Brugsch, p. 124.   ‡Brugsch, p. 122.

Sun. Joseph was now united in marriage to the daughter of the chief priest of his district. The names of his wife, Asenath, and of his father-in-law, Potipherah, belong to the ancient Egyptian language, and probably indicate the ancient lineage of this priestly family. In this manner was Joseph closely connected with the attempt of the Hyksos kings to extend the ancient Egyptian laws and religion over the delta region.

What were some of those laws? If we search among the inscriptions that belong to the time of Usertsen I., an early king of the Twelfth Dynasty, who ruled centuries before the time of Joseph, we find a report made by the "governor of the province of Mah." He writes: "I was a kind master, of a gentle character, a governor who loved his city. . . . . All the works for the palace of the king were placed in my hands. . . . . No child of the poor did I afflict, no widow did I oppress, *no landowner did I displace, no* herdsman did I drive away, from no 'five-hand master' (small farmer) did I take away his men for my works."* The tombstone of Mentu-hotep, another official of Usertsen, thus describes the royal servant: "A man learned in the law, a legislator, one who apportioned the offices, who regulated the works of the nome, who restored order in the whole land, who carried out all the behests of the king, and who, as judge, gave decisions and *restored to the owner his property*." Likewise, Mentu-hotep, as the king's representative, "imposed the taxes on the north country."†

Another king of this Twelfth Dynasty, Amen-em-hat III., constructed a great artificial lake, which the Greeks called Lake Moeris. In the valley called the Fayûm, that nestles between the hills on the western bank of the Nile above Memphis, this king built dams and excavated a basin, and into this he led the water of the Nile by a canal. Near this lake the king built the famous Labyrinth, a structure composed of twenty-seven palaces. From this magnificent residence he could direct the irrigation of the delta from the reservoir of Moeris whenever the Nile failed to supply the ordinary overflow water.

These facts, drawn from a period long prior to that of Joseph, indicate the existence in Egypt of fixed laws of

---

*Brugsch, p. 61.   †Idem, p. 63.

land tenure; a system of statutes deriving their authority from the will of the monarch; a judicial administration arranged under certain departments, the chief of which were *public works, taxation* and *war.*

Therefore, Joseph was not merely governor at Pithom, but Pharaoh's chief minister "over all the land of Egypt." The public policy inaugurated by Joseph may have been the attempt of the Hyksos king to fasten his power more completely upon his subjects. Concerning Pharaoh's dreams of the seven fat kine upon the bank of the Nile devoured by the seven lean kine, and of the seven good ears of corn devoured by the shrivelled ears, "Joseph said unto Pharaoh, The dream of Pharaoh is one; God hath showed Pharaoh what He is about to do. . . . . Behold there come seven years of great plenty throughout all the land of Egypt: And there shall arise after them seven years of famine . . . . . . and the famine shall consume the land."* Then went Joseph forth with royal authority to collect a double tax during the years of plenty. The ordinary revenue that went into the king's coffers seems to have been one-*tenth*. But Joseph collected one-*fifth* from the abundance of the first seven years; he "gathered corn as the sand of the sea, very much, until he left numbering; for it was without number."†

In due time sore famine spread "over all the earth." Throughout the seven years it continued. Joseph's storehouses supplied the need of all, but in selling the corn he advanced the royal authority of his patron. When money and cattle and herds and horses and asses were all given up for corn, then "Joseph bought all the land of Egypt for Pharaoh; for the Egyptians sold every man his field, because the famine prevailed over them: *so the land became Pharaoh's*." . . . . Only the land of the priests bought he not; for the priests had a portion assigned them of Pharaoh. . . . . . Wherefore they sold not their lands."‡ Thus Joseph declared that in future the people should hold and use the lands only as the king's tenants, on condition that they render to their lord a yearly *fifth*. "*And* Joseph *made it a law* over the land of Egypt unto this day that Pharaoh should have the fifth part, except the land of the priests

---

*Gen. 41: 25-30.   †Gen. 41: 49.   ‡Gen. 47: 13-22.

only, which became not Pharaoh's."* The probable meaning of this transaction is this, that the people in the time of Joseph's Pharaoh were made to recognize the fact that they must hold their land by royal permission. The priests remained in full possession of their estates. The religious order was still exalted above the military and civil orders, as the monuments fully affirm. Perhaps this Pharaoh was of the Hyksos dynasty, just now enforcing the ancient prerogatives of the native Egyptian kings and collecting a double revenue in order that he might build public canals for the irrigation of the land in time of drought.

We do know positively that the chosen family was now brought into close contact with a nation possessed of an elaborate system of law. The love of Joseph for his own people secured them a fertile land for a dwelling-place. Under God's own guidance came Jacob and all his family. "And Israel took his journey with all that he had and came to Beersheba and offered sacrifices unto the God of his father, Isaac. And God spake unto Israel in the visions of the night and said, 'Jacob, Jacob.' And he said, 'Here am I.' And He said, 'I am God, the God of thy father; *fear not to go down into Egypt; for I will there make of thee a great nation. I will go down with thee into Egypt; and I will also surely bring thee up again.*'"†

There are three reasons here apparent to account for the migration of this tribe into the land of Egypt:

(1) For the first time in its history the family of Jacob was treated as a distinct nation. The best of the land—the land of Goshen—was ceded to Jacob and his sons as a pasture-land for their flocks. As a nation upon terms of equality with the great empire of Egypt, Jacob was received as an ally and friend. Pharaoh received Jacob himself as he would receive a foreign monarch, and in accepting Jacob's blessing, the monarch of the Nile seemed to exalt his guest even above himself. It was Jehovah's favor alone, acting in miraculous manner through the exaltation of Joseph, that bestowed the same exalted dignity upon Joseph's brethren as a united nation.

(2) The family of Jacob was now planted in a sheltered home of great richness where it might grow and increase in

---
* Gen. 47: 26.   † Gen. 46: 1–4.

numbers and in wealth without molestation from enemies. It had become evident that the land of Palestine, as the permanent possession of Israel, must be fought for and held by force of arms. Of course, Jehovah would fight the battles of His people, but they must be numerous enough to garrison the land. There was need of a quiet seed-bed in which to grow. It was found in Goshen. There were they left severely alone by the Egyptians, "for every shepherd is an abomination unto the Egyptians." No intermarriages would be sought by these sons of Ham. The purity of the race and the strength thereof could be made to increase in no spot more rapidly than in the secluded home in Goshen.

(3) In connection with the Egyptians, the family of Jacob could learn the advantages of a system of statute laws. Among the Babylonians there were many customs that had the force of unwritten laws. But at that time the civil and canon law of Egypt was more thoroughly elaborated than in any other land upon the face of the earth. The sons of Jacob looked on while Joseph enforced the authority of one supreme monarch; and yet there were statutes to check the arbitrary wish of any Pharaoh inclined to play the despot. These heads of the tribes of Israel now, in fact, were entering upon a course of training. The supremacy of a king, connected with the supremacy of written law, were facts which Jehovah afterwards used at Sinai as means with which to burn into the hearts of the people of Israel His own authority as king and lawgiver.

Jacob's Dying Blessing on His Sons.

This supremacy of Jehovah in keeping His people pure and in making them to sit in the seats of honor among men was left to Jacob's family as their inheritance. As the sons gathered about the dying bed of the patriarch, his thoughts rested upon Palestine as the promised possession of his family. There he desired to be buried, and there he saw the line of his son, Judah, bearing the sceptre until the promised deliverer should come. He swore each of his sons to be faithful unto the God of his fathers. The gods of Egypt influenced Jacob only so far as to increase his trust in the promises of his own God. In this far-off land of exile, he died, pointing to the exalted strength of his own nation in the generations yet to come.* Likewise Joseph died and his embalmed body was kept in a coffin in Egypt. But Joseph's commands and Joseph's faith still lived in the hearts of his brethren and pointed them away from Egypt and her institutions unto better things. "God will surely visit you and bring you out of this land unto the land which he sware to Abraham, to Isaac and to Jacob."† As the years passed on, the covenant promise of Jehovah wrapped itself about the affections of this people more and more until the time was ripe for the divine power to draw them away from Egyptian influences and train them in pure religion and undefiled in their own home in Palestine.

---

* Gen. 48 and 49.   † Gen. 50: 24.

PART IV.

DIVINE REVELATION IN CONFLICT WITH HEATHENISM.

Exodus 1–19.

CHAPTER XIII.

ISRAEL IN EGYPT.

NOW have we reached a great crisis in the growth of Israel. The chosen family is ready to assume the garb and name of a distinct nation among the people of the earth. God's nation has come to years of maturity. Distinctive institutions, a home and a mission must be formally adopted. The home has already been marked out in the covenants between God and the three patriarchs of the race. The institutions and the mission are now to be assigned. Whence shall come the formal statutes and the national ideals to be used in guiding this nation in its future course? Not from the Babylonians and the Egyptians, nor from their gods, but from Jehovah himself. Jehovah has given the land of Palestine as a home. He must also declare the ideal way in which His people shall walk. In making known His will, it must be remembered, Jehovah uses human things and earthly as secondary agencies. The institutions of Egypt form one great means of instruction for Israel in the land of Goshen. The civil and religious statutes of the people of the Nile do not form the basis of the code of laws given to Israel at Sinai. That code is framed in the courts of heaven, and delivered to the people through God's servant, Moses. But the laws of the Egyptian play a part in educating the Israelites and in making them ready to understand and adopt God's law. They have learned in Egypt the necessity of some formal ritual, of some elaborate code of civil regulations ; and lo! now does Jehovah Himself hand down from heaven the law. It bears no relation to the law of Egypt, except that of contrast and opposition. In the lightning that flashes all around the sky, in the thunder that rolls from Sinai, the descendants of Jacob hear a divine form of speech declaring that they must be separate and distinct from all other nations upon the earth, and must be a nation holding intimate and peculiar relationship with

Jehovah. The story of this great transaction is recorded in the early chapters of the Book of Exodus—a great epic narrative, wherein we see Jehovah overturning the sun-god Ra, and leaving him forever conquered on the banks of the Nile.

The Growth of the People of Israel.

The number of years during which the Israelites sojourned in the land of Goshen was four hundred and thirty.* The aggregate number of people who departed out of that land, under the guidance of Moses, was six hundred thousand men able to march.† Supposing these to make up about one-fifth of the population, we find a vast host approximating three millions of souls fleeing out of Egyptian bondage. The historian begins his narrative by enumerating the heads of *families* that came into Goshen with Jacob. Now we know from the history of Abraham that the size of the household was great. He ruled over a family containing three hundred and eighteen armed servants. If we allow this number as a moderate estimate of those who made up each family in Jacob' tribe, we find that more than three thousand souls entered into Egypt in Joseph's time as the nucleus of the nation that numbered nearly three million in the time of Moses.

The early years of this long period are briefly described as a time of growth in numbers and in power. Joseph and all the people of his generation passed away, and the Israelites were still left in peace. They "were fruitful and increased abundantly, and multiplied and waxed exceedingly mighty ; and the land was filled with them." ‡

The Store Cities—Pithom and Raamses.

The increasing power of the Israelites within the Egyptian territory brought fear to the new dynasty of kings that began to reign some time after the death of Joseph. The "new king over Egypt, which knew not Joseph," § was a member of one of the royal families who reigned after the expulsion of the Hyksos line of kings. The ancient Egyptian princes had asserted their hereditary rights, had driven out the shepherd kings, and were now in constant terror by

---

*Exodus 12: 40. †Exodus 12: 37. ‡Exodus 1: 7. §Exodus 1: 8.

reason of these foreign dwellers in Goshen. The new king said unto the people, "Behold the people of the children of Israel are more and mightier than we : come on, let us deal wisely with them ; lest they multiply, and it come to pass that when there falleth out any war, they join also unto our enemies and fight against us, and so get them up out of the land. *

A distinct policy of oppression is outlined in this royal manifesto. The ultimate aim of the policy is to render the Israelites perpetual slaves. They must be kept in Egypt as serfs of the soil. Their old liberty is taken away. The allies and friends of Joseph's time are now treated virtually as slaves captured in war. Therefore the Egyptians "did set over them task-masters to afflict them with their burdens."†

In constructing the public works and fortifications of a military empire were the Israelites first employed. "They built for Pharaoh store cities, Pithom and Raamses." The spade of the excavator has brought these two "cities" to the surface, and now can we read the name of this Pharaoh who oppressed Israel. The story of this discovery dates back to Napoleon's invasion of Egypt. In making a survey of the Nile country, a French engineer was making his way along the site of an ancient canal running from Suez to Cairo. On the canal bank he found an elevated mound, marked by a half-buried monument of granite. The monument was a single stone, cut into the form of an arm-chair, on which were seated three figures in priestly garb. On the back of the chair was cut a series of hieroglyphics. But the secret of this strange form of speech was yet hidden, and for many years after the visit of the French engineer the place was known in the Arabic tongue as Tell-el-Maskhutah, " the mound of the statue."

Then came another engineer from France, De Lesseps, to dig the Suez canal. Midway between the two ends of the great ditch was fixed the house of the contractors; a little village soon sprang up here, and the modern name of Ismailiya still clings to the place. Twelve miles toward the south was Tell-el-Maskhutah. From that place were brought the three-figured statue, a red-stone tablet, two black-granite

---
* Exod. 1: 9, 10. † Exod. 1: 11.

sphinxes and a recumbent sphinx with a human head, and these were given the seat of honor in a public square at Ismailiya, a place which they continue to hold.

Ere this twelve-mile journey of the stone figures, enough of the inscription had been deciphered to show that the trio in the chair are none other than Rameses II., seated between the two sun-gods Ra and Tum. Hence arose the conjecture that the mound whence came the sculptured gods was Raamses, one of the "store cities" built by the enslaved people of Israel. Then at length in the year 1883 A. D., the scholar and explorer, Edouard Naville, came upon the scene to make known the whole truth.

First of all, Naville carefully read the inscriptions upon the objects at Ismailiya. He found all the stones dedicated to the god Tum. On both sides of the red-stone tablet this deity appeared. With a human head wearing the crown of all Egypt, and with a hawk's head wearing a solar disk, did Tum present himself. Then Naville, from these facts, drew the conclusion that the mound near the old canal is not Raamses, but *Pithom*. He was enabled to make this conjecture by supposing that the name Pithom is simply compounded of two words, Pi and Tum, "the abode of Tum."

In the year 1884, the work of Naville's spade proved his conjecture to be correct. An entire town was found beneath the sand at Tell-el-Maskhutah. The town is built in the form of a square, inclosed by a brick wall twenty-two feet thick, and measuring six hundred and fifty feet along each side. Nearly the whole of this space is occupied by solidly-built square chambers, divided one from the other by brick walls, from eight to ten feet thick, which are unpierced by window or door, or opening of any kind. About ten feet from the bottom the walls show a row of recesses for beams, in some of which decayed wood still remains, indicating that the buildings were two-storied, having a lower room which could only be entered by means of a trap-door, used probably as a store-house or magazine, and an upper one, in which the keeper of the store may have had his abode. Thus far the discovery is simply that of a "store-city," built partly by Rameses II.; but it further appears, from several short inscriptions, that *the name of the city was Pa-Tum or Pithom;* and there is thus no reasonable doubt that one of the two

THE STORE CITIES. 171

cities built by the Israelites has been laid bare, and answers completely to the description given of it."* The sacred historian in the book of Exodus further states that "the Egyptians made the children of Israel to serve with rigor: and they made their lives bitter with hard service, *in mortar and in brick.*† In corroboration, the walls at Pithom now show that the bricks were "laid with mortar in regular tiers." In addition to all this, some of the brick at Pithom were made with *straw* and some without it, an apparent confirmation of the practice enforced by the next king of Egypt when straw was for a time not furnished to the Israelite toilers.‡ Other inscriptions show that Pithom was the official capital and metropolis of a district known as Succoth, a Semitic word meaning "camp."§ The pasture-lands immediately around Pithom, in the district of Succoth, were the first rallying-place of the Israelites after the march from Raamses in the days of the exodus.‖ This second "store-city," Raamses, has also been brought to the light by Naville and identified with Phacûs, situated on a branch of the Nile, between Pithom and Tanis.

To sum all the facts together, modern learning and excavation have restored to our sight the toiling Hebrews under their cruel oppressor, Rameses II. The bitterness of their slave-life may be read in the colossal works carried to completion in these brick-fields of the delta region. Likewise, the inscriptions show us the motive of the king in constructing these military magazines. "Lest they join themselves unto our enemies and fight against us" was the fear of Rameses II., as set forth in Exodus. The hieroglyphics show that the fear of foreign enemies of the Semitic race, some of whom dwelt not far away to the eastward of the land of Goshen, filled the later days of Rameses with unrest. We have seen how he advanced into western Asia against the powerful Hittites. At Kadesh he defeated them, after great deeds of personal valor on his part. Over many a temple wall in Egypt was spread the epic poem of Pentaur, celebrating the prowess of the royal warrior. The cities of Canaan were captured at a later time, and many prisoners were borne away to the banks of the Nile. Then Rameses entered into peaceful alliance with the king of the Hittites and received the latter's

---

*George Rawlinson. †Exod. 1: 14. ‡Exod. 5: 10. §Brugsch, p. 96. ‖Exod. 12: 37.

daughter in marriage. Unto Zoan-Tanis, in the delta region, Rameses now returned, and there established a court of great splendor. He became a great public builder. His own statue was set up in every part of his kingdom. Temples arose in his honor at Abydos, Memphis, Thebes, and at Abou Simbel, in Nubia. Besides all these memorials, he has left his great line of military fortifications in the land of Goshen. Tanis was his capital. Branching out from this centre, there sprang up at his royal command a series of fortresses, commanding the highway across the Isthmus of Suez from Arabia into the delta region. Between Tanis and the head of the Red Sea were built the "store-cities," Pithom and Raamses, as the chief links in the great military chain drawn across this isthmus gateway. From his palace-towers Rameses looked out eastward and saw the tribes of western Asia ready to fall upon his kingdom. Between himself and these enemies he saw the growing population of Israel. By their toil he thought to build up breastworks against the threatening danger, and so the cruel edict went forth that Israel, in Egypt, should no longer be freemen but slaves in hard bondage.

At the same time the decree of Heaven seems to have gone forth that the plots of the King of Egypt should come to naught. The sacred historian does not make the distinct assertion, but the tone of the narrative undoubtedly indicates that God exerted His power in causing His people to increase under adverse conditions. The intention of the Egyptian king was to check the growth of Israelitish population. The methods of oppression which he used had no doubt worked successfully against other enslaved peoples. Not so with the children of Israel. "The more they afflicted them the more they multiplied and grew. And they were grieved because of the children of Israel."* The followers of Pharaoh were filled with mortification and with alarm at the failure of their scheme. "With rigor," therefore, did they press additional work upon the Hebrew slaves; "in all manner of service in the field"† did they compel them to toil. In digging canals, in draining swamps, in irrigating the hot plains, did these Hebrews continue to delve where malaria and pestilence lurked. But God preserved His

---

* Exod. 1: 12. † Exod. 1: 13, 14.

children and made them to increase. He had flung down the gage of battle before the princes of Egypt and before her gods. At every point He showed His might in bringing to naught the national policy of Pharaoh. As that policy increased in harshness God intervened with greater manifestations of might. He made the walls of Pharaoh's palace a place of refuge from Pharaoh's vengeance. He caused a leader of His people to be trained in the arts of war and peace in Pharaoh's schools. He used the royal power of Egypt in raising up Moses and then turned him against the empire of the Nile to crush the power thereof and to establish His own empire forever.

Moses and Pharaoh.

Failure followed the systematic oppression ordered by Pharaoh. The Hebrews did not sink beneath it, but increased the more. In his great anger, the king had recourse to systematic murder. The new-born male children of the Hebrews must die. Again did God interfere to thwart the scheme. The midwives, chosen as the instruments of murder, *feared God!* "Therefore God dealt well with the midwives: *and the people multiplied and waxed very mighty.*"* Then did Pharaoh enjoin all his people that they should become his tools in a wholesale slaughter of the newborn sons of the Hebrews. The king was determined to bury the race of Israel beneath the waters of Egypt. Then did God intervene with miraculous power to save Moses from the Nile and to make him great in the presence of the King.

The most prominent element in the life of Moses, even from the beginning, is the miraculous intervention of God in saving and in training him. Both his parents, Amram and Jochebed, were of the house of Levi. A temporary curse had been pronounced upon the family of Levi by Jacob,† but now did God take up a son of this house in order that He might change the curse into a blessing. Human ideas were not followed in the selection of a Hebrew leader. From a tribe resting under a shadow was he taken. Not the elder son, Aaron, but the younger son, Moses, was chosen, just as Jacob was preferred before Esau and Isaac before Ishmael.

---

*Exod. 1: 20.   † Gen. 49: 5–7.

174   THE ORIGIN OF THE PENTATEUCH.

The shrewdness of Moses' mother was the instrumentality used in preserving the young child from the edict of the Pharaoh. She probably knew the habits and disposition of the daughter of Rameses II. If we can trust the tradition handed down by Philo* this princess was married and childless. As a devotee of the Egyptian religion, a part of her daily worship consisted in bathing in the sacred stream of the Nile. A little boat of papyrus leaves was floated there, and within the boat was the young Hebrew child. The princess, with her maiden, discovered the boy. The babe's tears stirred up compassion in the heart of the Pharaoh's daughter. She recognized the features of the Hebrew; no doubt she remembered the cruel statute of the king. She evidently saw the skillful plan of the Hebrew mother, and at once made herself a party to it. Miriam, the sister of the child, was watching near. She ran to call the mother, and soon the child was in Jochebed's arms in her own home, but safe from the edict and now under the protection of the royal house of Egypt. "And the child grew and she brought him unto the Pharaoh's daughter, and *he became her son. And she called his name Moses.*"† What a wonderful thing had God wrought in Israel. The destined leader of this people saved from Egyptain cruelty by Egyptian hands, adopted into the royal household of the Pharaoh and bearing an Egyptian name! As the legal son of the Egyptian princess, Moses would naturally become "learned in all the wisdom of the Egyptians."‡ The early instruction of his Hebrew mother formed the basis of his education. His spiritual development never departed from the line marked out by this pious daughter of the house of Levi. But his mental growth was hastened by the wide range of learning known to the Egyptians. Heathen literature was the agency used, but God was the great Teacher of his servant Moses.

The Royal University at Heliopolis.

The monuments indicate the fact that the capital of Rameses II. was Zoan-Tanis, on a branch of the Nile, in the land of Goshen. This is supposed to be corroborated by the fact that Moses was there exposed on the river in a frail boat without fear of crocodiles—since these animals are not

---
* Vit. Mosis, 1: 4.   † Exod. 2: 10.   ‡ Acts 7: 22.

found at all along the Zoan branch of the Nile. Most probably, Moses was allowed to mingle from time to time with his father's people, there to learn more and more of the past history of his race, their hopes and their present grievances.* But his habitual place was at the king's court, under the supervision of royal tutors. The customs and the daily life of the Egyptians are clearly revealed on the monuments. Some facts in connection with the education of Moses may here be mentioned.

Figured upon the monuments are wrestlers and swordsmen. Athletic games like those of the ancient Greeks are pictured and written about. Most probably the "goodly child" of the house of Levi would excel in these manly sports.

Above all things Moses was taught to read and write the Egyptian language. Since this was expressed chiefly in signs and pictures, proficiency in writing meant skill in drawing. Great attention was paid to language as a science. The grammar and vocabulary of the hieroglyphic tongue were discussed by learned scholars. But in addition to all this, we find evidence bearing on a fact of great significance in the life of Moses. Already have we mentioned instances of Semitic words incorporated into the Egyptian language. Besides these, there are many documents of the time that show a clear knowledge of a Semitic dialect. It seems to have been a popular custom with the scribes of the time of Rameses II. to transliterate word after word from the Hebrew tongue. Then, the tablet found at Lachish by Mr. Birch, containing a letter to the king of Egypt in the Babylonian tongue shows that a Semitic dialect was used by the Egyptian officials before the time of Rameses II. Further than this, the mummy of Rameses himself, now in the museum at Cairo, shows traces of Semitic physiognomy. It seems probable that he was of Semitic extraction. Combining this evidence, we find almost conclusive proof that Moses learned to *write* in Egyptian characters his own mother tongue. If the Hebrews had not yet formed a written speech, what is more probable than the supposition that Moses elaborated and developed the language of the

---
* Exod. 2: 11.

Israelites while he was making wide studies in the literature of the people of the Nile?

In that day the chief seat of learning was Heliopolis, the "city of the sun," not far away from Zoan toward the south. This place was also the principal seat of the national worship of the sun. The religious and educational centre of Egypt was Heliopolis, at once the Oxford and the Canterbury of the Nile country. The Egyptian name of this sacred city was On. Here dwelt and worshipped Poti-pherah, the father of Asenath, the wife of Joseph. Here in Moses' time stood the four tall granite shafts erected by an earlier king of Egypt, Thothmes III. The mummy of this old king, now in the museum at Cairo, had already lain for years in the royal tombs near Thebes. Moses saw not him, but the Hebrew youth looked upon those obelisks which have become the trophies of western nations. One of these obelisks stands now in Constantinople, one in Rome, one in London and one in Central Park, New York. At the entrance to the great temple of the sun stood these towering stones, like petrified sunbeams, and between them passed the worshippers as they entered to offer sacrifice to the god of day. Perhaps Moses entered with them. Perhaps he learned the principles of the Egyptian creed and devoted many years to the study of the symbols used in its ritual. But he was simply learning how to use his tools. The teachings of this nature-religion found no lodgment in his heart. And yet the hold which this elaborate canon law had gained upon the affections of the Egyptian people, taught him the necessity of a full ritual as a permanent possession of his own race. By and bye, when God gave this ritual in all its minute details, the scribe was already fully taught to write it down.

This ultimate use of his intellectual acquirements was not yet revealed to Moses. But he labored on in the study of geometry, a science developed by the Egyptians in their numerous land-measurements. He was taught medicine and astronomy. He was trained in the principles and in the practice of law. Written laws in great number were possessed by the Egyptians. The use made of these by Moses we shall see in our study of the code issued at Sinai. Then, poetry was the subject of many a lesson in this university life at On. Perhaps Moses watched the professional scribes writing down the epic of Pentaur, celebrating the valor and the deeds of Rameses. Perhaps his soul was stirred within him, ready to break forth in lyric praises to the God of his fathers. All the known facts point to the conclusion that in this university course Moses became an educated Hebrew, rather than an Egyptian. He acquired facility in writing his own Hebrew language, and his mind was broadened by a close study of Egyptian science, religion and law, but his heart was all the while beating with loyalty for the unseen King above.

Moses as a Soldier of the Egyptian Empire.

The latest authentic biography of Moses is the brief sketch given by the martyr Stephen. Concerning that period of life which he spent in the Pharaoh's court, Stephen says that "Moses was learned in all the wisdom of the Egyptians, and was mighty in words and in deeds." * To be mighty in words and deeds would seem to imply administrative ability. Moses was evidently an official high in favor with the Pharaoh. The mechanism of practical government was learned by the Hebrew leader under the tuition of the king of Egypt himself. It was an administration characterized by "red-tape." The ruling-class was made up of multitudes, and the insolence of office was one of the burdens borne by the peasant class.

We have the authority of Josephus and of Artapanus for stating that Moses was a soldier of high rank in the Egyptian army. Whether he was old enough to assist Rameses against the Hittites, we know not. But the tradition handed down by Josephus affirms that Moses was the leader of an army that advanced into Ethiopia. Great success rested upon his movements; the Ethiopian king submitted and gave his daughter in marriage to Moses, and the Hebrew leader returned to celebrate a great triumph at the court of the Pharaoh.

When forty years of his life had run their course, Moses' technical education was completed. A successful soldier and statesman, high honor was accorded him by the Egyptians. But he had other plans than a career in the service

---

* Acts 7: 22.

of the Pharaoh. A higher mission was sending its light into his soul. Another king was calling him. His own brethren needed his abilities. He broke off from connection with Egyptian royalty. He "refused to be called the son of Pharaoh's daughter," * but turned away from Zoan as a mere Hebrew, the servant of God, with a great divine work opening up before him.

Moses the Self-Appointed Deliverer.

Moses did not escape the faults already noticed in the careers of Abraham, Isaac and Jacob. As in their case, so with Moses was the man's mistake made God's means of further revelations. Moses had the highest motives in breaking away from connection with the Pharaoh's court, but his impetuous haste in killing the Egyptian task-master can hardly be justified.

We are told that Moses, after passing his fortieth year, "went out unto his brethren and looked on their burdens." † No doubt he made a tour of the land of Goshen, along by the store-cities, Pithom and Raamses—through the canals then in course of construction, and across the fields where his brethren were driven to their rigorous toil by the lash. He saw "an Egyptian smiting an Hebrew, one of his brethren." ‡ The sympathy of the son of the tribe of Levi was aroused. The cause of these laboring Israelites was his cause. Then the impetuous haste of the successful soldier urged him to the slaughter of the cruel overseer. He did not pause to consider the legal methods open to him. The Egyptian law offered means of prosecuting injustice. But Moses seems to have constituted himself the deliverer of his brethren. He knew the promises of God unto His people. Now he rashly thought to use his own human ability and his own experience as a warrior, in order to set these Hebrews free. There is no evidence to show that Moses had as yet received a special revelation from God. He simply appointed himself as the agent of a deliverance which he believed God would work out for the descendants of Jacob. Moses soon saw his mistake. He was not received as a mediator by the Hebrews themselves. His unlawful deed became known even to the Pharaoh, who "sought to slay

---

* Hebrews 6.   † Acts 7, Exod. 2: 11.   ‡ Exod. 2: 11.

Moses." * At once he fled the land and took up his dwelling in Midian, beyond the Red Sea toward the east.

The motive of Moses in attempting a national deliverance for his brethren was a lofty one. It shows how deeply the lessons of Israel's past history had entered his soul. He realized that God had a better condition in store for them than this of Egyptian slavery. But he was mistaken in supposing that an Egyptian training in state-craft and in war could accomplish the proposed independence. He must have supreme power behind him. He must dwell in the solitudes of Midian for forty years to be taught of God. When the divine power shall fill his heart and his mind; when it shall be committed into his very hands; when he shall receive the explicit command to deliver this people as God's accredited agent, then shall the wisdom acquired at Heliopolis be of some value. But until God shall set His seal upon the Egyptian education and render it the subservient instrument of His will in the heart of a man consecrated solely unto Himself—until then, the skill and the knowledge of Moses are without power.

* Exod. 2: 15.

CHAPTER XIV.
JEHOVAH DECLARES HIS NAME.

Moses in Midian.

ACROSS the isthmus, now called Suez, into the Arabian desert, fled Moses. Beyond the Aelanitic gulf, among the Midianites, he found a home. A tribe of shepherds were these people of Midian, although they had already builded some cities along the shore of this arm of the sea. The priest and king of the tribe was Reuel, or Reguel, a name meaning "friend of God." These people seem to have believed in the God who had revealed Himself to Abraham, and in some measure they kept alive the worship practiced by the Hebrew patriarchs. One of the seven daughters of this priest became the wife of Moses, and then the late soldier of the Egyptian army became the leader of sheep in the desert country. The story of his life in these solitudes is not told. Stephen declares that he spent forty years in Midian.* As an indication of his love for his own people, we find him naming his first-born son in Midian, Gershom, a name meaning "stranger," for he said, "I have been a stranger in a strange land."† Not many years had passed ere Reuel died, and the leadership of the tribe was assumed by Reuel's son, Jethro. The latter was, therefore, the brother-in-law and not the father-in-law of Moses, since the Hebrew word used in Exodus 3: 1, may be rendered in either way. This man's flock was now kept by Moses, and "he led the flock to the backside of the desert and came to the mountain of God, towards Horeb." ‡ This statement means that he had wandered down the western shore of the Aelanitic gulf into the peninsula of Sinai, to the very mountain where God afterwards delivered to him the tables of stone.

These statements make clear to us the meaning of this period in the life of Moses. It was a time of personal communion with God in the midst of silent sand-wastes and

---
*Acts 7. †Exod. 2: 22. ‡Exod. 3: 1.

towering rocks. In the loneliness of the desert, as he sought for pasturage, God was teaching him. The Spirit of God was moulding into strength the mind and the heart already freighted with the teachings of Egypt. In later generations God continued to train His servants according to this very method. Elijah afterwards fled to this very rock of Horeb to receive comfort and new commands from the Lord. Our Lord Himself was in the wilderness for forty days, and His forerunner, John, spent his early life there. Paul, the Apostle, was three years in Arabia, possibly in these very wilds where Moses led his flock. Humility of spirit came to the impetuous soldier who had attempted to deliver his Hebrew brethren by means of his own strength. Confidence in the God of his fathers and in the covenant-promises increased with the passing years, for the second son borne by the daughter of the Midianite received from Moses the name Eliezer, meaning, "my God is an help." * Thus does his second-born child stand as the memorial of a great crisis in Moses' training. The truth of God's promises had taken hold upon his heart, and he was ready to turn unto high heaven for future guidance.

Meanwhile, a similar crisis had been reached in the story of the Hebrews in Egypt. Rameses II., King of Egypt, had died.† His successor was his son Meneptah II. This king continued the oppression begun by his father, "and the children of Israel sighed by reason of the bondage," and they cried, and their cry came up unto God by reason of the bondage.‡

Most probably the Hebrews had been fascinated by the civil and religious institutions of Egypt. Perhaps they had ceased the strict observance of that divine worship practiced by the patriarchs. But now they awaked as if from a long sleep. The persecutions of two successive kings recalled the instances of deliverance wrought by the God of their fathers. Accordingly they turned unto Him. It was an act of national supplication to the God who had made the covenants with Abraham. "And God heard their groaning, and God remembered His covenant with Abraham, with Isaac, and with Jacob. And God looked upon the children of Israel, and God had respect unto them."§

---

*Exod. 18: 4.   †Exod. 2: 23.   ‖Exod. 2: 23.   §Exod. 2: 24, 25.

The narrative thus far reveals the conditions upon which God based His proposed revelation of Himself. Moses, the individual, and Israel, the people, were first brought to a sense of their personal dependence upon Him. Their oppression by heathen power turned them unto the God who had made covenants with their fathers. Unto Him alone did they now turn for help. He was ready to answer them with a stretched-out arm.

The Burning Bush.

The most striking element in the vision of Moses in Mt. Horeb was the personal manifestation of God. The individual voice of God in the person of His Son, spoke and revealed His plans. Truths before unknown to Moses were now revealed. The line of his own thought was broken off, and a page from God's purposes was handed down through the medium of the One Person who appeared in the form of a flame of fire. The silence of long years was broken, and the communication between man and God, once clearly established in Abraham's day, was again resumed. Resumed, too, according to a more definite method. Not only did Moses see with his own eyes the form of the bush all aflame, but he heard with his ears the message of the Holy One. It was not a vision of the night, but of the day, for Moses was commanded to stand with unshod feet as in the presence of Him who demands worship as the preliminary condition of all revelation of Himself. As the Holy One God had revealed Himself in the days of Noah and of Abraham. As the Holy One he now received Moses into His presence. The personal relationship established between this man and his God, was upon the basis of the primitive revelations made unto the patriarchs. In fact, God continued to break the silence by saying, "I am the God of thy father, the God of Abraham, the God of Isaac, and the God of Jacob. And Moses hid his face, for he was afraid to look upon God." *
A spirit of reverence filled the heart of Moses, and therefore did God continue to make Himself known. The revelations were all made upon the basis of the Abrahamic covenants. "My people, the children of Israel," is the refrain that runs through all of God's declarations.† To discharge His cove-

---

* Exod. 3: 6.   † Exod. 3: 7-10.

nant promises unto them had He come. The "cry" of His people had come up unto Him. The "home" of His people stood ready for them, a home long before promised to them. The time for the fulfillment of the contract was at hand; the measure of the suffering of His people was full. God said to Moses, "Come, now, therefore, and I will send thee unto Pharaoh that thou mayest bring forth my people, the children of Israel, out of Egypt."*

God's Covenant Name is Jehovah.

The great change wrought in the character of Moses by forty years of shepherd life is indicated in his humility. Once he thought to set himself forth as a national liberator. Now, when God speaks, Moses draws himself back. We have here an indication that the narrative is not fabricated by human wisdom to show that Moses conceived the vision in his own imagination. The revelation ran counter to his thoughts. He no longer hoped to play a great personal part in the history of his own people. When God called upon him to serve as the agent of His plans, "Moses said unto God, 'Who am I, that I should go unto Pharaoh?'"† Then follows the declarations concerning God's abiding presence. Moses not only doubts his own fitness as God's messenger, but he also asks more particularly concerning the character of the God of his fathers. "What is His name?" cries Moses.‡

"And God said unto Moses, 'I AM THAT I AM;' and He said, Thus shalt thou say unto the children of Israel, 'I AM hath sent me unto you.' And God said, moreover, unto Moses, Thus shalt thou say unto the children of Israel, '*Jehovah, God of your fathers*, God of Abraham, God of Isaac, and God of Jacob, hath sent me unto you; *this is my name forever, and this is my memorial unto all generations.*'" §

The Hebrews dwelt in the midst of a people who had many gods under varying names. As the Almighty had God appeared unto Abraham. Now He declares, by the use of the name Jehovah, that He is yet the same God as of old. The term, "I Am That I Am" means the same as the word Jehovah, and this simply indicates that God is The Eternal One. The covenants with Abraham were made upon the

---
*Exod. 3: 10.   †Exod. 3: 11.   ‡Exod. 3: 13.   §Exod. 3: 14, 15.

basis of God's Almighty power. His eternal existence and unchangeable nature were clearly implied in those contracts as conditions of their fulfillment. In the revelation now made to Moses, a new covenant is not made, but the old covenants are renewed. The basis of such revelation must be that God is the same God making again the same covenants. This fact is expressed in the declaration that God is Jehovah—the Eternal—"the same yesterday, to-day and forever." It is the official name under which God continues to expand and amplify His revelations from age to age. It is a name which we have found already in the narrative in the Book of Genesis, placed there by the author of that book as indicating this same fact, that from the very beginning God is Jehovah, the Maker of progressive revelations unto His people. But in God's own specific declarations to the primitive peoples of the days of Adam and Noah, He manifested Himself as the Almighty Creator and Ruler.

To prove unto Moses and the people of Israel that He is now, in their day, as He was in the day of Abraham, still the same God of Almighty power, He works certain miracles. These wonders are given as His credentials. In those former days He wrought wonders to deliver their fathers—Abraham and Jacob—and now does He work wonders to show that He is in truth Jehovah—that is, the self-same God during all time.

In the name of Jehovah, the rod, or shepherd's staff of Moses, is changed into a hissing serpent. Moses flees from before it, but, at the Lord's command, he takes it up, and lo! the serpent becomes again the rod in his hand. This is done in order to vindicate the divine assertion, "that *Jehovah*, God of their fathers, God of Abraham, God of Isaac, and God of Jacob, hath appeared" unto him.*

Moses and Aaron in Egypt as the Representatives of Jehovah.

For many days Moses resisted the call of Jehovah. He seems to have made the mistake now of too much humility. He carried this so far as to indicate a lack of confidence in God's power. In fact, the first of God's miracles were designed to drive Moses from this position by showing that Jehovah is still the all-powerful.

---

* Exod. 4: 1, 5.

At first Moses offered the objection of his own lack of fitness.* Then he demurred on the ground that the people would not believe his story of the divine vision.† Instantly the rod in his hand was changed to a serpent—then his hand was made leprous and again made whole within a moment; and the promise was further made that water poured out by his hand upon the ground should be changed into blood. All these wonders were given as signs that God had given him commission.‡ Even then Moses continued to resist. His own unfitness again was brought forward. "And Moses said unto the Lord, 'O my Lord, I am not a man of words, neither heretofore nor since thou hast spoken unto thy servant; but I am slow of speech and of a slow tongue.'" § To such extent was this obstinacy now carried that the Lord saw fit to punish Moses. He took the man at his word. No longer should he be alone as mediator between God and His people, but Aaron was sent as spokesman for Moses.‖

The commission aroused Moses to a sense of duty. The rite of circumcision had been neglected even in his own household. During the journey to Egypt with his wife and sons, he circumcised the children. In the wilderness came Aaron to meet him and then started these two servants of Jehovah upon their mission.

A public assembly of all the Hebrew people was called by their own elders. In their presence appeared Moses and Aaron. "And Aaron spake all the words which the Lord had spoken unto Moses, and did the signs in the sight of the people. And the people believed: and when they heard that the Lord had visited the children of Israel, and that He had looked upon their affliction, then they bowed their heads and worshipped."¶ The divine credentials were received. The worship practiced by the patriarchs was revived. The people as a nation were united under the standard of Jehovah, ready to be guided unto their promised home. It was now left unto Moses and Aaron to throw down the gage of battle before the sun-worshippers of the land of Egypt.

Into the presence of Meneptah, at Zoan, came Moses and Aaron. Startling to his royal ear was the demand, "Thus saith

---
*Exod. 3: 11. †Exod. 4: 1. ‡ Exod. 4: 2, 9. § Exod. 4: 10. ‖ Exod. 4: 11, 17. ¶ Exod. 4: 29–31.

Jehovah, God of Israel, let my people go that they may hold a feast unto me in the wilderness." * In the name of Jehovah and in the name of common justice came the demand. Meneptah recognized neither Jehovah nor justice. Jehovah declared that the people were His, and, therefore, unlawfully oppressed by the king of Egypt. Meneptah returnd the answer of all despots when a demand comes in the cause of liberty. "Who is Jehovah, that I should obey His voice to let Israel go? I know not Jehovah, neither will I let Israel go." † Instead of liberty to depart even three days from the presence of the Egyptians, Meneptah enforced greater burdens upon the Hebrews. They were sent to gather straw in addition to the labor required in making the ordinary tale of bricks. Then came the people of Israel to lay the blame upon Moses and Aaron, and these in turn came to chide Jehovah.‡ At this juncture came Jehovah's formal declaration of war against the power of the king of Egypt. His covenant was recalled and all the promises renewed. Again upon the ears of Moses came the declaration that God is Jehovah. "Wherefore, say unto the children of Israel, I am Jehovah, ... and I will redeem you with a stretched-out arm and with great judgments."§

Then again into the presence of the Pharaoh was Moses sent. Although his old obstinacy returned and he hesitated at the very crisis of the dispute with the king,‖ yet Jehovah continued to urge him forward until he dared a second time to face King Meneptah. When Moses was now four-score years of age, and Aaron was yet older by three years, these representatives of the living God entered the palace of the Pharaoh at Zoan-Tanis to present their formal credentials as ambassadors from the court of Jehovah. As they stood before the royal throne of Egypt, demanding the release of Jehovah's enslaved children, at the same time the divine commission was presented. Aaron bore the rod of authority. Down before the king he cast it. Immediately it became a writhing, living serpent. A symbol of power was there presented which the Pharaoh could not mistake. The serpent was perhaps the basilisk or cobra, which was carved on the diadem of every king of Egypt as the sign of royal authority. Upon Meneptah's own crown at that very moment was displayed

---

* Exod. 5: 1. † Exod. 5: 2. ‡ Exod. 5: 4–23. § Exod. 6: 1–8. ‖ Exod. 6: 9–37.

this serpent-symbol. Here upon the floor, at Jehovah's command, a little rod of wood became the symbol of power. Then came Meneptah's magicians. Jehovah permitted their rods to become serpents also. But Aaron's rod swallowed up their rods. Egyptian power must submit to Jehovah's power.* Pharaoh was defied in his own palace. An omen was there displayed that Jehovah would crush his kingly authority forever. But the Pharaoh's heart was hardened. The obstinacy of his temper blinded his eyes, and he accepted the challenge of battle. Henceforth must we look for the active manifestation of Jehovah's authority through his mediators, Moses and Aaron. Now came the stern conflict wherein God spake and the power of Ra, the sun-god, and of his son, the sovereign of the Nile, was overwhelmed.

---
*Exodus 7: 1-9.

CHAPTER XV.

JEHOVAH'S NAME VINDICATED IN THE PRESENCE OF THE SUN-GODS OF EGYPT.

Zoan, the Capital of the Delta.

THE year 1884 A. D., saw the ancient Zoan brought to the light. A vast heap of ruins in the centre of the eastern portion of the delta region was excavated by Mr. W. M. Flinders Petrie, and there lay the capital of Meneptah, the Pharaoh of the exodus. In later times the city came to be known as Tanis; for when the Septuagint scholars came to that passage in Psalm 78: 12, "Marvelous things did He . . . . . in the field of Zoan," from their knowledge of the locality and the place, they rendered the statement thus: "Marvelous things did He . . . . . in the field of Tanis." The spade of Mr. Petrie corroborated the testimony of the Septuagint scholars. He found Tanis to be the remains of a splendid capital, the ancient seat of Rameses II., and of his son Meneptah—the same city once called Zoan in the days of the exodus.

Fragments of domestic ware, of royal trappings, of religious paraphernalia, were scattered abroad throughout the streets of the buried Zoan; but the chief of all the ruins were a temple, a palace and a royal statue. Like all the other sanctuaries of Egypt, the great temple was sacred to the sun, and Meneptah bore the proud name of "the son of the sun," "the living Horus." The king before whom Moses and Aaron appeared was considered a living god upon earth, the representative of Horus, the sun upon the morning horizon. Wonderful was the palace wherein dwelt this reputed son of the beams of morning light. But more wonderful still was the figure of Meneptah's father, King Rameses II., which stood in the court-yard of the palace. Not in one piece did Mr. Petrie find this statue, for later kings had sawn it asunder, and built the fragments into various walls. Enough of these were found to show the proportions of the figure.

Surmounted by its double crown, this stone king towered up to the height of one hundred and twenty feet. There stood he yet in the days of Meneptah. There stood he as the representative of the cruel, haughty, despots of Egypt, who claimed to represent the unseen deities of the heavens. There stood he in the midst of a scene of great natural beauty, thus described by an Egyptian poet of Moses' time:

"I arrived in the city of Rameses-Meri-Amen, and I have found it excellent, for nothing can compare with it on the Theban land and soil. Here is the seat of the court. It is pleasant to live in. Its fields are full of good things, and life passes in constant plenty and abundance. Its canals are rich in fish; its lakes swarm with birds; its meadows are green with vegetables; there is no end of lentils; melons, with a taste like honey, grow in the irrigated fields. Its barns are full of wheat and durra, and reach as high as heaven. Onions and sesame are in the enclosures, and the apple tree blooms. The vine, the almond tree, and the fig tree grow in the gardens." *

What abundance is here described for filling up those flesh-pots afterwards seen in the wilderness in the dreams of the Hebrews! This capital of the delta, this royal city of King Meneptah, was now to become the scene of conflict between powers heavenly and powers infernal.

Wonders in the Field of Zoan.

"Against all the gods of Egypt I will execute judgment; I am Jehovah."† Thus spake the Lord near the close of the conflict waged upon the banks of the Nile. "I am Jehovah; speak thou unto Pharaoh, King of Egypt. . . . . See, I have made thee a god to Pharaoh."‡ In this manner spake the Lord in the beginning of the battle. It was in very truth a great battle between the one true God, the Lord of Hosts, and the powers of the false gods. Moses and Aaron were simply the standard-bearers and ambassadors of Jehovah, while King Meneptah represented the sun-gods of Egypt. Moses wrought miracles as "signs" and "wonders,"§ showing the power and might of Jehovah. The magicians of Meneptah attempted to imitate the deeds of the messengers of God, and failed at the critical point.

---
* Brugsch, pp. 299, 300.   † Exod. 12: 12.   ‡ Exod. 6: 29; 7: 1.   § Ps. 78: 42, 43.

From this view of the history of the Exodus we discover how great is this epoch in the growth of divine revelation. Here Jehovah speaks in miraculous manner to entire nations. Hitherto His miracles have been wrought simply to guide and to teach individuals, the single heads of families, like Abraham and Jacob. But now we have the age of miracles. The finger of God reaches down into the mechanism of the earth, and moves it at His will in such manner that the Hebrew nation beholds the "signs" of His presence, and the Egyptians look upon the "wonders" which He can work. No such age as this has since dawned upon the earth. The incarnation of Jesus Christ represented another period of miracle-working, but His deeds were those of healing and blessing. The day of judgment upon the visible manifestation of the power of Satan came in the time of Moses. Once for all upon the banks of the Nile was the lesson taught that Jehovah is God above all gods.

Just here springs up the question, Were these sun-deities of Egypt real spiritual beings? John Milton in *Comus* and in *Paradise Lost,* has stated his opinion that all these heathen deities were the fallen angels, cast out of heaven along with Satan. In our own time, Dr. Charles Robinson,[*] with others, has accepted virtually the same view. Against the gods of Egypt as veritable spiritual powers did Jehovah exercise His power. "They moved Him to jealousy with strange gods, with abominations provoked they Him to anger. They sacrificed unto demons which were no God, to gods whom they knew not, to new gods that came up of late, whom your fathers dreaded not."[†] These gods, say this school of interpreters, belonged to that hierarchy of spirits called "demons" in the New Testament. Therefore, say they, the deeds of the magicians of Meneptah represented real effects and not slight-of-hand results. The limited number of magical effects possible to these sorcerers was only the natural limitation that was set to the power of the emissaries of Satan. This may have been the case. But it seems more probable that the deeds of Meneptah's troupe were simply the handiwork of skillful sorcerers. The serpent produced by them when Moses' rod was transformed was only a live serpent, made torpid for a moment, so that it could be passed off as

---

[*] The Pharaohs of the Bondage and the Exodus.   [†] Deut.

a stiff rod. The wisdom of Egypt was the only power behind the supposed gods. These deities had their being only in the imagination of men. The powers of earth, air, and sky were personified and worshipped, and the source of all existence was traced to the sun. His regular course across the sky day by day, the shade into which all other objects fell during his absence, had elevated the king of light as the supreme object of reverence, and the giver of life and of law. Now fell the judgments of Jehovah to fix a new law upon the course of nature, and to show another source of life beyond the sun. The wisdom of men was paralyzed, the powers of earth, air, and sky, became dead or alive at His command, and the supposed gods of Egypt vanished into nothingness when His name was declared.

The Seven Days' Death of the Nile-god.

The first stroke of the warlike sword fell at the hour sacred to King Meneptah himself. One of his special titles was "the living Horus." Now, this name was given to the sun just as he darted his earliest beams across the eastern desert into the land of the Nile. He represented the return of life after the death-like darkness of night. It was perhaps the daily custom of the monarch who represented the morning-sun, upon an earthly throne, to go forth at this hour of growing dawn in solemn religious ceremonial to the brink of the river Nile. Old Nilus himself was a holy stream, another representative of the sun, for he gave life unto all the land. An ancient hymn to this water-god has come down to us:

" Blessed be the good god,
The Nun-loving Nile.
The father of the gods of the holy Nine dwelling on the waters.
The plenty, wealth, and food of Egypt.
He maketh everybody live by himself;
Riches are on his path,
And plenteousness is in his fingers;
The pious are rejoiced at his coming.
Thou art alone and self-created,
One knoweth not whence thou art.
But on the day thou comest forth and openest thyself,
Everybody is rejoicing.
Thou art a lord of many fish and gifts,
And thou bestowest plenteousness on Egypt."*

---
* Records of the Past, X., p. 37.

The morning-ceremonial of Meneptah was simply a conclave of earthly gods in honor of the coming of their heavenly original. But this particular day saw astonishment written upon the faces of the Nile's adorers. When the assembled attendants were about to bow the knee to both the king and the Nile, they beheld the standard of Jehovah upheld there by Moses and Aaron. Defiance was written in their faces and the words of challenge were upon their lips. In the name of Jehovah, God of the Hebrews, was formal demand made that the Pharaoh should let His people go. Since obstinate refusal was still the policy of the king, then Aaron "lifted up the rod and smote the waters that were in the river, in the sight of Pharaoh and in the sight of his servants; and all the waters that were in the river were turned to blood. And the fish that was in the river died; and the river stank and the Egyptians could not drink of the water of the river; and there was blood throughout all the land of Egypt."* Not merely the stream of the Nile was thus touched with death, but all the water that stood in ponds, or pools, or in vessels. The only source of water in the land was the river; and whether in the channel or outside, the life-giving fluid was changed to the condition of a stream of death.

The greatest of all the earthly gods of the land was changed in its very nature. It oozed along its slimy banks as the very symbol of death. No longer did it bestow blessing and prosperity. No longer did it gladden the hearts of men. It ceased to be the artery of commerce, the highway for vessels of burden. The very sight of it sent a thrill of horror deep into the soul of every Egyptian. The sun came up in all his splendor and glory, but he awakened no flash of recognition in bright waters. The claims of the Nile to be the sun's representative—to be the origin of life unto all the land and all the people thereof—these claims were stamped as false forever. The word of Jehovah by the mouth of His servant Moses had sent ignominy and defeat throughout all Egypt. At the first onset Jehovah was triumphant over the Nile-god. He spared the lives of the people during this week of the god's death. They digged in the sands along the river-bank, and thus in the bosom of the earth were permitted still to find drink. The magicians of

---

* Exodus 7: 14-21.

Meneptah again deceived his sight by marvellous tricks. The spectators of their skill seemed to see the water changed to blood. At least, Pharaoh made their performance his excuse for not yielding in presence of Jehovah's wondrous miracle. He stiffened his heart into obstinacy. The old cruelty found its seat in his breast, and as he became accustomed to the sight of the dead river-god, he persisted in refusing to allow the Hebrew people depart out of his realm.

The Plague of Frogs.

The second plague was another blow directed at the Nile-god. From this giver of all good there now came forth a loathsome pest. After the Nile-water had become again clear and sweet, Moses stood in the Pharaoh's presence with the old demand, "Thus saith Jehovah, Let *my* people go that they may serve *me*."* But the heart of the king was as yet hardened, and he refused to obey Jehovah. Then was the wonder-working rod of Aaron outstretched over "the river," and "the frogs came up and covered the land of Egypt." † The word used in the Hebrew narrative indicates a species of frog still common in Egypt. It is small in size, makes progress chiefly by crawling, and literally fills the land with the din of its croakings. A fearful gift from the Nile-god was this loathsome animal, especially since he came in such numbers as to invade the houses of the Egyptians, their bed-chambers and their beds, even their ovens and their kneading-troughs.‡

If the worshippers of Nilus had supposed their god recovered from his seven-days' death by his own power, such a supposition must fall to the ground when the river sent forth a curse and not a blessing. His sanctity and power as a deity were overthrown.

But this second plague reached farther than simply to touch with paralysis the fabled character of the Nile-god. The frog himself was worshipped. In the district of Benihassan, made memorable by the inscriptions of the kings of the twelfth dynasty contemporary with Abraham, the god Chnum was held in special reverence. This deity's wife bore the name Heka, and was represented as having the head of a frog. Throughout the whole land the frog seems

---

* Exod. 8: 1.   † Exod. 8: 6.   ‡ Exod. 8: 3.

to have been numbered among the symbols of the resurrection.* The regular appearance of this animal in the month of September out of the waters of the river seemed to betoken life of a different order springing out of the source of all Egyptian life. But now the little animal came in such multitudes as to indicate the horror of death rather than the vigor of another life. The symbolism had lost its significance and another deity of Egyptian imagination was slain.

Further than this, the family of King Meneptah himself seem to have been special worshippers of the frog. A vignette in Mariette's "Fouilles d'Abydos" † portrays an act of worship on the part of Meneptah's grandfather, Seti I., who offered wine in two vases to a frog enshrined in a small chapel, with the legend, "The Sovereign Lady of both worlds." Perhaps Meneptah kept up the adoration for this great deity. Not only as a family-god of this nineteenth dynasty, but as a representative of the animals as widely worshipped in Egypt, the frog lost his ancient sacred honor by the visitation of Jehovah's might.

The magicians came at the Pharaoh's call, and in some mechanical manner brought up frogs upon the land. But their powers served only to increase the plague, not to diminish it. Now first did Pharaoh cry out and ask for deliverance. The dishonor of the frog-deity seems to have touched him more to the quick than did the disgrace of the Nile. "Intreat Jehovah that he may take away the frogs from *me* and from *my people*, and I will let the people go that they may do sacrifice unto Jehovah."‡ A distinct advantage in the conflict was gained by Jehovah, even in the opinion of the Pharaoh. He had been brought to the point of acknowledging Jehovah's power. From this time onward, so far as Meneptah was concerned, the strife lay between his conviction and his wishes. Even now, when he saw a respite granted, and the plague stayed at Moses' prayer, his obstinate heart got the better of his judgment, and he refused to let the Hebrews go.

The Curse upon the Soil of the Earth.

Without previous announcement, Jehovah now touched the sacred soil of the Nile valley, and it became a plague of lice [Hebrew Kinnim—a word found nowhere else.] The

---

*Speaker's Com. on Exodus, p. 280. †Part II., Vol. I., p. 30. ‡Exod. 8: 8.

earth herself was one of the gods of the Egyptian pantheon, and bore the sacred name Seb. Seb and Nut, "the earth," and "the sky," were father and mother of Osiris and Isis, chief deities in one of the myths of the sun-god. The black, fertile soil of the Nile basin was held in special reverence as a part of this great earth deity. At Jehovah's command "Aaron stretched out his hand with his rod, and smote the dust of the earth, and it became lice in man and in beast; all the dust of the land became lice throughout all the land of Egypt." *

The extreme limit of the power of the magicians was reached in the presence of this third plague. After unavailing efforts to imitate the miracle, they turned away in awe, crying unto the Pharaoh, "This is the finger of God."† But the king hearkened not unto his minions. His heart was set in its course of obstinate resistance.

By degrees the plagues were working their way into the very centre of Egyptian religious rites. Jehovah's power began its manifestations by smiting the gods who had their habitation within and along Egypt's great life-artery, the river Nile. The stream itself, the frog that dwelt in the stream, and the rich earth that bordered it were all worshipped as gods, and were all now smitten and made into curses by the finger of Jehovah. In addition to the blows directly aimed at these deities, there fell a withering curse upon the priests and their ceremonies. Extreme cleanliness was enjoined upon the priestly order. Four times during the twenty-four hours they bathed the whole body in pure water. Once in every three days' time, they shaved the body in order to preserve absolute cleanliness. Therefore, when the Nile ran blood, for seven days the priestly rites were profaned by unclean priests. When the frogs invaded the land, they brought unwholesome filth into the very shrines and up to the altars, and now, when the lice were upon man and beast, what a cry of horror must have ascended at sight of the sacred officials and the sacred animals covered with the loathsome pest!

A late traveller, Sir Samuel Baker, refers to a pest now prevalent in Egypt similar to this third plague. The insects swarm "as though the very dust were turned into lice."

---

* Exod. 8: 17.   † Exod. 8: 18, 19.

196   THE ORIGIN OF THE PENTATEUCH.

Increased in numbers by Jehovah's power until the very sorcerers had to cry, "This is the finger of God," how disastrous to Egyptian superstition must have been the blow! The highest order of men in the kingdom were shorn of their *prestige*, and all the sacred animal-gods lost their hold upon the popular reverence at the visitation of this pest that swarmed up from the bosom of the holy earth.

The Atmosphere Breeds a Plague, but not upon the Hebrews.

The trio of plagues upon water, creeping animal, and soil were past, and the Pharaoh took courage to play the worshipper once more. Again in the early morning light he stood by the Nile. "Let *my* people go that they may serve Me" rang out upon the quiet air. The Pharaoh was startled and then dismayed to see Jehovah's messengers before him. Once again he saw that rod of power waved, and lo! the air-god brought forth swarms of pestilential insects. The god Shu, son of the sun-god Ra, was the personification of the atmosphere. Upon the wings of the atmosphere's breath there now came swarms of dog-flies, or perhaps they were beetles. If the latter, then a veritable deity of the land was thus changed to a biting pest. The sun-god himself, in the character of creator (Chephra), is represented in the form of a beetle. This symbol of creative power swarmed as an agent of destruction. But not upon the land of Goshen came this fourth plague. Jehovah guarded His own people from the attack of these winged Egyptian deities and turned them only against their own worshippers. Even the Pharaoh for the moment lost faith in Chephra and cried out unto Moses, Go, but sacrifice to your God within the borders of Egypt.

Then the religious character of the warfare was brought to the front in the answer of Moses. It is not meet to offer up slain animals here in this beast-worshipping land, cried the Hebrew. "We shall sacrifice the abomination of the Egyptians to Jehovah our God, ... and will they not stone us?"* The creeds of the Hebrew and of the Egyptian presented a complete antagonism. Egypt's animal-gods were demanded by Jehovah in sacrifice unto Himself. His worship meant the utter annihilation of the Pharaoh's

* Exod. 8, 26.

ritual. In sullen compliance the Pharaoh gave permission, and then at once withdrew it. His heart was made bitter by the dishonor cast upon his supposed gods, and he still refused to let Israel go.*

Curses upon the Cattle and upon the People.

For the fifth time and for the sixth fell Jehovah's plagues upon the Egyptians, but upon the Hebrews in Goshen fell they not. From across the border returned the Pharaoh's messengers to say that Israel had escaped the curse of murrain upon the cattle upon the specific day before named by Jehovah. Upon "the cattle in the field, upon the horses, upon the asses, upon the camels, upon the oxen, and upon the sheep" of the Pharaoh's people came this disease, so that "all the cattle of Egypt died."† The chief part of the property of his subjects was destroyed. The royal herds died along with the horse and the ass and the ox of the poorest subject. In many districts were some of these cattle of the field worshipped as gods. Indiscriminate death was now visited upon these supposed givers of life.

Man's own person was at length touched in the sixth plague. Borne along by the air-god came the ashes of the furnace, inflicting boils by the very touch of a grain of dust. Moses was casting defiance in the very face of all the gods of Egypt when he stood before the Pharaoh and cast the ashes toward the face of the heavens. Upon the magicians, upon the persons of the royal family, the sons of the sun, upon the persons of the priests fell this curse-bearer out of the surrounding atmosphere. The gods seemed to be looking down in mockery upon the suffering multitudes whom they were supposed to deliver. There may have been some connection between this act of Moses in scattering ashes and an old practice current among the Hyksos kings of offering human victims to the god Sutech and then scattering the ashes of the victims. This deity (Sutech) was of Canaanitish origin and corresponded virtually to the god Baal, or Bel, the sun-god of the Babylonians. His worship was brought into Egypt by the shepherd kings, and at Heliopolis human sacrifices were at one time offered to him. Sutech was incorporated into the Egyptian pantheon as

---
* Exod. 8: 25-32. † Exod. 9, 1-7.

Set, son of Seb, the earth. Set represented darkness, as opposed to Horus, the morning light. Now, when we remember that Meneptah's grandfather, Seti, "the follower of Set," was named after this god, we can readily see what dread memories would be called up to Meneptah by the defiant Moses as he sowed the ashes to the wind. The source of a dread curse upon all the people had this evil god become—a god whose very name formed part of the royal inheritance of King Meneptah. The power of Jehovah went abroad through all the land with the scattered ashes, proclaiming the overthrow of the patron deity of the house of Meneptah, of Rameses, and of Seti. But the Pharaoh's heart became more and more like stone, and he refused to let Israel go.

The Pharaoh's Heart Hardened.

After the sixth plague the magicians confessed their defeat and retired from the contest. But the Pharaoh yet continued his stubborn resistance to the will of Jehovah. Henceforth the narrative declares that the heart of the monarch himself was the arena of battle. The Pharaoh persisted in his opposition, heedless of the remonstrances offered by his own people, temporarily touched but not permanently affected by his own fears, and finally indifferent to the warnings of Jehovah. When Moses now again stood in the Pharaoh's presence the message delivered was more than ever a personal one. "Thus saith Jehovah, God of the Hebrews, Let my people go that they may serve Me. For I will at this time send all my plagues upon thine heart and upon thy servants and upon thy people, *that thou* mayest know that there is none like Me in all the earth. For now indeed had I stretched forth my hand and smitten thee and thy people with the pestilence. Then hadst thou been cut off from the earth; *but in very deed for this cause have I made thee to stand for to show thee My power and that My name may be declared throughout all the earth.*"

The specific purpose of Jehovah in this great struggle reached out to the ends of the earth and concerned His own power and His own name; but the Pharaoh had been raised up to serve as an instrument in God's hands. Not an instrument unwilling, nor an instrument irresponsible, but one that lived and acted his own will upon the field of battle. His temper fluctuated. His mind was subject to temporary changes, but the underlying principle of stubborn hate and willful cruelty hurried the king into open blasphemy against the God of hosts. This is termed in the sacred narrative the hardening of the Pharaoh's heart.

From first to last in this biography of Meneptah we find just nineteen references made to the hardening of his heart. Eleven times is the statement made that God was the author of the hardening; thrice is it declared that Pharaoh hardened his own heart, and in five cases occurs the simple assertion that the king's heart was hardened. Now, the revised version comes to our assistance with a more exact rendering of the different Hebrew words used to describe this process of growth in evil. The first phase of the hardening was due to the Pharaoh himself. When the demand came to him that he should let Jehovah's people go forth from illegal slavery, the avarice of the Pharaoh gained control and he stiffened his own temper into dull, stupid obstinacy, so that his "heart resisted." This resistance continued long after the magicians surrendered and repented. Their advice to the king was rejected, and the Pharaoh bent himself more and more to the task of keeping Israel in bondage. He might have repented along with his servants, but he was not at all inclined to submission. "Let these men go and serve Jehovah their god. Knowest thou not yet that Egypt is destroyed?"* Thus cried the servants of the Pharaoh after the plague of thunder and hail and fire had fallen "upon man and upon beast and upon every herb of the field throughout the land of Egypt."† Death and ruin were spread throughout the land by the hail-stones that were sent to teach the king the impotence of his own gods and to show him "how that the earth is the Lord's."‡ For a moment, indeed, the heart of the king seemed to yield, for in the midst of the terror inspired by the plague he cried to Moses and Aaron, "I have sinned this time; the Lord is righteous and I and my people are wicked."§ But when the fear was past the king "sinned yet more and hardened his heart, he and his servants."‖

---

* Exod. 10: 7.   † Exod. 9: 22.   ‡ Exod. 9: 29.   § Exod. 9: 27.   ‖ Exod. 9: 34.

Then at the word of the Lord the heavens became dark with a great cloud of locusts, sent to "eat the residue of that which is escaped, which remaineth unto you from the hail."* At the approach of the cloud of insects the hearts of the Pharoah's servants were turned to complete submission, and they spake to the king in the words quoted above. The sky —home of their gods—was turned into the home of curses multitudinous by the power of Jehovah. For another brief moment, fear gained control of Meneptah. "Go serve Jehovah, your god; go now, ye that are men,"† he said, to Moses. Ready to compromise, but not to surrender, was the stubborn old king. And then as the locusts, objects of worship before among the Egyptians, became a creeping pest that "covered the face of the whole earth so that the land was darkened,"‡ and all verdure was destroyed, "Pharaoh called for Moses and Aaron in haste; and he said, I have sinned against Jehovah, your god, and against you. Now, therefore, forgive, I pray thee, my sin only this once, and entreat Jehovah, your god, that He may take away from me this death only."§ Moses did entreat the Lord, and a mighty wind came to sweep all the locusts into the Red Sea. At this juncture, "the Lord hardened Pharaoh's heart so that he would not let the children of Israel go." ‖ The judicial sentence of Jehovah began to fall upon a heart that continued obstinate. Up to this time had Pharaoh closed the doors of his own heart against justice and mercy. He had added falseness to cruelty. He had broken his word as a man and as a king. He pretended submission unto God and when the plague was removed became more defiant and rebellious. Even in this last appeal for Jehovah's forgiveness the Pharaoh was not sincere. The demand for Israel's departure had never yet been granted. To ask forgiveness, with that divine injunction unheeded, was simply a cry of defiance mingled with a request for lighter punishment. It was the same course as if an open rebel should keep his flag aloft and his sword drawn and at the same time should ask his lawful sovereign to hurl a smaller number of darts against him. Meneptah's heart was all the while resisting Jehovah's demands, and at last there came a time when Jehovah declared that the falseness and sternness of the king

---

*Exod. 10: 5. †Exod. 10: 8, 11. ‡Exod. 10: 13, 15. §Exod. 10: 16, 18. ‖Exod. 10: 20.

should be tolerated only a little while longer. What was it that Jehovah did when he hardened Pharaoh's heart? Exactly the same thing that he did all the while from the beginning, viz., making demand for Israel's release and sending plagues upon the obdurate king. There was no exercise of external constraint upon the Pharaoh. Until the very last the king was still free to yield. Until the last he remained stern and stubborn. Until the very end, we are told, now that Pharaoh hardened his own heart, now that Jehovah did the hardening. What, then, can be the meaning of these statements? Only this, that the cruel Meneptah hardened his own heart from first to last; that his stubborn resolution grew in intensity until his harsh purpose was fixed and hardened. All that Jehovah did was simply to declare that this trial of Meneptah should be decisive—that the process should continue in the same manner until the end. He determined that the demand should be kept before the Pharaoh until the king should cease to vacillate and to make false promises and should either yield or turn his own heart to very stone in its stubborn defiance. Meneptah deliberately chose the latter course. Nor are we surprised when we see the stern, coarse features of his father, Rameses II., in the museum at Cairo. Meneptah did exactly as we should expect such a tyrant to do. He declared himself the open and determined enemy of God. God's hardening of the Pharaoh's heart means nothing more nor less than this, that He determined that Meneptah must show himself in his true colors before all the world. God demanded that the king of Egypt must choose the side on which he would stand, and then must he stand there boldly to take all the consequences. The Lord did not choose for the Pharaoh, nor does He make choice for any man, but He did declare that this rebel against His law, this oppressor of His people should stand forth from his covert of superstition and cruelty and falseness in order that God's power might be shown in overcoming such a leader of the powers of darkness. For such a purpose did Jehovah raise up Meneptah, the king of Egypt.

This interpretation of the Pharaoh's career is in exact accord with the part played by Moses. At first, the same command came unto Moses that came to Meneptah. Moses was bidden to lead Israel out of Egypt, and the king was commanded to let Israel depart. In effect, these orders were identical. The first act of Moses was like the first act of Meneptah. Moses refused to lead the people, and the king refused to let them go. Then three miracles were wrought before Moses, and he repented and yielded himself as God's servant. These same miracles were wrought before the king, but his heart began to resist and he began to declare himself as God's enemy. Exactly the same treatment was used by Jehovah in the case of Moses and Meneptah. The different results were due to the character of the men themselves. Each was free to choose his course in life; the one made choice of obedience, the other of disobedience. In both cases did Jehovah show only love and mercy. As Theodoret declares: "The sun by the action of heat makes wax moist and mud dry, hardening the one while it softens the other, by the same operation producing exactly opposite results; thus from the long-suffering of God some derive benefit and others harm, some are softened while others are hardened." *

The part that God's mercy played in the history of Meneptah is striking. Ample time for reflection and repentance was allowed the king. Nearly a year was occupied in sending the ten plagues. The first one came about the middle of the month of June, at the time of the annual overflowing of the Nile; the fourth plague of swarms of insects was sent early in the month of November when the inundation was abating and the first traces of vegetation appeared on the deposit of fresh soil.† Then in December appeared the fifth plague of the murrain of beasts, and about the middle of February, when "the barley was in the ear and the flax was bolled,"‡ or in blossom, came the seventh plague of hail. Now was the time growing short. Probably in March appeared the locusts. All the more like rock was the Pharaoh's heart, in spite of these opportunities. Yet twice again will the Lord call, if perchance the king will hearken and yield. Yet another month will He permit the time to run wherein Meneptah may repent and be obedient unto the Lord ere the power of Jehovah shall be visited upon the king and upon all the gods of Egypt.

---

* Quoted in Speaker's Com. on Exodus.   † Speaker's Exodus, 8: 20.   ‡ Exodus 9: 31.

The Darkness that Could be Felt.

The ninth plague fell upon the land of Egypt without a word of warning. The heart of Meneptah had become like stone even while he was yet speaking the mockery of an insincere petition for pardon. "And the Lord said unto Moses, stretch out thine hand toward heaven, that there may be darkness over the land of Egypt, even darkness which may be felt."* The hand of the patriarch was raised and down upon the people came the folds of a thick darkness that continued to envelop them for three days. "They saw not one another, neither rose any from his place for three days: but all the children of Israel had light in their dwellings." †

What a time of deep horror was that period of darkness along the Nile! The total eclipse of Egyptian faith! Ra, the sun-god, chief of all the gods, was apparently blotted out of existence. The source of all life and the giver of all good had himself ceased to exist. Not a single ray of light pierced the awful gloom. The sense of sight was gone and eyeballs ached. In stillness, in silence and in black darkness sat each one in his place, bowed to the earth in gloom that could be felt with the ends of the fingers; yea, and felt far more by the tendrils of the heart. It was the darkness of despair in the Egyptian's heart, for all his gods were gone when Ra had lost his light-beams. At one blow the Jehovah of the Hebrews had blotted out the heavens, the home of all the chief deities, the divine light-bearers, Horus, the morning sun, and Ra, the noonday sun, and Tum, the evening sun, were all alike shrouded in a pall of darkness, the symbol of death.

The plague of darkness dried up the Egyptian religion at the fountain—cut it up by the roots. It was sent in such manner that the Egyptians recognized the hand of Jehovah. They saw the blow of the One God aimed at the flimsy structure of their superstition. Some have supposed that a natural occurrence, a storm of sand from the desert, was heightened in its effects so that it produced the impression of supernatural agency. After the vernal equinox in Egypt, travellers tell us, a periodical gale sweeps up from the southwestern desert for two or three days at a time

---
* Exod. 10: 21.   † Exod. 10: 23.

during the space of fifty days. This wind "fills the atmosphere with dense masses of fine sand, bringing on a darkness far deeper than that of our worst fogs in winter. While it lasts 'no man rises from his place; men and beasts hide themselves; people shut themselves up in the innermost apartments or vaults.' So saturated is the air with the sand that it seems to lose its transparency, so that artificial light is of little use.* Here we find an analogy for a darkness that could be felt! The hand of God was in it, however, for the darkness came not upon the land of Goshen and, moreover, the Pharaoh had never seen the like before. It was a visitation from Jehovah, in his opinion, for he cried out upon the instant unto Moses: "Go ye; serve the Lord; only let your flocks and your herds be stayed ; let your little ones also go with you."†

The old king was deceptive and scheming to the last. He wished to hold the property of the Hebrews as a pledge of their return. But in proportion to Meneptah's falseness, the courage of Moses grew apace. "Our cattle also shall go with us; there shall not an hoof be left behind; for thereof must we take to serve Jehovah our God."‡

It was a clearly-drawn issue between Jehovah on the one side and Meneptah and Ra on the other; service unto the one or unto the other and not a hostage left behind to indicate a divided obedience. And yet, with the sun-god's complete eclipse fresh in memory, Meneptah rushed blindly onward in his stubborn contest and brought down the last crushing blow of Jehovah upon every household among the Egyptians.

Judgment against all the Gods of Egypt.

"I will pass through the land of Egypt this night, and will smite all the first-born in the land of Egypt, both man and beast; and against all the gods of Egypt I will execute judgment; I am Jehovah."§ Thus ran the divine proclamation announcing that the great battle was about to terminate. The tenth and last visitation of God's power upon the land in the form of plague was the death of the first-born. This was a final assault against the gods of Meneptah and his people. Herein was summed up the meaning

---

*Speaker's Com. Ex. 10: 21.   † Exod. 10: 24.   ‡ Exod. 10: 26.   § Exod. 12: 12.

of the whole strife. It was the God of the Hebrews against the deities of the Nile and universal death was now to be sent upon those objects of worship which had hitherto been brought low in shame and disgrace. The powers of nature were the primary objects of reverence. These had already been made to show their complete subjection to the power of Him who created them. But each of these nature-deities had its animal representative. Every form of animal life, from man down to the lowest insect, was held sacred in one place or another as the type of some patron deity. The eldest son of the king was the divine son of the sun and heir to the royal throne. The lowest form of beetle life was the type of some heavenly being. The death that came unto the first-born among all these grades of animate existence marked the complete triumph of Jehovah. These imagined deities, who had their being solely in the crude superstitions of the people of the Nile, were sealed unto everlasting contempt. The hand of Moses was used as the agent of this desolating curse. Jehovah Himself came in person and "smote all the first-born in the land of Egypt, from the first-born of Pharaoh that sat on his throne unto the first-born of the captive that was in the dungeon; and all the first born of cattle. And Pharaoh rose up in the night, he and all his servants and all the Egyptians; and there was a great cry in Egypt; for there was not a house where there was not one dead."*

For the time, Meneptah and his people were overcome. They were ready to acknowledge the infinite power of Jehovah. The Pharaoh saw how vain were all subterfuges. He must yield the field of battle. "And he called for Moses and Aaron by night, and said: "Rise up and get you forth from my people, both ye and the children of Israel; and go, serve Jehovah as ye have said. Also take your flocks and your herds, as ye have said, and be gone; *and bless me also.*"† The Pharoah's heart was paralyzed with fear; his opposition was, for the moment, at an end, because he could see no further method of resistance. God's judgment upon the gods of Egypt was complete. The slaughter of the Hebrew children at the time of the birth of Moses, a measure taken to continue the power of Egypt's kings and her gods, was now

---
*Exod. 12: 29, 30.   †Exod. 12: 31, 32.

brought back upon the head of Meneptah, the son of the murderer, Rameses. The long resistance of the Egyptians against God, and against His people, was now punished in this awful visit of the midnight death-messenger. And now, when the Hebrews asked of the Egyptians, "Jewels of silver and jewels of gold and raiments," these were all given with gladness. For the conscience of these people of the Nile seems to have been aroused. They hastened to make some reparation for the long years of oppression they had visited upon Israel. Willingly did they give their treasure unto these brick-makers as compensation in part for their enforced toil, and in order that they might hasten the departure of a people, who were under the guidance of a God who struck fear to their hearts. The Egyptians believed in God and trembled, but to love Him and trust Him, as counsellor and guide, far too hardened in sin were their hearts to yield obedience of that kind.

CHAPTER XVI.

FROM HELIOPOLIS TO SINAI.

The Sacrifice of the Passover.

THE institution of the formal religious life of the Hebrews took place in the same night with the death of the firstborn of the Egyptians. The offering of sacrifices as practiced by Noah and Abraham, had probably been left in abeyance by the Hebrews in Egypt. Perhaps they were not permitted to offer up those animals that were held sacred by the people of the Nile. Perhaps they forgot that reverence toward God which had marked Jacob and Joseph. But now were they called back to the religious rite of the patriarchs in the sacrifice enjoined upon them. At the same time were they led a step forward in the matter of ritualistic forms, when a *symbolic* character was attached to the sacrifice. The God who delivered Moses and his brethren, was the same God who taught Abraham; but now began he to teach the Hebrew children in accordance with a more advanced method. The period of *symbolism* in Revelation, was inaugurated in the sacrifice of the Passover. Not a symbolism that was gradually developed by the use of a graded system of types and shadows. Fully developed in the very beginning was this divine method of Revelation. The first sacrifice ordained in Egypt was a type of the Lamb of God, slain from the foundation of the world.

Ten months had elapsed since the beginning of the plagues. The month Abib or Nisan was at hand, corresponding to our April. Although June was the opening month in the Egyptian calendar, yet unto the Hebrews there was now ordained a different opening of the year. "This month [Nisan, or April] shall be unto you the beginning of months; it shall be the first month of the year to you."* The formal dedication of this sacred month was to be marked by a sacrifice, and by the departure of Israel from Egypt.

---

* Exod. 12: 2.

A lamb without blemish, a male of the first year, from the sheep or from the goats, was to be selected by each household on the tenth day of the month. In solemn assembly, the congregation of Israel, each household gathered together, slew the lamb on the evening of the fourteenth day of the month. The blood of the lamb was sprinkled by the father of each family on the two side-posts, and on the upper door-post of the house. That same night they ate the flesh of the lamb, roast with fire; with unleavened bread and with bitter herbs did they eat it. With girded loins and feet ready shod, and with a staff in the hand did they eat this feast—for lo! just as they were concluding the solemn festival, the word of the Lord came, and they were off upon the great journey.

This sacrifice was the formal renewal of their vows to be the children of the God of Abraham. It was God's formal acceptance of them as His own forever. "The blood shall be to you for a token upon the houses where ye are; and when I see the blood, I will pass over you and the plague shall not be upon you."* A *sign* of mercy unto Israel was the blood of the sacrifice. "And this day shall be unto you for a memorial, and ye shall keep it a feast to the Lord throughout your generations; ye shall keep it a feast by an ordinance forever."† The entire feast itself, the eating of the lamb, was to be unto Israel a symbol of national deliverance, afterwards completely fulfilled in the deliverance wrought by the death of the Son of God, the true Lamb. Even now and unto all generations will God's people celebrate this feast in the communion of the Lord's Supper.

The religious life of Israel as a nation began with the sacrifice of the Passover. The strength that came to them through the flesh of the lamb in symbol and from God, in fact, served to start them upon the journey away from the bondage of Egypt.

The Gathering at Succoth.

To the pasture-lands, in the district of Succoth, near the store-city of Pithom, came the nation of Israel. The last interview between Moses and Meneptah took place probably at the fortified store-city, Rameses, and from that point to

---

* Exod. 12: 13.   † Exod. 12: 14.

Succoth the largest body of the Hebrews followed their leader. During the sojourn of more than four centuries the tribes that sprang from Jacob's sons had multiplied until the men alone were in number six hundred thousand. An aggregate population of more than three million people is thus indicated. "A mixed multitude went up also with them; and flocks and herds, even very much cattle."* The fragments of old Semitic people dwelling in Egypt from the time of the Hyksos onward were driven out with Israel. The bones of Joseph were carried along by Moses. The command of the patriarch and the command of Jehovah were upon them. They had registered a solemn vow to keep this day forever as a memorial that "By strength of hand Jehovah brought us out from Egypt, from the house of bondage."†

In booths, made of green branches, the Hebrews encamped upon the fields of Succoth. The obelisks of Heliopolis, the sacred city of the Pharaoh, were left behind them, many miles to the westward. The desert lands of the wilderness were not far away to the eastward. Perhaps the traditions handed down from the time of their fathers, concerning the days and times of wilderness travel, were now passed from mouth to mouth. In orderly array they soon began to move. "And they took their journey from Succoth and encamped in Etham, in the edge of the wilderness. And Jehovah went before them by day in a pillar of cloud, to lead them the way; and by night in a pillar of fire, to give them light. To go by day and night, he took not away the pillar of the cloud by day, nor the pillar of fire by night, from before the people."‡ The pillars of the temple of the sun were left in their silence, mockeries erected by human superstition to indicate the divine power of the beams of the sun. But now the pillar that indicated God's presence as a living leader and guide went before to lead them unto liberty of mind, body and spirit.

The Passage of the Red Sea.

At Etham the Hebrews were still upon the wilderness road that led northeastward to Palestine. Their expectation pointed to a journey through that long desert pathway,

---
*Exod. 12: 38.   †Exod. 13: 14.   ‡Exod. 20: 22.

traversed years before by Abraham and Jacob. But now the Lord spake and commanded them to turn directly toward the south. They were to remain yet within the pasture-lands of Succoth and to journey along the eastern border of Egypt. Soon the sparkling waters of the Red Sea came into view. Not across the swamp district of the Bitter Lakes that lay just to their left hand were they permitted to pass. Such a course would have brought them into the wilderness itself, and then the Red Sea might very soon have been placed between them and the land of Egypt. They kept those Red Sea waves beyond them toward the eastward as they wound slowly down among the hills. "Speak unto the children of Israel that they may turn and encamp before Pi-Hahiroth, between Migdol and the sea, over against Baal-Zephon; before it shall ye encamp by the sea."* Near the modern Suez were the people encamped. From the military point of view they were in a trap—surrounded by sea and mountain on every side save that by which they entered. The Red Sea stretched many a mile to the left hand and to the right as they looked toward the land of Midian and of Palestine. Just behind them rose up the tall summit of Mount Atakah, and the same barrier extended its rocks toward the sea-shore on their right flank so that further progress toward the south was checked. Then, as they looked backward along the way by which they had come, lo! the little hilltops were crowned with the banners of Meneptah's host, coming after them in hostile pursuit. "They are entangled in the land, the wilderness hath shut them in."†

The false king's heart had again become hardened with the passing of his terror. Not all the children had died on that night of the Passover. Six hundred chosen chariots and all the chariots of Egypt and his horsemen and his army called he together, and away he hurried to bring back these flying bondmen. The avarice of the king and of his people was again uppermost and the prey must not escape.

A great cry ran through the multitude of the Hebrews when they saw the warlike array behind them. So far as the eye of man could see there was no escape. Murmuring at once arose. "They said unto Moses, 'Because there were no

---

* Exod. 14: 2.   † Exod. 14: 3.

THE PASSAGE OF THE RED SEA. 211

graves in Egypt, hast thou taken us away to die in the wilderness?'" "And Moses said unto the people, 'Fear ye not; stand still and see the salvation of Jehovah, which he will shew to you to-day.'"* The murmuring and the sarcasm against Moses were soon made to cease, for Jehovah began to show His power.

The great pillar of cloud began to move from front to rear. As a great wall of thick darkness it lifted its folds now in front of the Egyptian host and concealed Israel from view. As the night came on the army of the Pharaoh was in the midst of darkness, but Israel was in the light, for the cloud was now unto them a pillar of fire. Hidden away under this cloak of fire Israel saw the finger of God uplifted to deliver. "And Moses stretched out his hand over the sea; and Jehovah caused the sea to go back by a strong east wind all that night, and made the sea dry land and the waters were divided. And the children of Israel went into the midst of the sea upon the dry ground; and the waters were a wall unto them on their right hand and on their left." † Thus did they escape by the miraculous power of Jehovah. A path was swept dry for them along the bed of the sea, and from Africa to Asia they crossed. Probably a mile in width was the arm of the sea at this point, and by the morning all the host of Israel, with their cattle, had passed over. Angered at the sudden escape of their prey, the Egyptians dashed madly in pursuit. But "Jehovah looked unto the host of the Egyptians through the pillar of fire and of the cloud and troubled the host of the Egyptians." ‡ "The clouds poured out water; the skies sent out a sound; their arrows also went abroad. The voice of thy thunder was in the heaven; the lightnings lightened the world; the earth trembled and shook. Thy way is in the sea, and thy path in the great waters, and thy footsteps are not known. Thou leddest thy people like a flock by the hand of Moses and Aaron." §

In the soft sand of the sea-bed sank the chariot wheels. Their movement was clogged and they "drave heavily." When the army turned at last to escape by fleeing backward toward the Egyptian shore, then dashed the waters upon them. "And the waters returned and covered the

---
* Exod. 14: 11, 13.   † Exod. 14: 19, 22.   ‡ Exod. 14: 21.   § Ps. 77: 17-20.

chariots and the horsemen, and all the host of Pharaoh that came into the sea after them; there remained not so much as one of them, ... And Israel saw the Egyptians dead upon the sea-shore."*

Was Meneptah drowned along with his soldiery? The narrative does not so affirm. Probably this coward of a king was not at the head of his troops and did not die here at the hand of Jehovah. His mummy has not been found and the latter end of this cruel monarch seems wrapped in obscurity. But the deliverance of Israel was marvellous and complete. The passage through the sea stands as the typical miracle in an age of miracles. It was the climax of the wonders in the field of Zoan. It was the crowning work of Jehovah in delivering his people from bondage. A whole nation was baptized in the cloud and in the sea. Away from the idolatry of Egypt to the service of God—away from national slavery to national freedom had they escaped. This day of passage marked the birthday of a new moral life in an entire race of people. From this time forth is it to be shown that not only individuals like Abraham and Moses may be guided by Jehovah, but also an entire people who fill up a great quarter of the earth.

Bread from Heaven.

The new nation found itself in an unknown land. The people knew Moses and they knew Jehovah in part, but naught else did they know. And yet the great need of this race was knowledge and discipline. Now were they to make great progress in the knowledge of their God and of His method of dealing with men. All the practical questions that confront men in this life came unto these Hebrews. The question of bread for daily life; the question of national existence when menaced by enemies; the question of national growth and prosperity as based upon a form of government; the question of religious creed and ritual; all these problems were now to be solved by the Hebrews first among all the nations of the earth. They had come up from the Nile, where they had witnessed a dismal failure in all these matters on the part of the Egyptians. Divine revelations from Jehovah Himself were given them now through Moses as

* Ex. 14: 26-30.

the final solution of these problems for the Hebrews and for all other nations upon earth.

The peninsula of Sinai was now the home of the Israelitish host. This region is triangular in shape, and thrusts itself like a wedge into the Red Sea, dividing it into two long arms of water—the Gulf of Suez and the Gulf of Akabah. The peninsula belongs to that great stretch of desert land between Egypt and Palestine known as the "wilderness of Shur." This peninsula itself is built up of sand and stone into a veritable three-cornered house. The land is elevated in the centre, rising by degrees as it approaches the south until it culminates in the mountain peaks that tower up above the sea.

Looking toward this rugged triangle from the North we see first a flat desert country, thrusting itself like a wedge into the peninsula, even as the peninsula like a wedge thrusts itself into the waters of the sea. This flat desert forms a vast table-land, reaching from point to point of the two gulfs, and lying two thousand feet above the sea-level. It is known as the desert of Tih or "wilderness of wandering," and was the scene of part of the subsequent meanderings of these Hebrew tribes. The underlying basis is limestone, while a carpet of flint-stone is laid across the broad plateau. Without water and without trees is this great waste. But not here do we find the Israelites encamping during the early days of their new freedom.

Passing farther to the south we come to the edge of this plateau. Along the side, toward the southwest, overlooking the gulf of Suez, is a perpendicular cliff upholding the great flat region of limestone. Down at the base of this cliff, along the shore towards the south, marched the people of Israel under Moses. Soon we find on the waste above a change in the character of the soil. A broad strip of sandstone country stretches itself across the triangle from east to west. Further south there arises up a great cluster of granite mountains, filling the entire corner of the peninsula and lifting their height in varied measure above the whole country. These peaks of quartz and black slate seem to have been tumbled together in chaotic mass. Between them are valleys deeply-cut, and widening in many a turn. Hidden away in the bosom of these hills is much mineral wealth, once extensively mined by the Egyptians. Away from the sandy shore of the Suez, along the deep and narrow gorges of this mountain range, did the Hebrew hosts climb up into the heart of these hills as into God's own house. The presence of Jehovah's glory was found far away in the wild and rugged retirement amid the everlasting mountains.

Ere reaching this scene of the giving of the Law, great lessons concerning Jehovah's watchfulness over his people had already been imparted. Only three days had they journeyed when the pangs of thirst seized upon the multitude. God's power was at once made manifest. The miracles wrought upon the Nile were duplicated, only with opposite effect. There was a land of fruitfulness made like unto a desert-land. Here was a waterless waste made to furnish a fountain of sweet water. For when Moses cast a tree into the waters of Marah, they were made sweet. The same power was behind this miracle as that which changed the Nile water into blood, for after the wonder was wrought, this message was sent through Moses unto Israel, "I am Jehovah that healeth thee."*

In the midst of the peninsula, between the limestone table-land of Tih, and the granite mountains of Sinai, is the waste region called the "Wilderness of Sin." This desert land was reached by the wanderers "on the fifteenth day of the second month after their departing out of the land of Egypt."†

Hunger began now to oppress the Hebrews. The fleshpots of Egypt rose up in their memories to recall the fleshly advantages of the home of slavery. Murmuring ran through the host. The bread and the meat of the land of Goshen seemed to be of greater value in their eyes than the spiritual growth of the nation. Then spake He who had made the land of the Nile desolate as a punishment upon the Egyptians. Jehovah gave His children bread and meat from heaven. The meat came in the flocks of quails which God caused to fly over the desert to the Hebrew encampment. Great flocks of the quail frequent the Sinai region at certain seasons. But now did God show miraculous power in bringing the birds in number innumerable at the hour of need.

---

* Exod. 15: 26.   † Exod. 16: 1.

And then the Lord caused bread to rain from heaven! And the bread was called manna, like unto the food-juice of a tree still found in Arabia. Manna, as now known, is the sweet juice of the tamarisk tree. It exudes from the trunk and the branches, and is found upon the twigs, or upon the fallen leaves beneath the tree.* But the manna sent unto Israel was found scattered over the surface of the desert after the passing of the morning dew. The supply was exceeding great, more than a forest of tamarisks could furnish, and moreover it fell not upon the Sabbath-day. The people used it as they would use meal, grinding it, or baking it— and so was bread afforded them during forty years. It was not the soil of the country, but it was Jehovah who fed His people.

The Rock of Rephidim.

The tents were struck, and the hosts departed from the sandstone country of Sin, and pushed southward into the valleys and gorges that wind through the granite mountains of the range of Sinai. And they pitched camp in Rephidim, and there they found no water. The privations of the wilderness life pressed sorely, and the murmurings of the people increased to such extent that Moses cried unto Jehovah, "Yet a little while and they will stone me."†

Moses carried still "the rod of God" in his hand. The same staff that had been outstretched over the Nile and over the land of Egypt to plague the Egyptians, was now stretched out to bring blessing upon Israel. At Jehovah's command, Moses took the elders of Israel forward in advance of the multitude until he came to a great, dry rock. Then did Moses smite the rock with his rod and water gushed out. The need of the people was supplied from the parched mass of granite by the power of Him who delivered Israel from bondage. This wondrous miracle was also a prophecy of "the spiritual rock which followed them, and that rock was Christ."‡ Thus did the symbolic method of teaching advance in clearness along with the daily sustentation of the nation. Thus did Jehovah declare that their physical life itself must draw its support from Him, of whose strength and power the granite rock is only a symbol.

---

* Speaker's Com. I.: 321.   † Exod. 17: 1-5.   ‡ 1 Cor. 10: 4.

Like a rock also did Jehovah stand against Amalek. This shepherd tribe was the most powerful among the heathen nations of the wilderness. They were accustomed to pasture their flocks along the slopes of the Sinaitic mountains. The flocks of the Israelites, as they came nibbling and lowing through the gorges, threatened to cut off the pasture lands from the flocks of the Amalekites. Therefore this fierce people grasped their spears and made a bold attack against the pilgrims from Egypt. These brick-makers from the Nile were not accustomed to the sounds of war. But Joshua seems to have possessed an instinct for battle. Moses gave him commission to select a fighting band and to lead them forward in the vale of Rephidim against the Amalekites. But it was Jehovah, the Rock of Rephidim, who fought in behalf of Israel. All that long day until the going down of the sun the battle raged in the valley. Upon the mount above, Moses interceded with God in prayer. This action of the leader is set forth in the narrative as the holding up of Moses' hands. Aaron and Hur were present, and they "stayed up his hands, the one on the one side, and the other on the other side."* But in the hand of Moses was that same rod of God, the symbol of divine intervention in behalf of Israel. As upon the banks of the Nile and of the Red Sea, as at the rock whence flowed the living stream, so here upon the battle plain was Jehovah present to give His people victory. Amalek was routed with a great slaughter, and from that day until their complete extinction they remained as the type of the enemies of God's people. It was a victory directly due to the power of God alone. He here declared His veritable existence, as real as the existence of the Rock of Rephidim itself. He here declared Himself as the source of all strength unto His people, merciful and gracious in the hour of sore need.

The Mountain of Fire.

Rephidim was probably the valley now known as Wady es Sheikh. Perpendicular rocks on each side wall in this grassy vale. Amalek fled in confusion and left the entire range of valley and mountain to the people of Israel. They now turned still southward until they came upon the broad

---

* Exod. 17: 12.

plain of Er Rahah. Here they found themselves in the presence of towering granite peaks that rose upward into heaven like perpendicular pyramids. Immediately in their front was the summit of Ras Sufsâfeh. At the base of this mountain, and in this very plain, perhaps, Moses had led the flocks of his Midianitish father. This father (Jethro) was even now with them as the adviser of Moses and as a worshipper of God. In this part of the wilderness Jehovah had appeared in the burning bush. The name Sinai is supposed to mean "acacia," the species of bush or shrub that covers this great wilderness chain of mountains. The people were here in the presence of the living God.

The group of mountain peaks were scattered here and there like granite pyramids, far grander than those on the Nile. The approach to this heart of the mountain-world had been along narrow ways lined with towering rocks, more imposing than the avenues lined with obelisks and statues, guarding the approaches to the temples of Egypt. The silence of the everlasting hills rested like a veil of heavenly blessing upon this great sanctuary. It was God's temple wherein they now dwelt, and the signs of God's presence were there. The cloud of glory had gone before them and it now rested upon the mount and lifted its tall pillar into the heavens. And Jehovah came down to declare Himself unto His people.

First of all, God sent a message unto the people out of the mount. "And Moses went up unto God, and Jehovah called unto him out of the mountain, saying, Thus shalt thou say to the house of Jacob and tell the children of Israel: 'Ye have seen what I did unto the Egyptians and how I bare you on eagles' wings and brought you unto myself. Now, therefore, if ye will obey my voice indeed, and keep my covenant, then *ye shall be a peculiar treasure unto me above all people;* for all the earth is mine. And *ye shall be unto me a kingdom of priests and an holy nation.*" *

To establish the *priest-relationship* between Himself and this nation is Jehovah's great purpose in the deliverance and the training of Israel. They have been brought away from the idols and the altars of Egypt in order that the true knowledge of God may be known among them and that the

* Exod. 19: 1-6.

true worship of Jehovah may be established. After this announcement follow the signs of God's personal presence. The people are sanctified and barriers are placed about the mount so that they can see but dare not touch the great rock. The idea of God's holiness is made to fill the very atmosphere, and to be written upon the mountains. "And it came to pass on the third day, in the morning, that there were thunders and lightnings, and a thick cloud upon the mount, and the voice of the trumpet exceeding loud; so that all the people that was in the camp trembled. And Moses brought forth the people out of the camp to meet with God, and they stood at the nether part of the mount. And Mount Sinai was altogether on a smoke, because *Jehovah descended upon it in fire;* and the smoke thereof ascended as the smoke of a furnace, and the whole mount quaked greatly. And when the voice of the trumpet sounded long and waxed louder and louder, Moses spoke and *God answered him by a voice.*" *

Like a great altar the mountain burned, and the smoke of the fire ascended continuously as the smoke of a great furnace. The symbolic meaning was clear. The Israelites saw not only lightnings and heard thunderings, whereby God manifests His power, but they saw a great mountain burning like a sacrificial altar, and they heard the voice of Jehovah Himself, and they received the message that they were to be dedicated unto Him as a nation of priests.

Here was the most stupendous event in the world's history, save the birth of Jesus Christ. Here first the infinite God spake to a whole race of people in terms intelligible. The silence of the supposed gods of Egypt and of Babylonia was made an open shame in the presence of the whole world. Overwhelmed in utter ruin were the sun-gods of the Nile, and now did Jehovah reveal Himself in those personal attributes that underlie His very being. He spake, and He was heard and understood. He declared Himself in His power and holiness, and all the people stood in awe, for here they perceived a standard of purity far above any that had been dreamed of in the philosophies of men. The mountain of fire stood before them, as a symbol of Him who rules in a world unseen and eternal.

---

* Exod. 19: 16-19.

The Song of Moses.

Aside from the occasional spirit of murmuring that possessed the people, and the intense heaviness of awe that now rested upon them in the presence of Jehovah's majesty—the great undercurrent of sentiment that now flowed from heart to heart among the Israelites was that of buoyant exultation. They were the victors in a great contest. The Egyptian religion and civil administration had gone down beneath the powers of their God. They were lifted each day up to new heights of triumph. At the foot of Sinai, no doubt, they still chanted the great song of victory written by Moses and sung by Miriam and the Hebrew women just after the passage of the Red Sea. Upon this feeling of exultation was based the first beginnings of Hebrew epic poetry. "The Book" in which Moses wrote the story of the battle of Rephidim as a memorial,* was, perhaps, the same book in which he wrote down the song of triumph at the Red Sea. This refrain, which gives a glimpse of Moses as an inspired penman, inditing the sentiments which Jehovah set in the hearts of His people on account of their deliverance, may be fittingly set down here at the close of the story of conflict. The hymn itself was sung by "Moses and the children of Israel," while Miriam and her attendant maidens, to the accompaniment of timbrels, sang the chorus:

I.

Sing unto the Lord, for He hath triumphed gloriously;
The horse and his rider hath He thrown into the sea.

My strength and song is JAH;
And He is to me for salvation.
He is my God, and I will praise Him;
My father's God, and I will exalt Him.

Jehovah is a man of war;
Jehovah is His name.

Pharaoh's chariots and his host hath He cast into the sea,
And his chosen captains are sunk in the Red Sea.
The depths covered them; they sank to the bottom as a stone.

Chorus by Miriam and the women.

Sing unto the Lord, for He hath triumphed gloriously;
The horse and his rider hath He thrown into the sea.

---

* Exod. 17: 14.

II.

Thy right hand, Jehovah, is glorious in power;
Thy right hand, Jehovah, dasheth in pieces the enemy.
In the greatness of thy height, Thou overthrowest them that rise up against thee.
Thou sendest forth thy wrath which consumeth them as stubble.
With the blast of thy nostrils the waters were piled up;
The floods stood up as an heap:
The depths were congealed in the heart of the sea.
The enemy said, "I will pursue, overtake, divide the spoil;
"My lust shall be satisfied upon them;
"I will draw my sword; my hand shall destroy them."
Thou didst blow with Thy wind; the sea covered them;
They sank like lead in the mighty waters.

(*Chorus as before.*)

III.

Who is like unto Thee, Jehovah, among the gods?
Who is like unto Thee, glorious in holiness,
Fearful in praises, doing wonders?
Thou stretchedst out Thine hand, and the earth swallowed them.

(*Chorus.*)

IV.

Thou, in Thy mercy, didst lead forth the people which Thou hast redeemed;
Thou didst guide them in Thy strength to Thy holy habitation.
The peoples have heard; they tremble;
Pangs have taken hold on the dwellers in Palestine.
Then were the dukes of Edom amazed;
The mighty men of Moab, trembling took hold upon them;
All the inhabitants of Canaan are melted away.
Terror and dread shall fall upon them;
By the greatness of Thine arm shall they be still as a stone
Till Thy people pass over, O Jehovah,
Till the people pass over which Thou hast redeemed,
Thou shalt bring them in and plant them in the mountains of Thine inheritance,
The place, O Jehovah, which thou hast made for Thee to dwell in,
The sanctuary, O Jehovah, which Thy hands have established.
Jehovah shall reign forever and ever.

Chorus.

Sing unto the Lord, for He hath triumphed gloriously;
The horse and his rider hath He thrown into the sea.*

---

* Ex. 15: 1, 18—Translation from Rawlinson's "Moses."

PART V.

THE DIVINE CHARTER OF DELIVERANCE FROM HEATHEN SUPERSTITION.

[*Exodus 20–40, Leviticus, Numbers, Deuteronomy.*]

CHAPTER XVII.

THE NATIONAL COVENANT. JEHOVAH MADE KING.

[*Exodus 20–40.*]

THAT part of the Pentateuch still left us for discussion is a written constitution confirming unto Israel the freedom wrought out for the nation by Jehovah Himself. Here we find the first charter of liberty ever recorded in the language of men. This charter from Jehovah has served as the basis of all charters since that time; the foundation of civil and religious freedom throughout the whole earth, so far as that principle has been recognized, was laid in the covenant between God and His people at Sinai. The fundamental idea of this charter is deliverance from bondage.* The charter itself is simply a written guarantee from Jehovah that the deliverance granted unto Israel shall continue their own forever upon condition of obedience unto Him as their king. The absolute sovereignty of Jehovah is acknowledged by Israel, and a formal oath is registered that they will abide forever by the statutes of the charter. Let us now proceed to the task of bringing out these great truths by a minute examination of the sacred record.

The Invisible Redeemer.

Jehovah descended upon Mount Sinai in the midst of fire and thunder and earthquake. He answered Moses in a voice that could be heard. He called Moses up into the mount to meet with Him. There was lacking no sign of Jehovah's personality. His character as a living Being was written in all these manifestations of power. The convulsions of nature that had brought desolation to Egypt were reproduced here in the midst of the mountains. The purpose of this method of revelation is clear. That purpose was to impart unto Israel the fact that the God who spake on Sinai and the God who spake on the banks of the Nile

---
* Ewald—History of Israel.

was one God and the same. The unity of the Godhead was impressed upon Israel and made a fundamental article in the great charter. The first stage in the historical revelation of the character of God was brought to a climax in this transaction. As Jehovah, God spake to Moses in this same mount and gave him commission to deliver Israel; as Jehovah, He now spake and claimed Israel as His people because of this deliverance of them. "I am Jehovah thy God, which have brought thee out of the land of Egypt, out of the house of bondage."*

By way of contrast with the character of the gods of Egypt, Jehovah gave further evidence of the unity of His nature. While granting ample evidence of His existence and of His active exertion in behalf of Israel, yet He had always dwelt in the pillar of cloud unseen. Here in the mount He remained behind the veil. Bounds were set about the mount so that the people might not even touch it. They could not come near the hill of fire lest they gaze upon Jehovah. Death would be the instant result of such intrusion. His dwelling-place is unapproachable, except upon conditions set forth by Himself. Sanctified by a three days' purification must all the people be before they might even come near the mount. "An holy nation" were they to become. But now they could not see God because of impurity of heart. It was the holiness of Jehovah that was thus revealed as the basis of his character. Because of that holiness He cannot be seen by human eyes. The invisible God who can reveal Himself to the hearts and affections of His people is a spiritual God. In these ideas of holiness and spirituality we have a complete contrast with the gods of Egypt. The sun-god was known chiefly on account of his visibility. Types of the sun-god were worshipped far and wide; his *personality* was as naught, for it was dissipated among the many gods who represented him. Holiness and spirituality were not attributes of the gods of the Nile country, and hence were they worshipped under the form of images that could be touched. There was nothing in the nature of these heathen deities that fenced them off from contact with the nature of flesh. On the other hand, this very attribute of holiness was the ground-reason why Jehovah was veiled from the gaze of

---

* Exod. 20: 1

men. The hearts of those men must be radically changed from beastliness to purity before they could come into His presence. "Holiness to Jehovah"* was to be the badge of their approach toward Him.

Thus have we reached the idea of deliverance from spiritual bondage as the underlying idea of the exodus of Israel from Egypt to Sinai. The One Holy God has *redeemed* His people. Their redemption is recorded in the history of the mission of Moses and the triumph of Jehovah over the gods of Egypt. The yoke of Meneptah has been lifted from their necks. The lash of the task-master has been removed. They have been taken from an environment of bondage to one of freedom. All of this is summed up for them in the truth that their Holy God has delivered them from the multitude of Egyptian nature-gods. They dwell no longer under the shadow of sun-gods and animal-gods, but they live in the presence of an invisible redeemer. In order that they may not bring the spirit of idolatry into the worship of Jehovah, He remains hidden from view. They cannot see His form, nor His face, and cannot, therefore, make an image of Him. No doubt the Israelites would have made idols like unto the idols of Egypt, for very soon they did compel Aaron to mould a golden calf. The teaching of a long sojourn in Egypt had left deep impressions upon the Hebrews, and the nation would very soon have fallen into a ritual like that of the sun-worshippers. But this was made impossible by the fact that their God remained unseen. They began their religious life as a nation by cutting loose from a people whose gods were manifested in forms and shapes that could be seen and by entrusting themselves and all their interests to the orderings of the invisible One.

The Sealing of the National Covenant.

The people of Israel accepted their deliverer as their God, the personal object of worship, and in thus doing they set themselves forever in opposition to the polytheism of Egypt. But, in addition, they accepted their divine deliverer as king, and upon that acceptance was based the theocracy. In this form of government were incorporated certain principles in direct contrast with the despotism of

---

*Ex. 28: 36.

the Pharaohs—principles that have been recognized in the establishment of every form of free government throughout the world. The very beginning of free government, the preservation of the rights of the individual, was here made in the establishment of the theocracy at Sinai. The victory of Jehovah over the sun-gods was made perpetual and embodied in the charter granted unto Israel. In the light of this divine constitution it was made clear that despotism in government is to be held forever as a crime against man and a sin against God.

In its primary character the theocracy was a covenant between Jehovah on the one side and the Hebrew nation on the other. A contract was formally proposed by Jehovah, was accepted by Israel and ratified by a solemn ceremony and by an oath sworn by the whole people in public assembly.

The covenant was made through the mediation of Moses, after many messages transmitted between Jehovah and the people. When first the pilgrims approached Mount Sinai, Moses went on in advance and up into the presence of Jehovah. There, in declaring the purpose of this great national deliverance, that is, to make of Israel "a kingdom of priests and an holy nation," Jehovah announced to Moses the sole condition upon which this purpose depended, viz.: that Israel should "keep my covenant." *

When this condition was announced, what said the people? "Moses came and called for the elders of the people, and laid before their faces all these words which Jehovah commanded him. And all the people answered together, and said, All that Jehovah hath spoken we will do."

Thus did Israel formally accept the covenant, and this acceptance was made legal and complete when "Moses returned the words of the people unto Jehovah." †

After this preliminary condition was completed, then began the ratification of the covenant more in detail. All the while must it be remembered that Israel was acting from choice. No constraint was laid upon the nation. They were willing and eager to enter into solemn compact with Him who had delivered them from Meneptah's tyranny.

---

* Exod. 19: 1–6.   † Exod. 19: 7, 8.

On the third day, in the morning, "Moses brought forth the people out of the camp to meet with God."* Not the elders merely, but the entire population were led forth to make the covenant. Then it was that "all the people saw the thunderings and the lightnings and the noise of the trumpet and the mountain smoking; and when the people saw it they removed and stood afar off." †

While thus in awe and fear, afar stood the people away from the mount; Moses himself "drew near unto the thick darkness where God was." ‡ Then God spoke the words which He afterwards engraved with His own finger upon the two tables of stones.§ Also He gave other commandments which Moses was commanded to write in the book of the covenant.‖ "And Moses came and told the people all the words of Jehovah and all the judgments: And all the people answered with one voice and said, All the words which Jehovah hath said will we do."

Thus a second time did the people formally agree to accept the covenant, and this agreement was made after they had heard in detail from Moses all the terms of the compact.

As a third step in the ceremony, "Moses wrote all the words of Jehovah."¶ A written constitution must this covenant be. We find here nothing like the "contrat social" of which Rousseau dreamed as the basis of society and of which he adduced no written fragment whatever. The scribe who wrote down the words of Jehovah as the basis of the first great national compact was the author of the epic of triumph at the Red Sea—the chosen mediator between God and His people.

In accepting this written charter, a great religious ceremonial was enacted. Moses "rose up early in the morning and builded an altar under the hill, and twelve pillars, according to the twelve tribes of Israel.

"And he sent young men of the children of Israel which offered burnt-offerings and sacrificed peace-offerings of oxen unto Jehovah.

"And Moses took half of the blood and put it in basins; and half of the blood he sprinkled on the altar.

---

*Exod. 19: 17. †Exod. 20: 18. ‡Exod. 20: 21. §Exod. 20: 1; 21: 1. ‖Exod. 24: 3.
¶Exod. 24: 4.

"And he took the book of the covenant and read in the audience of the people; and they said:

"All that Jehovah hath said will we do and be obedient."*

While thus the people stand as a great mass-meeting, gathered to accept a divine form of government, let us remember the binding character of the ceremonial symbolism stamped upon the whole transaction. The altar built by Moses is a symbol of the presence of Jehovah. The same meaning attaches to this altar that belonged to the altar built by Abraham. In that case, Jehovah was present to make covenant with an individual; in this case he is present to enter into covenant with the nation descended from that individual. It is the covenant of Abraham renewed as a national compact.

Likewise, the twelve pillars are a symbol of the presence of the twelve tribes with whom Jehovah is making the covenant. Now let us observe the symbolic union of the two parties in the ceremonial that follows.

The burnt-offerings placed upon Jehovah's altar by the young men, signify the complete dedication of the people of Israel unto Jehovah. Thus freely do they give themselves to be His.

The peace-offerings are a figure of their communion with Jehovah. It is a kind of Old Testament Lord's Supper, wherein the nation comes into spiritual contact with their king and redeemer.

This sacramental union was made still more complete, in symbol, by the casting of the blood of these sacrifices upon the altar and upon the people. First, upon the altar Moses cast half the blood. This signified that Jehovah initiated the covenant and awaited the agreement of the people. No haste was made. Due time for deliberation was granted. The book of the covenant was read to the people. This book was the same as that written by Moses at the command of Jehovah. It contained the terms of the covenant, aside from the ten commandments already accepted. This book probably contained the "judgments" recorded in Exodus 20: 22—23: 33. With full knowledge of what they did— with full knowledge of the charter of freedom granted on condition of obedience—the people of Israel took the solemn

---
* Exod. 24: 4-7.

oath. "And Moses took the blood and sprinkled it on the people, and said, Behold the blood of the covenant which Jehovah hath made with you concerning all these words."*

The whole nation had accepted the charter. Jehovah's kingship was proclaimed and Jehovah's law was enacted in solemn assembly of the whole people. "There went up Moses and Aaron, Nadab and Abihu and seventy of the elders of Israel:

"And they saw the God of Israel:

"And under His feet it was like a work of bright sapphire-stone, and like the heaven itself in clearness.

"And upon the nobles of the children of Israel He laid not His hand: also they saw God and did eat and drink."†

These men were the representative heads of the families of the nation. Up into the mountain they went to eat the feast of the covenant. They ate, in God's presence, the flesh of the peace-offerings. The feast itself was an act of solemn worship. They recognized the presence of their deliverer and king. They "heard the voice of the words, but saw no similitude."‡ Not even here did they see the form or face of God. But a great vision unfolded itself in such manner as to overwhelm the sight with its glory. The pavement of His throne shone upon them like sapphire, and His voice filled the air, and the sense of His presence overwhelmed mind and heart. Sight was extinguished in the blaze of glory, and no form appeared therein; but so far as it is possible for men to see Jehovah and live, these elders and priests saw the God of Israel. He did not smite them, for this communion of feasting was a gracious approach of God unto His people in order that they might learn to love the giver of law. Not stern was Jehovah in giving statutes, for the law was not the arbitrary imposition of a powerful despot. The law was based upon the covenant between the king and the people. The nation willingly accepted the commandments and the judgments of Jehovah because they had love for their Redeemer and reverence for their king.

The Tables of the Covenant.

At the feast that completed the covenant Moses again heard the voice of God. "And Jehovah said unto Moses,

---
*Exod. 24: 8.   †Exod. 24: 9, 11.   ‡Deut. 4: 12.

Come up to me into the mount and be there; and I will give thee tables of stone with the law, even the commandments which I have written, that thou mayest teach them. . . . . And Moses went into the midst of the cloud and gat him up into the mount; and Moses was in the mount forty days and forty nights."* Without meat and without drink, Moses dwelt forty days and nights in the midst of the cloud upon the mount. During his absence the spirit of Egyptian idolatry was revived in the memories of the people. They desired an image of their God. A golden calf like unto the sacred bull of Egyptian worship was made by Aaron, and they bowed the knee unto the idol. As an image of Jehovah Himself they seem to have regarded it. But in this idolatry they violated the terms of the covenant. They had already heard the ten commandments and had given assent; but even now while Moses was receiving the written form they violated the covenant. And Moses petitioned Jehovah to forgive these pledge-breakers and still to keep them as His nation.

"And Moses turned and went down from the mount, and the two tables of the testimony were in his hand; the tables were written on both their sides; on the one side and on the other were they written.

"And the tables were the work of God, and the writing was the writing of God, graven upon the tables."†

When Moses reached the camp the awful truth of the broken covenant burst upon him. Righteous indignation stirred his heart and he cast down the tables of stone and brake them into pieces, for since the compact was violated no longer was there need of the testimony.

Now again were the people to be purified. The molten calf was ground into powder and the children of Israel were made to swallow the powder mingled with water. Then the standard of Jehovah was raised and a general amnesty proclaimed in Jehovah's name. "Who is on Jehovah's side?" rang through the camp. The penitent and the obedient flocked unto Moses. The tribe of Levi came as one man. The act of idolatry was disavowed by the people as a nation. Those who persisted in their sin and the love of it were put to the sword. Of such there were about three thousand

---

* Exod. 24: 12-18. † Exod. 32: 15, 16.

men, and these all fell at the hands of their brethren, who desired to disavow the great sin against Jehovah. Thus were the covenant-violators blotted out, and the whole nation stood penitent before Jehovah.*

Again into the mount went Moses. There his great heart outflowed in intercession for his brethren. His own name out of the book of life might be blotted if Jehovah would only again receive the people into favor. And Moses found grace in God's sight and was granted a near vision of His glory. There was given to Moses a new revelation of the name and nature of Jehovah.

"And Jehovah passed by before him and proclaimed, Jehovah, Jehovah God, merciful and gracious, long-suffering, and abundant in goodness and truth,

"Keeping mercy for thousands, forgiving iniquity and transgression and sin, and that will by no means clear the guilty; visiting the iniquity of the fathers upon the children and upon the children's children unto the third and to the fourth generation."†

Here stands revealed the love of the deliverer. The nature of their God is mercy and forgiveness. Even His justice is made subordinate to His love and is to be exercised only upon those who persevere in rejecting Him.

The covenant was renewed upon this basis of human penitence and divine mercy. Moses prepared again two tables of stone and Jehovah "wrote upon the tables the words of the covenant, the ten commandments."‡

The tables were called the testimony. Direct evidence from the finger of Jehovah were they. Not in symbolic form was this law given, but in definite statements written by God Himself. Neither in form nor in spirit were they ever to pass away. They establish and guard the rights of Jehovah and the rights of the nation as the basis of the covenant. The first four commandments specify the prerogatives of Jehovah as sovereign, and those prerogatives must be safely guarded. The next six commandments specify certain sanctities and privileges between man and man. Violation of Jehovah's rights in any form—whether profanation of His person by following other gods or making images, or profanation of His name and His day—is to be

---

* Exod. 32. † Exod. 34: 6, 7. ‡ Exod. 34: 1, 28.

punished by death.* Here is written the law of high treason as now incorporated in the forms of government throughout the world.

The sanctity of parentage, of life, of personal purity among men is guarded by the death penalty.† All these penalties, it is true, are not incorporated in the testimony. The safeguard there set forth is the sovereign mandate of Jehovah Himself. All these commandments must be obeyed simply because they represent the will of the lawgiver and because they are the only basis upon which He will establish His covenant. Covenant-breakers, and, therefore, rebels against God, are all those who violate any one of the ten words of the testimony.

The Book of the Covenant.

The tables of the covenant were written by Jehovah Himself; the book of the covenant was written by Moses. The people of Israel heard the commandments of the first before they were recorded, and gave assent thereto. The "judgments" of the book were read from the manuscript form and Israel swore an oath to obey them.‡ The exact contents of this book are contained, probably, in Exodus 20: 22—23: 33. The tables and the book together held the terms of the great compact.

These two portions of the covenant had the same authority stamped upon them. Both came from God. The one was the testimony of Jehovah; the other was made up of "the words of Jehovah." The one came directly from God; the other came from God, through the agency of Moses.

The tables are called "the law, even the commandment;" § the book is said to contain "the judgments," ‖ that is, the decisions of the law in detail. The primary principles of the covenant were written upon the tables in order that they might stand in that form forever; the interpretation of those principles in connection with some of the conditions of life among the Hebrews was set forth in the book. The tables contained the law in its divine and eternal form; the book contained the same law in symbolic and changeable form. This brings us back, in fact, to the relationship existing between Jehovah and Moses. As mediator, Moses

---
*Exod. 21.   †Exod. 21.   ‡Ex. 34: 3-7.   § Ex. 24: 12.   ‖ Ex. 21: 1.

was prophet and type of all the prophets and type of Christ Himself; the work of Moses was the establishment of the theocracy, type of the reign of God and of His Christ in the hearts of all men in all the ages of the world.

The symbolism of the book of the covenant is apparent from the examination of a few of its statements. The first injunction deals with the matter of divine worship. It gives an interpretation to the Hebrew nation of that day of the meaning of the first and second commandments. "And Jehovah said unto Moses, Thus shalt thou say unto the children of Israel, ye have seen that I have talked with you from heaven.

"Ye shall not make with me gods of silver, neither shall ye make unto you gods of gold."*

But the question would naturally spring to the lips of the Hebrew, "If not by means of idols, as the Egyptians taught us, then how shall we worship Jehovah?" Altogether by the sacrifice of victims upon the altar. So ran the answer. "An altar of earth thou shalt make unto me."† The commandment enjoining worship was intended to remain in force forever; but the commandment enjoining the altar of earth was meant to be binding only until the coming of Christ.

A second fact that indicates the symbolism of the book of the covenant is the attachment of temporal penalties to some of the statutes. This penal legislation was enacted according to a definite principle, and that principle was "life for life, eye for eye, tooth for tooth, hand for hand, foot for foot, burning for burning, wound for wound, stripe for stripe." ‡ Hence, the death penalty was attached to the first eight commandments.§ Nothing less than human life could be used to measure the value of God's own sanctity and the sanctity of human life itself and of human purity. And yet a great change has taken place in the form of this legislation. Christian legislation, which professes to observe the spirit of divine law, does not punish idolatry; but the death penalty here has been transferred to crimes against the state itself or its monarchical head. Idolatry was treason against God; the penalty against such treason is now

---
*Exod. 20: 22, 23. †Exod. 20: 24. ‡Exod. 21: 23–25. §Exod. 22: 20; 32; 24: 16; 31: 14; 21: 15; 17; 21: 12; 21: 16; Lev. 20: 10.

left to God; but treason against the human monarch is visited with death. In like manner, blasphemy, Sabbath-breaking, dishonor to parents, adultery and theft are now punished in lighter methods than the use of the death penalty. Murder alone must still be expiated by means of the life-blood. The reason for this change is not that these crimes are less heinous now than at that time; but the conditions of life have changed, and moreover, as chief reason, the milder legislation of the sermon on the mount has superseded the Mosaic code. That such a change in form could take place is clearly shown in the symbolic character of the book of the covenant.

Another indication of this future change in the form of penalties is found in Leviticus xxvi., closely linked with the book of the covenant. "If ye will not hearken unto me, and will not do all these commandments,

"And if ye shall despise my statutes, or if your soul abhor my judgments, so that ye will not do all my commandments, that ye break my covenant, I also will do this unto you."* If thus the people disobey, then God will visit upon them all the temporal calamities that follow in the train of (1) disease, (2) famine and (3) defeat.† The meaning of all this can only be that God retains within His own power the final punishment of all disobedience; but that in Moses' time the penalty of death must be imposed by the rulers among the people as indication to a primitive race of the heinous nature of disobedience.

The book of the covenant is closed by a reference to the presence of Jehovah in the midst of His people. The angel of the covenant will represent Him and go before the nation to lead them in the way. "My name is in him," ‡ said Jehovah. As a leader in the wilderness and a leader in battle will this angel be, if the people continue to obey. He shall bring them into the land promised unto Abraham.

Thus, by means of the ideas embodied in altars and angels and promised homes, does Moses explain unto Israel the principles of that theocracy which belongs to the realm of the human soul, and which shall extend forever in the place where God reigns in the heavens.

---

* Lev. 26. † Lev. 26. ‡ Exod. 23: 21.

The Ark of the Covenant.

(*Exodus* 25-31; 35-40.)

After the covenant was ratified at the foot of Mount Sinai, Jehovah called Moses into the midst of the cloud and gave him directions for making the ark of the covenant and the tabernacle of the testimony. The ark was designed to hold the stone tables of the covenant; it was to be surmounted by the cherubim, and above it was to rest the cloud that symbolized God's presence. Within the tabernacle was this ark to rest, in symbol that God dwelt in the midst of His people, making His abode in a tent constructed like the tents of the children of Israel.

The ark of the covenant was the chief part of this sanctuary, since it represented Jehovah Himself in plighted union with Israel. The tabernacle itself was subordinate in importance to the ark, even as the house is subordinate to him who dwells therein. The construction of the ark and its establishment in the tabernacle brought to a close the great national covenant. Let us, therefore, review the order of events that were terminated by the placing of the ark in its sacred dwelling-place.

First of all, the voice of Jehovah uttered the ten commandments from the summit of Sinai. Then, next in order, Moses wrote down the short list of legal interpretations in the book of the covenant, and, then, Israel swore to obey the commandments and the book. They accepted the law, and also the principles of its interpretation as written by Moses.*

After the making of the covenant in fact, then was it ratified also in symbol. Immediately after the oath of the people had been sanctified by the blood of the covenant, Moses was commanded to make the ark,† that was to contain the tables of the ten commandments, with the mercy-seat above. Next was he commanded to make the holy table and the holy candlestick to be set in the holy place of the sanctuary; and after all this was he commanded to make the tabernacle itself.‡ As matters connected with the tabernacle, instructions were given him concerning the brazen altar and the court and the ministers of the whole sanctuary.§ Following

---
*Exod. 19: 24. †Exod. 26: 10-16. ‡Exod. 26. §Exod. 28, 29.

all these instructions concerning the dwelling-place of the law, the tables of the law were last of all given to Moses.

During eighty days and eighty nights was Moses in the mount in the presence of Jehovah.* When he returned from this long conference, the seal of God's presence was visible upon the very countenance of Moses, for the skin of his face shone in the presence of the people, and he wore a veil over his features in sign of the glory revealed to him alone. It was the glory of the completed covenant reflected in the face of him who had represented Israel. That same glory was now to be given a permanent abiding-place over the ark of the covenant. Moses at once called the people to the work of making a symbolic house of God upon earth.

In Exodus 25–31, we have the manual of divine direction as to how the ark and its tent shall be made. In Exodus 35–40, we have the manual of construction, where all the commandments of Jehovah are obeyed and the work is completed.

In the order of construction, the tabernacle was first made. The architect was Jehovah Himself, for He gave unto Moses in the mount the pattern of it.† The chief constructors were Bezaleel and Aholiab, who were called by Jehovah unto this special work, and were men filled "with the spirit of God, in wisdom, in understanding, and in knowledge and in all manner of workmanship."‡ All the assistant workmen were "wise-hearted," "in whom Jehovah put wisdom and understanding."§ Moreover, the material used in the construction was the free-will offering of the people in obedience to the command of Jehovah. In design, in material, in construction, the sanctuary was Jehovah's.

In three parts was the sanctuary made. Curtains of fine twined linen and blue, and purple, and scarlet, were bound together by clasps of gold to form the inner dwelling-place. In this great web were embroidered figures of cherubim, or human forms with wings, symbolizing the highest type of human adoration before God.‖

As a protection for this inner abode of curtains, there was made a tent of goat's hair, and then, as a covering for the tent, there was stretched a canvas of red ram-skins, and above that, a covering of badger's skins.¶

---

* Exod. 24: 18; 34: 29. † Exod. 25: 9. ‡ Exod. 35: 30-35. § Exod. 36: 1. ‖ Exod. 36: 8-13. ¶ Exod. 36: 4-19.

Within the inner dwelling-place there was set up a rectangular structure of acacia boards, resting in silver sockets and coupled together with bars and rings. Then a partition vail and a door-way vail of the same material with the curtains themselves, completed the tabernacle. The sanctuary now awaited its holy furniture, in order that a peculiar significance might belong to the entire structure.

The ark of the covenant was made by Bezaleel himself. A rectangular chest of acacia wood, overlaid with gold, and borne by rings and staves; this formed the base. The covering of the chest was a solid plate of gold with two cherubs standing upon it, all beaten from one piece of metal. This was the mercy seat.

As accompaniments of the ark were the table of shewbread and its vessels, the seven-branched candlestick, the altar of incense, the brazen altar, the laver and the court.* These were merely the implements of the holy ritual, of which the ark was to be the centre. Then were made the dresses of the priests of the same blue and purple and scarlet material.†

At last came the great day of dedication. "In the first month in the second year, on the first day of the month," Jehovah's symbolic residence among His people was consummated. The tabernacle was upreared. Like a royal palace it stood in the midst of the camp, with its royal trappings of blue and purple and scarlet. In these imperial surroundings was Jehovah coming to dwell.

Then was brought the symbol of Jehovah's presence. In the ark were placed the stone tables of the covenant, and upon the ark was set the mercy seat.‡ Along with the tables was placed the omer of manna.§ Hence did it become the ark of the covenant, or the ark of the testimony. This ark was placed in the inner chamber of the tabernacle, beyond the dividing-vail. Then in their proper order and place were arranged the vessels of the sanctuary, and next followed the sanctification of Aaron and his sons as priests. "Holiness to Jehovah" was inscribed on Aaron's breastplate as he came forward to enter into God's service. The lamps were lighted, the altars began to smoke with the burning of incense and the burning of the sacrifice. Moses

---

*Exod. 37: 10.—38: 31. †Exod. 39. ‡Exod. 25: 16. §Exod. 16: 33, 34.

and Aaron stood in official robes at the door of the sanctuary, for their part of the work was finished.*

"Then a cloud covered the tent of the congregation, and the glory of Jehovah filled the tabernacle. And Moses was not able to enter into the tent of the congregation, because the cloud abode thereon, and the glory of Jehovah filled the tabernacle."†

The great covenant was now completed, and the ark rested in the midst of the camp as the visible symbol thereof. The ark was shut away from the sight of the people behind the vail of the most holy place of the tabernacle. None but Moses at first, and then the High Priest could come before the ark. There God dwelt in the cloud that hovered over the mercy seat between the cherubim. "And when Moses was gone into the tabernacle of the congregation to speak with Him, then he heard the voice speaking unto him from off the mercy seat that was upon the ark of testimony from between the two cherubim; and he spake unto Him."‡

In the covenant was the voice of Jehovah accepted by Israel as their law; the ark of the covenant was the sacred seal and symbol whence came the voice of Jehovah at all times unto the representative of the nation. The ark was borne along upon the march, and thus Jehovah dwelt continually with Israel to vouchsafe guidance forever. For even so did He promise: "I will dwell among the children of Israel and will be their God.

"And they shall know that I am Jehovah their God that brought them forth out of the land of Egypt that I may dwell among them; I am Jehovah their God.§

Jehovah the Sovereign King.

We are now in a position to understand that the national covenant at Sinai was something more than the establishment of a form of government. The covenant was primarily a revelation of the nature and character of God. As such it forms an integral part of that revelation which is recorded in the story of creation and of the patriarchs and in the story of the exodus from Egypt. This will appear when we array in order many facts imbedded in the sacred record. All these facts centre about the great truth that Israel, in the covenant, accepts Jehovah as sovereign king.

*Exod. 40. †Exod. 40. ‡Exod. 25: 20-22; Numb. 7: 89. §Exod. 29: 45, 46.

Jehovah is king because He is deliverer. This is the first truth presented by the narrative of the covenant. It is the leading fact in the history. It is also the one great fact that binds together the Book of Genesis with the other four books of the Pentateuch into one unbroken history. For in the story that begins in Genesis God appears unto Abraham and declares, "I will surely bless thee and thy seed after thee."* In the same narrative, carried on in Exodus, God appears to Moses and thus speaks: "I am Jehovah, God of your fathers, God of Abraham, God of Isaac, and God of Jacob, and I am come down to deliver My people."† Then again at the Red Sea Israel sings thus unto God: "Jehovah is . . . . become my salvation. . . . He is . . . . my fathers' God, and I will exalt Him."‡ At Sinai the great sequel is declared: "I am Jehovah thy God which have brought thee . . . out of the house of bondage."§

The entire history is simply the story of deliverance promised and deliverance completed. The whole work is wrought by the same God who is accepted as eternal king because He hath chosen Israel as His people and has delivered them with an high hand.

But this unity of the nature of Jehovah is apparent from other facts than the announcement of His name. At the same time the deliverance wrought is far greater than a temporal deliverance from the task-masters of Egypt. All this appears from the character of the ten commandments. Obedience unto these will bring deliverance not merely from earthly despots, but first of all from the bondage of sin. Very naturally, therefore, we find no new revelation in the details of the subject-matter of the commandments.‖ Every duty enjoined in them is found revealed in the Book of Genesis and the early part of the Book of Exodus.

The first three commandments concerning the unity and sanctity of God's person and the sanctity of His name, that neither of these shall be desecrated by polytheism nor by image worship nor by blasphemy; these three injunctions underlie the entire history recorded in the Book of Genesis. Time and time again are they repeated in didactic form— in visions, in deliverances, in punishment of the enemies of God's people. They are fundamental principles involved

---
*Gen. 15. †Exod. 3: 15, 8. ‡Exod. 15: 2. §Exod. 20: 1. ‖Speaker's Com. I.: 433.

in the revelations recorded in the early parts of the Pentateuch.

The fourth commandment was observed before the people arrived at Sinai, even while they were marching through the sands and rocks of the upper peninsula.* And this was true, because the obligation to sanctify God's day is based upon His example of sanctifying the seventh day after the six days of creation. This reason held good among the patriarchs unto whom was revealed the fact that God is the creator, and it was assigned as the reason for the observance of God's day in the fourth commandment.† In the legislation that follows the announcement of the commandments, the sacredness of the Sabbath seems to be a touch-stone. The Sabbath day and the sabbatical year are incorporated in the book of the covenant;‡ the Sabbath is to be kept holy even in preparing material for the sanctuary.§ Afterwards, when Moses expounds the law unto Israel, he expresses a second reason for observing the sacredness of the Sabbath; that reason is the deliverance wrought for the people in the exodus.‖ Thus was the Sabbath declared to be a sacramental bond between Jehovah and His people. It was an old and recognized duty made into a badge of the covenant. The rainbow existed before Noah's time, but became with him the sign of a new covenant. The Sabbath was a holy day from the close of creation, and as such was binding on all nations whether they recognized it or not. After the covenant at Sinai it had the added significance that it became a token of deliverance from Egypt, and of deliverance from sin forever. "It [the Sabbath] is a sign between me and you throughout your generations; that ye may know that I am Jehovah that doth sanctify you."¶

The remaining six commandments concerning the sanctity of certain properties and privileges of the individual man—all these are likewise incorporated in the early parts of the Pentateuch. The duties enjoined in these six commandments are amply illustrated in the lives of the patriarchs.

Hence, the covenant is based upon the patriarchate and the exodus, not merely as a historical sequence, but in the

---

* Exod. 16: 29, 30.   † Exod. 20: 11.   ‡ Exod. 23: 10-12.   § Exod. 35: 1-3.   ‖ Deut. 5.
¶ Exod. 31: 13-17.

matter of fundamental principles. The corner-stone of the covenant is the character of Jehovah—a character already revealed through long dealings with his chosen tribes, and now manifestly shown in keeping the promises made centuries before unto the fathers of this people. It is the same Jehovah who chose their fathers, because He loved their fathers, that has now chosen them because He loves them. It is the same Jehovah who showed mercy unto Noah and unto Abraham, and unto Jacob, who has now shown mercy unto them, and who is willing to show mercy unto their children, even to the third and fourth generations of them that love Him. It is the same God who overwhelmed the world of wicked men in the flood, who has now shown His right arm in strength to overwhelm the Egyptians in the Red Sea. This same Eternal Being is now accepted as the absolute and sovereign king over Israel, because of His love, and because of His might in delivering them, and in revealing Himself as the source of physical and spiritual, of individual, and of national life.

This sovereignty of God is recognized in direct terms in the stone tables. He is accepted as the only God in all the earth. He is accepted as the only object of worship. He is accepted as the only source of authority in all affairs of men, temporal and eternal. The people receive the law as the word of their absolute king.

But this sovereignty is yet more specifically recognized in every part of the terms of the covenant. All the duties imposed upon the nation are assigned because of His ownership of all the earth, and particularly His ownership of Israel. "Ye shall be a peculiar treasure unto me above all people; *for all the earth* is mine." * Israel is God's costly possession, set apart from His other possessions unto the particular destiny of holiness and blessedness. God owns His people and, in consequence, they are in debt to Him to the extent of implicit obedience unto all His laws.

(a) The first instance of this claim of ownership on the part of Jehovah is the example just cited where He claimed the entire nation as His property. As a symbol of this fact, that all the people themselves belong to Him, Jehovah commanded that all the first-born of men should be consecrated

---

* Exodus 19: 5.

unto Him by a formal, priestly ceremony.* These were to be His ministers, representing the fact that the entire nation was to be a kingdom of priests. In the practical administration of the ritual, however, the tribe of Levi was set apart to serve in the temple, in the place of these first-born among men. † This ownership of men was symbolized, also, in the laws concerning Hebrew slavery. "If thou buy an Hebrew servant, six years he shall serve: and in the seventh he shall go out free for nothing." ‡ Eternal slavery was not countenanced, because such a system would imply that man might have absolute ownership of man. But slavery was thus limited in order to show that all men are Jehovah's personal property. Another symbol of God's ownership is to be found in the laws concerning diet. God's people must be clean in their manner of eating if they would be holy in their lives. With the flesh of unclean beasts they might not defile themselves, nor by contact with dead flesh of any sort whatsoever. §

(b) Ownership of cattle was likewise claimed by Jehovah. The first-born of beasts were to be set apart unto Him as victims. The firstling of the ass, being an unclean animal and not fitted for sacrifice, might be redeemed with a lamb. In like manner, the horse and the camel and every unclean beast might be thus redeemed by an offering of other sort.‖

(c) "The land is mine; for ye are strangers and sojourners with me."¶ Thus spake Jehovah concerning His ownership of the soil. His people are simply His guests. Hence did He declare the law concerning the reversion of all lands to their original possessors after the lapse of fifty years. Each individual was to be granted a portion of land as God's tenant. His possession was thus based on God's gift. If the man should sell the lease, it would revert to him at the next sabbatical year. No man could use money in purchasing the inheritance of many men and thus build up a great private domain. The land was Jehovah's and He chose to keep it in the hands of these families unto whom it was at the first assigned.**

(d). "The first fruits for Jehovah" were required of every harvest, of the vintage, the threshing-floor, the wine-press,

---

*Exod. 13: 2, 11, 12. †Numb. 2: 12. ‡Exod. 21: 2. §Lev. 11 and 17. ‖Numb. 18: 15. ¶Lev. 25: 23. **Lev. 25: 23.

the oil-press, the first baked bread of the new crop, and the first fleeces of the flock. All these gifts must be brought to the temple and there offered unto Jehovah as the subsistence of His priests.* In this way was the entire fruit of the earth dedicated to Jehovah, just as the nation was consecrated to Him in the dedication of the first-born.

(e). The tithe.—In addition to the first-fruits of all the products of the earth and the heave-offerings that were presented along with those first fruits, Jehovah ordained that unto the Levites should be given a tenth of all the possessions of the other tribes of Israel. "Behold, I have given the children of Levi all the tenth in Israel for an inheritance, for their service which they serve, even the service of the tabernacle of the congregation." † This tribute was recognized among the patriarchs when Abram rendered a tithe to Melchizedek and Jacob promised tithes unto God if he should be permitted to return to his father's house. But now was it made a part of the covenant that a tenth of all property should be rendered unto Jehovah for the support of His ministers, the entire system symbolizing the fact that God is the absolute owner of all the possessions of men. Therefore, God required a second tenth from the nine parts left after the first tithing, to be offered to Him as a feast in the sanctuary. In every approach unto Jehovah on the part of His subjects, they were required to present not only themselves, but a part of their substance in sign of the fact that Jehovah, the king, possesses and holds forever all that which He has created and which He sustains by His divine power.

Jehovah established His kingship throughout upon the principle of unlikeness to the royalty of the land of Egypt. The Egyptians worshipped the sun as chief god; Jehovah declared Himself as the creator of the sun. The Egyptians worshipped local deities and bowed down to their images; they regarded the reigning sovereign as "the living image and vice-gerent of the sun-god;" ‡ the Pharaoh's statues were upreared in every spot as objects of worship, and the king's palace was in reality a great temple; but the Israelites were commanded to worship the One only God, their sovereign king, who had conquered Egypt's king; and that

---
* Exod. 23: 19; Numb. 15 and 18; Lev. 23. † Numb. 18: 21. ‡ Renouf., p. 167.

worship was to be rendered not with images, but with simple obedience to His laws. Since the Israelites were to become an holy nation, unlike all other nations, the foundation of such character was laid in the revelation of Jehovah as one who is unlike all other gods.

Although images of God were forbidden, yet did He not withdraw Himself from communion with His people. He spake with Moses in the mount; He revealed His glory there to Moses and the elders, and He appeared in the cloud above and within the tabernacle. While He thus drew near to His people in a manner far beyond the conception of Egyptian worshippers, yet did He declare His character to be unlike anything known among the Egyptian gods. "Under the name of god, the Egyptians did not understand, as we do, a being without body, parts or passions. The bodies of the gods are spoken of as well as their souls, and they have both parts and passions; they are described as suffering from hunger and thirst, old age, disease, fear and sorrow. . . . . All the great gods require protection. Osiris is helpless against his enemies, and his remains are protected by his wife and sister."* Jehovah reveals Himself as a spiritual being. The character of the Egyptian gods is not at all imitated. A new principle, absolutely unknown to all heathen mythologies, is declared as the basis of Jehovah's character. As spirit, He is unseen and eternal; as a person, He loves His people and speaks unto them through the mediator, Moses.

Among the Egyptians different representatives of the gods ruled upon the earth. Many animals were worshipped as deities; the kings themselves sprang from the sun; the serpent was carved on the monuments as a symbol of royal power. In contrast with all this diversity, Jehovah alone dwelt in the midst of His people in the tabernacle; in contrast with all the symbols of power that surrounded the Pharaoh, Jehovah's tent was constructed in great simplicity and the symbols of mercy were used as the signs of His presence. It is true that the tabernacle was made of curtains of purple, scarlet and gold, the trappings that belong to royalty in all ages; the tabernacle was thus a palace wherein the King of Israel held His court; but, on the

---

* Renouf., p. 89.

other hand, the king's house was only a tent in the midst of the camp of tents. Then, the mercy-seat was the specific place of His presence; the cloud of glory was the specific sign of His presence, and that cloud had been and continued to be the sign of deliverance. By means of sacrifices, offered upon the altars that stood in the ante-chambers, could the God of mercy be approached.

Chiefly, however, from the political point of view, do we observe the contrast between the character of Jehovah and that of the Pharaohs. Politics and religion with all these ancient peoples were virtually the same, but we may speak of the political character of the king as pertaining to the origin and exercise of his authority as a ruler. The Pharaohs inherited their power, and that power was despotic. The Pharaoh owned his people—body and soul—because his father had owned them and had handed them down to his son as he bequeathed his lands and his cattle. Jehovah's kingship, however, rested upon the covenant made at Sinai. His sovereignty was accorded Him in this great national compact. Jehovah's character as creator and deliverer was revealed unto the people; an appeal was thus made to their reason as individual men; the law was revealed as containing the will and purpose of Jehovah, and then the nation, by assenting to the terms of the covenant, chose Him as their king. They yielded unto Him the intelligent obedience of men who were free to consent or free to refuse. The new principle, the dignity of the individual man, was thus declared. The power of earthly despots over the life and interests of their subjects was denied; the foundation for all free government was laid in this covenant wherein an entire nation swore to obey Jehovah alone as their sovereign king.

CHAPTER XVIII.

THE NATIONAL ADMINISTRATION. THE PRIESTS AS MINISTERS OF STATE.

[*Book of Leviticus.*]

The Kingdom Visible.

THE Book of Exodus has shown us how Jehovah established Himself in the tabernacle as a king in the midst of His people. His form and His face were never seen, but the symbols of His presence were always visible. His power was real and absolute and touched the physical and spiritual life of all Israel. This spiritual, invisible authority was now enthroned in a visible form of administration. Jehovah's government was regularly and definitely organized. Aaron and his sons were selected as His priests or ministers of State. Moses was the great mediator or prophet of Jehovah. Directions were given concerning the selection of a king from the people. This official was not chosen until many years later in the history of Israel, and then the king was simply Jehovah's representative as the executive head of the divine government. The supreme authority of Jehovah was, therefore, to be carried into effect through three heads of administration—priest, prophet, and king. Each of these heads of departments had his peculiar official functions. Each one of them was an Israelite to the manor born. Each administered the duties of his office by the use of certain symbols that set forth the authority of Jehovah over the officer and over the people. The invisible king made Himself known through a form of government which was constituted entirely of visible symbols.

Jehovah's royal tent was the centre of the civil and religious life of the people. His voice spake from the cloud over the mercy-seat and gave orders to march or orders to halt; orders to fight or orders to rest; orders to come into His presence at the door of the tabernacle and there receive blessing, or else receive punishment for sin. Two priests,

Nadab and Abihu, were consumed by "fire from Jehovah" for their impiety.* Again, fire from Jehovah's tabernacle consumed two hundred and fifty men, and the earth opened to swallow Korah and his company for their rebellion against the government.† These and other instances show that Jehovah was the chief *executive* in this administration of his authority. An earthly representative of Jehovah as the executive was not chosen in the period contemplated in the Pentateuch. The Israelitish kings, beginning with Saul and David, were all types of the messianic king, Jesus Christ, who came in the fullness of times to be the chief ruler in the kingdom of Jehovah.

The official next in authority to Jehovah Himself was the prophet. This term describes the work of Moses in establishing the theocracy. God spake with him face to face. God's law was given through him. Moses performed *executive* duties at times, but only as the representative of Jehovah. The peculiar relationship between Moses and Jehovah, and also between Moses and the people, will be discussed in a later part of this volume.

The visible machinery of the divine government was chiefly established in the work of the priesthood. Here we find the application of God's power to the minutest matters in the Hebrews' daily life. This power was administered by the priests, His ministers or servants. Their acts were authoritative only as sanctioned by Jehovah and only as performed in strict compliance with the regulations imposed in His law. In addition to serving Him in the active discharge of official duties, the priests also were representatives of the people in the presence of Jehovah.

The law of the priestly administration is written in that part of the Pentateuch called Leviticus. The book was probably not thus named originally, but simply formed a part of the law of the theocracy. Only a brief discussion of this priestly law can here be given. It will be sufficient to indicate its general character and its organic connection with the Book of Exodus. The reasons for asserting such a connection are not far to seek. (1) The central theme of Leviticus is the national altar and its ministers—that altar which was established at Sinai during the period of time

---

*Lev. 10: 2. †Numb. 16: 31, 35.

embraced in the history recorded in Exodus. (2) Leviticus, therefore, deals with the establishment of Jehovah's kingship in its practical administration around the altar—that kingship which was proclaimed in Exodus. (3) The point of time contemplated in Leviticus is that which immediately follows Jehovah's entrance into the tabernacle, as given in the closing words of the Book of Exodus. No sooner had He taken up His abode therein than "Jehovah called unto Moses and spake unto him out of the tabernacle of the congregation."* We have, then, in Leviticus, a continuance of the history already considered. In the Exodus Jehovah spake in the fire in the land of Egypt and in the thunder on Mt. Sinai, and thence gave the tables of stone and the book of the covenant. But now, at the foot of Sinai, from the tabernacle there erected, He speaks to Moses and reveals the law of the altar and the sacrifices whereby the people must show daily reverence for their king.

The National Altar. (*Leviticus 1-7.*)

The tabernacle was divided into three parts. The inner division, or holy of holies, contained the ark of the covenant. This was the central object in the sanctuary, for it was the throne of the invisible King. There dwelt Jehovah between the cherubim; there did the mercy-seat cover up the law. The sacred veil, made of three royal colors, shut off this central shrine from the holy place, and then just outside, in front of the tabernacle, was the court. These three divisions of the sanctuary marked three degrees in the approach of the people into Jehovah's presence. In the outer court was placed the altar of burnt-offerings, otherwise called the brazen altar, and in the holy place was set the altar of incense, or the golden altar, and on the one side of this altar the table of shew-bread, and on the other side the golden candlestick.†

To the brazen altar, in the outer court, came the people, bringing animal sacrifices, and these were offered to Jehovah in whole or in part in the fire of the altar. To the golden altar in the next court, or holy place, came only the priests, representing the people, and there they offered the

---
*Lev. 1: 1.   † Exod. 27: 40.

holy incense unto Jehovah. Into the holy of holies went the high priest alone and only once during the year.

The form of the tabernacle bore a general resemblance to the form of the Egyptian temple. "The pattern" of the first, however, was revealed to Moses in the mount. It was not copied from the sanctuaries of the sun-god. Rameses II. had built many of these at Zoan, at Memphis, Heliopolis, Thebes, and one was hewn from the cliff at Abou-Simbel, in Nubia. The latter contained an inner chamber, or shrine, approached through three other pillared chambers or halls. The furniture of the inner chamber consisted of an altar and images of four Egyptian gods, one of these gods being Rameses himself.* Further, we know that these figures of the gods were taken from the shrine on festival occasions and borne at the head of the procession through the streets. The idea of the divine Holiness was absent in this Egyptian ritual, while it is stamped on the Hebrew ceremonial and on the very arrangement of the sanctuary. The ark of the presence could be approached only once a year by the high priest with the blood of atonement. The Egyptian altar stood in the presence of the images, but the Mosaic altars were curtained off from the ark. The Egyptian religion was altogether legal and ritualistic. Nothing was there found to stir up the love and obedience of the heart. On the other hand, a moral and spiritual character was written upon the Hebrew ceremonial. The arrangement of the altars themselves was sufficient to teach submissiveness of spirit in the offerings upon the outer altar by the people, and the efficacy of intercessory prayer in the burning of incense upon the second altar by the priests. In the symbolism of the entire tabernacle, the Hebrew had before him a living connection between his own soul and the ceremonial of the sacrifice. The inward and spiritual grace was always surely called for by the outward and visible sign. Against the merely empty form in sacrificial worship, the whole tabernacle and its laws cried out.

While the Egyptian temples had served as object-lessons to keep before the minds of the Israelites the general meaning of divine worship through the use of altars and symbols, yet the spirit of the Mosaic ritual was something entirely

---

* Brugsch, p. 298.

new, except as it was only the completion of divine revelations already begun in the time of the patriarchs. The Mosaic system of worship was altogether of divine origin. The only real connection between it and the Egyptian system was this, that the latter had made the Hebrew people familiar with a national system of sacrifice by a national, hereditary priesthood. One national altar, however, was established at Sinai, in contrast with the multitude of altars in the land of the Pharaohs.

In the character of the offerings brought to the altar, the Mosaic code introduced a new principle. The sin-offerings required by Jehovah created a revolution in the old system of animal sacrifices. The oblations which were sacrificed on the altar were animal and vegetable. The animal sacrifices were burnt-offerings, peace-offerings and sin-offerings. The vegetable sacrifices, or incense and meat and drink offerings, always accompanied the first two of the above-named animal sacrifices.

Five animals might be used in sacrifice, the ox, the sheep, the goat, the dove and the pigeon, all of these belonging to the class of clean animals.* Moreover, each animal offered in sacrifice must be perfect, without spot or blemish, without deformity or disease.† These conditions of acceptable sacrifice came down to Moses from Abraham, for in the sacrifice of the covenant the patriarch of the Hebrew race offered " an heifer of three years old, and a she-goat of three years old, and a ram of three years old, and a turtle dove and a young pigeon."‡ When we remember that Noah sacrificed burnt-offerings after the flood; that Jacob sacrificed peace-offerings at Mizpeh; that other patriarchs "built an altar and called upon the name of Jehovah," and that Jethro offered burnt-offerings and peace-offerings when he met the Israelites in the wilderness, it will appear certain that the sin-offering was the one new and distinct sacrifice instituted by Jehovah at Sinai.

The burnt-offering was wholly burnt upon the altar. First into the outer court was the animal led and presented to the priest; then was it bound fast to the north side of the brazen altar. The man who presented the offering then laid his hand upon the head of the animal in token that he thus

---

*Lev. 11. †Lev. 22. ‡Gen. 15: 9.

dedicated himself unto Jehovah. Then was the animal slain, and all his parts were burnt upon the altar and the blood was sprinkled round about the altar.

The peace-offering was presented unto Jehovah in the same manner, except that only a part of the animal was burned upon the altar, the remainder being shared between the priest and him who offered the animal. The sacrificial meal was then eaten, in token of communion with Jehovah.

The burnt-offering was the great symbol of self-sacrifice unto Jehovah. The flesh was supposed to ascend in the fire of the altar up towards heaven, signifying the surrender of the body, soul and spirit of the sacrificer unto his God. Complete submission and acknowledgment of dependence upon Jehovah was thus set forth as the key-note of the entire religious ritual. In the peace-offering there was the symbol of self-surrender and also the symbol of communion with God. These two great rites of dedication and consecration were used by Moses in the formal ratification of the covenant at Sinai. They were incorporated into the system of sacrifices there ordained, but they belonged to the past as well. In fact, they are two links of blood that bind the administrative ritual of Leviticus to the preceding history of the patriarchs.

Egyptian and all other heathen sacrifices bore a general resemblance, in respect to the method of presentation, to the peace-offerings alone. But the sacrificial feasts of heathen priests were little better than the ceremonies of sorcerers against evil demons. While the feast of the peace-offering followed the spiritual submission unto the Supreme Jehovah already made in the whole burnt-offering.

But a new meaning was stamped upon the ceremonial of the sacrifice by the law in the establishment of the sin-offering. No doubt, the patriarchs had a sense of their own sinfulness in their approach to the altar of Him who is Holy. But it was left for the law to set forth sinfulness and its propitiation as the matter of chief concern between man and God. And Jehovah spake unto Moses, saying: "Speak unto the children of Israel, saying, if a soul shall sin through ignorance against any of the commandments of Jehovah, ... let him bring for his sin which he hath sinned, a young bullock, without blemish, unto Jehovah for a sin-offering."* The commandments are here represented as "holy, and just, and good,"† even as Jehovah is holy. A sin against any one of his statutes is a sin against Him, and unto Jehovah must the sin-offering be brought. The burnt-offerings and peace-offerings were voluntary, but this sacrifice was commanded in every case of the violation of the law. This offering marks the completion of the national altar as the centre of the administrative system. The sin-offering is meant to preserve the majesty of the law. It is intended to symbolize the holiness of the lawgiver; it marks the necessity of the law itself, and likewise marks its purpose. This sin-offering, and with it the entire ceremonial of the altar, points forward to the time when sin shall be removed by Jesus, the one great sacrifice, who is likewise the Priest presenting Himself as a sin-offering.

The method of presenting the victim in the sin-offering was after the manner of the other offerings except in the treatment of the blood of the sacrifice. After the slaughter of the beast by the man who had committed the sin, then came the priest to take charge of the offering. The sacrifice must be presented by a mediator, consecrated to this particular office. The mediator took the blood of the victim. This blood was the symbol of the life of him who offered it. The violator of law thus offered to Jehovah the life which had been forfeited by the sin. The priest smeared some of the blood upon the horns of the altar. In minor offences a subordinate priest smeared the blood on the brazen altar. In the sin-offering for the high priest and for the nation, the blood was placed on the altar of incense, and likewise sprinkled seven times within the tabernacle. For certain offences a trespass-offering was presented, like unto a sin-offering.‡ After the sprinkling of the blood, the priest placed in the fire of the altar the fat portions of the victim, and these were accepted as "a sweet savour unto Jehovah." As concerning the sinner and his sin, it was declared that in this manner the "priest shall make an atonement for him, and it shall be forgiven him."§

The sin-offering was placed first in order in the sacrificial service. When the sinner had been restored to his position as a loyal subject by the atonement of the sin-offering, then

---

* Lev. 4: 1–3. † Rom. 7: 12. ‡ Lev. 7: 7. § Lev. 4: 31.

must he dedicate himself unto Jehovah in the whole burnt-offering and in the peace-offering.

The administrative system of the national altar touched the spirit of the worshipper through every symbol used. The violator of the sanctity of the law was led back through a graduated ceremonial into communion with Jehovah. The soul and the body of the believer were typified in the blood and the flesh of the victim. Between the sinner and his God stood the mediating priest. The entire system was only a shadow of that which was to come when the divine administration should be centred in one person. In Christ, the Mediator and the victim are combined in the suffering and triumphant Son of God. In Him we have "the blood of the everlasting covenant."*

The National Priesthood.
(*Leviticus 8–10.*)

Through Moses were given Jehovah's directions concerning the order and the character of the offerings. Through Moses Jehovah now inducted the priests into office.

The sanctuary, commanded at the time of the giving of the law, stood complete. The divine order issued at Sinai concerning the dress and consecration of the priesthood was written among the statutes in the Book of Exodus.† "And Jehovah spake unto Moses, saying, Take Aaron and his sons with him, and the garments and the anointing oil, and a bullock for the sin-offering, and two rams and a basket of unleavened bread;

"And gather thou all the assembly together towards the entrance of the tent of meeting."‡

The entire body of the Hebrew people was brought to the door of the tabernacle to witness this inauguration of the kingdom visible. They looked on while Moses solemnly consecrated Aaron and his family as ministers of state. First were they cleansed with water in sign of their spiritual cleansing. Then did Moses invest Aaron with the official robes of God's minister—the coat, the girdle, the robe, the ephod, the breast-plate, the mitre, and, last of all, upon Aaron's forehead, he bound the crown, the golden band inscribed "Holiness to Jehovah."

---

* Heb. 13: 20. † Exod. 28, 29, 40. ‡ Lev. 8: 1–3.

Then took Moses the holy oil and with it anointed the tabernacle and all the sacred furniture, the ark and the altars. Then upon Aaron's head he poured the oil, in symbol of the fact that the high-priest's authority and power thus came from Jehovah. The chief minister and the sanctuary were now formally set aside and consecrated for divine use.

After this the sons of Aaron were clad in their robes of office, and then followed the sacrifices of the consecration. Moses acted the part of priest as Jehovah's representative. The hands of Aaron and his sons were laid upon the victims as they were brought. The blood of these was sprinkled by Moses upon the altar, but the blood of the last, or peace-offering, was sprinkled upon the ear, thumb and toe of each minister of state. This ceremony symbolized the complete service to be rendered by the priest now reconciled and consecrated unto Jehovah in these sacrifices. Each day for seven days were these ceremonies repeated until the seals of office were thus given to Aaron and his sons.

Even yet was Aaron under the direction of Moses. At the command of the latter, Aaron offered sacrifices for himself and for the people, and then both Moses and Aaron entered the tent of meeting, and when they came forth they blessed all the people who stood in waiting. "And the glory of Jehovah appeared unto all the people. And then came a fire out from before Jehovah and consumed upon the altar the burnt-offering and the fat; which, when all the people saw, they shouted and fell on their faces."* The inauguration was thus made complete by Jehovah Himself. His sanction fell upon the sanctuary and upon the priests and upon the people. His administration was established when the "fire from Jehovah" came to consume the sacrifice. Further, when Nadab and Abihu, in an unseemly manner and at an improper time, advanced with irreverent spirit to offer incense to Jehovah, that same "fire from Jehovah" consumed them. The infinite power of God was behind all this ceremonial. This sanctuary contained His throne, and these priests were His ministers of state, and the fire burning upon the altar might be made to burn up in its flame any one who should fail to reverence the symbols of God's visible kingdom.

---

* Lev. 8: 23, 24.

Ordinances Concerning Holiness.

(Leviticus 11-15; 17-22.)

A large part of the statutes written in Leviticus are concerned with the practical means to be used in attaining unto holiness in the daily life. These precepts may be characterized in general as the application of Jehovah's spiritual law to the natural world. The basis of this practical legislation is found in the purpose which Jehovah has already declared concerning the entire law, that He will make of this people "an holy nation" if they will render Him obedience.

"I am Jehovah, your God, which have separated you from other people. Ye shall therefore put difference between clean beasts and unclean, and between unclean fowls and clean; and ye shall not make your souls abominable by beast, or by fowl, or by any manner of living thing that creepeth on the ground, which I have separated from you as unclean.

"And ye shall be holy unto me; for I, Jehovah, am holy, and have severed you from other people that ye should be mine."

In accordance with this injunction, Jehovah spake unto Moses and Aaron and specified those creatures in the kingdom of animal life whose flesh might be used as food.*

(1) Among quadrupeds, the people might eat only the flesh of those which completely divide the hoof and chew the cud.

(2) Among the fishes, only those which have both scales and fins might be eaten.

(3) Among the birds, those that live upon animal food are prohibited; at least, nineteen of this class were named as unfit for use.

(4) Among flying insects, only those that possess two long legs for leaping, like the grasshopper, might be used as food.

(5) All creeping things were to be an abomination as concerning their use for food.†

It is clear from these statutes that the division between clean and unclean animals had reference only to their dead bodies. Animal life of all kinds was made sacred by the

---
*Lev. 20: 24-26. †Lev. 11.

law. All *living* things were clean. On the other hand, all bodies of men, or beasts that had died of themselves, were unclean and polluting to the touch. These laws were based upon this great distinction, that life is a holy thing while death is the symbol of unholiness and pollution.

In order to provide the Hebrews with animal food, Jehovah ordained that certain creatures might be slain and their bodies prepared according to a fixed method. This method was in reality a religious ceremonial. The animals thus treated were regarded as made free from the taint of death. Before the door of the tabernacle must the animal be brought and there slain. The blood, wherein was the "life of the flesh," was all drawn off and sprinkled on the brazen altar by the priest. The blood was not to be eaten. Each animal slain for food became in this manner a kind of peace-offering unto Jehovah.* The daily life of His people was brought into vital connection with His divine power. It is a fact that the animals prescribed for food were those that feed on vegetable life, and are hence conducive to health in men. But the spiritual law is the primary reason why these animals were chosen, and the sanitary law is only secondary in the purpose of Jehovah. His statutes were imposed upon Israel for the furtherance of their moral and spiritual life, and it was afterwards found to be a fact that these same statutes promote the physical well-being.

For the same reason, Jehovah ordained certain purifications for the removal of particular cases of taint and defilement connected with the daily life of His people. These cases were (1) defilement from secretions; (2) defilement from leprosy, and (3) defilement from a corpse.† The removal of impurity and pollution caused in any one of these three ways was to be the work of Jehovah Himself, through the means of a particular religious ceremonial. Until its removal, this uncleanness excluded the individual from the services of the sanctuary, and, in the case of leprosy, cut him off from the camp. The presence of God as giving life and absence from Him as the symbol of death was thus signified in these ceremonials. Furthermore, the sinful character of men in their natural condition was set forth. Herein did the Mosaic law of uncleanness among animals

---
* Lev. 17. † Lev. 11, 12-15; Numb. 19.

and men pass beyond the meaning of similar laws in vogue among the Egyptians and other heathen. Those laws were based solely on sanitary reasons, but the laws of Jehovah carried always a deep spiritual lesson.

In Leviticus 18-22, we find certain laws for the regulation of the private life of the individual members of the nation and the priests. "Ye shall be holy, for I, Jehovah your God, am holy." * Thus spake Jehovah to priest and people alike concerning marriage and the offering of sacrifices and concerning other duties of the private life. His divine superintendence extended even into the secret places of each Hebrew's daily career, and, in all things were they commanded to be holy.

The Holy Festivals.

These statutes reach a climax in the ordinances concerning the public worship of Jehovah in the stated feasts.† The book closes with strict injunctions to abstain from practical idolatry, to be careful in the performance of all vows, and, above all, to observe the public worship of God in all regularity after the order prescribed in "the appointed times." ‡

For the sake of clearness, it may be well just here to mention all the specified times of public worship according to the ritual of the altar. First in order among all was "the continual burnt offering," or the regular morning and evening sacrifice, whose upward-ascending smoke was like the continual waving of Jehovah's royal banner over His obedient people. Next in order was the weekly Sabbath, named here first among the feasts as "an holy convocation."§ Already had the Sabbath been declared the sign of the covenant, as a rest-day to Jehovah.‖ It was to be marked by a doubling of the common daily sacrifices, as a symbol of the sanctification of the daily life of the people. It was now ordained in Leviticus as the centre of the sabbatical system, made of the sabbatical year and the year of jubilee.¶ The covenant was brought thus into practical connection with Israel's life in the rest allotted to the soil itself and in the liberty granted unto all in bondage. A holy life

---
*Lev. 19; 2; 21-6.   †Lev. 23: 27.   ‡Lev. 26: 27.   §Lev. 23: 3.   ‖Exod. 20: 10.   ¶Lev. 25.

and a free life was to be that of God's people, sanctified unto Him in all these feasts and ceremonials.

The third feast was that of the passover or of unleavened bread. This feast was ordained in Egypt at the beginning of the exodus and is here named as a part of the great system of covenant festivals concerning the holiness of the nation. Passover was the name given to the first day and unleavened bread to the seven continuous days of feasting. This feast was celebrated at the beginning of the wheat harvest, and the sheaf of grain first ripe was then offered as a wave-offering to Jehovah.*

After this came the " feast of harvest." † It was celebrated at the end of harvest, in acknowledgment of God's bounty shown in the ripened grain. This festival was also called the " feast of weeks," since it occurred seven weeks after the passover; ‡ likewise was it called "the day of the first-fruits," since an offering was then made of bread baked from the first fruits of the harvest.§ The most familiar name of this feast is the Greek designation, " Pentecost" (fifty), assigned to it because of the period of fifty days that separated it from the passover feast. In the Acts of the Apostles, Pentecost marks the outpouring of the Holy Spirit and the ingathering of the first-fruits in Christ's work of redemption.‖

Next in order we name two feasts, the festival of the new moon and the feast of trumpets. The first-named was celebrated at the beginning of each month, and might have been mentioned in connection with the daily and weekly sacrifices.¶ The feast of the trumpets marked the new year's day of the civil year. It was " an holy convocation " on the first day of the seventh month of each year.** The tenth day of this seventh month saw the celebration of the great Day of Atonement. This festival had peculiar significance, and will require special discussion.

The last of the great festivals of the year was the feast of ingathering†† or the feast of tabernacles.‡‡ This was the celebration of the harvest-home at the close of the fruit-bearing season. It was the last of the three great festivals —Passover, Pentecost and Tabernacles—at which every

---

* Lev. 23. †Exod. 23: 16. ‡ Exod. 34: 22. § Lev. 23: 17; Numb. 28: 26. ‖ Green's Hebrew Feasts, 243. ¶ Numb. 28: 11. **Lev. 23: 23. ††Exod. 23: 16. ‡‡ Lev. 23: 34.

male Israelite was to present himself before Jehovah at the sanctuary. In tents made of green boughs the Hebrews were to sojourn for seven days as a memorial of the life in the wilderness—as a memorial of that period of transition from the nomadic life to the agricultural life, wherein they should be made glad by gathering in corn and wine.* An eighth day was added to the seven booth-dwelling days, and in New Testament times this was known as the great day of the feast."† All the joys and hopes of the year were mingled together in this culminating of the calendar of festivals. Thus, in these sacred feasts, was the entire daily life of the Hebrew consecrated to Jehovah. Every season of joy, every occasion of temporal prosperity, every period of patriotic fervor—all of these were holy times of praise and thanksgiving before the sanctuary of Jehovah. Church and state were completely joined together because the secular and religious life of the Hebrew were one and the same, and in all things Jehovah was the supreme king.

These feasts are mentioned in four diffrent places in the Pentateuch. In the book of the covenant, Exodus 23, and its reproduction in Exodus 34, they are briefly set forth as part of the terms of the great contract between Jehovah and His people. In Leviticus 23, they are mentioned chiefly as days of holy convocation in connection with Jehovah's administration of the covenant. As given from this point of view of public worship, certain particulars in the method of observance are added. Numbers 28 and 29, detail the more elaborate ordinances connected with these feasts, as they were commanded by Jehovah just before the entrance into Canaan. When Joshua had been chosen as the successor of Moses, then through the latter was this more complete public ritual set forth before the people.‡ Deuteronomy 16, contains the farewell injunction of Moses unto Israel, when the generation that received the law at Sinai was now dead. The new generation knew the three forms of the festival statutes just mentioned, and Moses simply reiterated the commandments concerning these great feasts, dwelling upon certain particulars suggested by the prospective occupancy of Canaan. These four forms of the festival statutes simply present four different points of view from which they are

---

*Deut. 16: 13. † John 7: 37. ‡ Numb. 27: 18-23.

enjoined. Certain critics claim that these four aspects are four successive stages in a long period of development; that they are different laws enacted at different times upon this subject of public worship. This claim is advanced more particularly in regard to the feasts of the Passover and Tabernacles.* This hypothesis is without foundation because of two considerations: (1.) The central point in each of the four forms of the festival statutes is the same injunction of a national worship of Jehovah around the one national altar in the sanctuary established at Sinai. (2.) The purpose of this worship is always the same, "the holiness of the people." Their daily life must be consecrated to Jehovah in furtherance of his great plan announced at Sinai, to make them "an holy nation." There is absolutely no development whatever in the essential method of celebrating the feasts, nor in the ultimate purpose of those feasts concerning the religious character of the people. The minor injunctions concerning details of their celebration are those that naturally fall in with the change of circumstances.†

The Blood of the Atonement.
[*Leviticus 16.*]

The climax of symbolism used in the administration of Jehovah's visible kingdom was reached in the ceremonial of the day of atonement. The sin-offering was the specific addition to the national altar made by the Sinaitic code, and the day of atonement concentrated into its one day of worship the meaning of all the sin-offerings of the year. In presence of the symbols used on this day the Hebrew was made to see that Jehovah's government exhausted not its strength in the enactment of a few legal and moral precepts, but that His administration dealt directly with his individual life; with his body and with his soul. This foundation truth was set forth in the character of the chief element of the ritual. That element was blood.

The purpose of the ceremonial was "to make an atonement for the children of Israel for all their sins (and uncleanness) once a year."‡ Like all sin-offerings, this great atonement was the concession of the mercy of Jehovah unto

---
*Kuenen: "Religion of Israel." Wellhausen: "Geschichte Israels." †Green's Hebrew Feasts, p. 82. ‡ Lev. 16: 16, 34.

the weakness of His people. They had entered into covenant relationship with him, swearing a solemn oath that they would keep His law. But weakness would lead many to violate that oath and transgress the law. Thus would the covenant be broken between those individuals and Jehovah. How could it be reëstablished? How could the violated law be vindicated? How could the law-breakers be restored to fellowship in the kingdom? How could he be made at one with God? Only by means of the life-blood of the animal-sacrifice. Jehovah ordained that the penitent transgressor might bring the life of the animal as a substitute for his own forfeited life. This statute was based upon the principle announced that the soul of the animal, as distinguished from the body of the animal, is in the animal blood. "The soul of the flesh is in the blood; and I have ordained it for you upon the altar, to make atonement for your souls; for the blood it is which makes *at-one-ment* by means of the soul."*

Four different methods marked the treatment of the blood used in the sacrifices. In making the burnt-offerings, the peace-offerings, and the trespass-offerings the priests were commanded to "bring the blood and sprinkle the blood round about upon the altar." There was a certain degree of the idea of atonement in these offerings. But in the sacrifice of the sin-offering there were three distinct modes of treating the blood—(1) the priest with his finger put some of the blood upon the horns of the two altars ; (2) with his finger sprinkled some of it before the vail, (3) and poured out the remainder at the base of the altar of burnt-offering. The day of atonement was signalized by the same method of distributing the blood of the sacrifice; but it was sprinkled upon a part of the tabernacle furniture that was unapproachable except upon this one day of the year. The mercy-seat within the holy of holies was the central object in the ritual of this holy day. It was regarded, it would seem, as the most sacred of Jehovah's altars for this crowning act in the penitential service of the Hebrews' religious life. The parts of this ritual may be briefly mentioned. (1) The *place* of offering was in the very presence of Jehovah Himself. The high priest on this day made his one

---
* Lev. 17: 11.

yearly approach "into the holy place within the vail before the mercy-seat which is upon the ark."* The holy of holies, the divine king's presence-chamber was this. In His own holy personality did He there abide as the ruler of His people. This day marked His sovereignty as the forgiver of sin. "I will appear in the cloud upon the mercy-seat."† Into such intimate contact with the life of His people did Jehovah here bring Himself that if the high priest should venture to come into this throne-room on any other day of the year the priest would die.† But in the sacrifices of at-one-ment came the priest to sprinkle the blood seven times upon the mercy-seat on its east side, and then seven times upon the floor in front of it.† Thus into living contact with Jehovah Himself was brought the penitent soul of every Hebrew. The life blood of the animal without blemish was placed upon Jehovah's throne in place of the life of the transgressor of the law, and from that mercy-seat passed forth the divine power to touch and heal the heart of the repenting sinner.

(2) The *offerer* of the atonement sacrifice was the high priest alone. First of all, he was commanded to wash with water his entire body, not merely his hands and feet as in ordinary sacrifices. Then was he arrayed in "holy garments" of pure, "holy linen." Further than this must he offer a bullock as a sin-offering, "an atonement for himself and for his house (verse 6). This official was of divine appointment and had received the oil of anointment, but for his own sins must he make atonement ere he could stand before the mercy seat as the mediator between Jehovah and His people. He must "offer up sacrifice, *first* for his own sins and then for the people's."‡ In very truth, at Sinai in this beginning of Hebrew national life, we find established as mediator Aaron, a type of the great high priest who is "holy, harmless, undefiled, separate from sinners,"§ who now in these last days of revelation has, once for all, "entered into that within the vail." Three times did the high priest enter within the vail in completing the sacrifice. First he entered with a censer full of burning coals from the brazen altar, and therewith caused a cloud of incense to cover the mercy-seat as a vail between himself and Jehovah (verses 12, 13).

---
*Lev. 16: 2.   †Lev. 16: 14, 15.   ‡Hebrews 7: 27.   §Heb. 7: 26; 6: 19, 20.

A second time he entered bearing the blood of the priest's sin-offering. Then a third time did he enter with the blood of the goat that represented the whole nation. In like manner was this sin-offering for the people sprinkled upon the mercy-seat, and also upon the golden altar and upon the brazen altar (verses 15–19). The sacrificial blood hallowed anew these altars as meeting-places between God and man at the same time that the blood was the medium of reconciliation. After these ceremonies, the priest sent away the second goat to Azazel, and thereupon put off his linen garb, bathed himself and resumed his golden raiment. It was only left that he should offer the closing burnt-offerings, with the fat of the two sin-offerings. His mediatorial work for that day was completed.

(3) The *efficacy* of the atonement was complete. This was symbolized in a striking manner by presenting *two* goats as a sin-offering for the people. One of these goats was slain and the blood was borne within the holy of holies to atone for the sins of the nation—as already explained. Thus was the nation reëstablished in the covenant. But what had become of the forgiven sins? Did their consequences still remain in force within the hearts of the people? Nay, not thus did Jehovah administer His forgiving power. The sins could be removed by Jehovah, and He taught this very truth that the reconciliation wrought through the blood of the sacrifice was so complete that the sins were borne away. The two goats represented the two essential parts in the atonement—the making of peace with Jehovah and His complete removal of the effects of all transgression. This second part was symbolized in the goat for Azazel. He symbolized the act of a living being after death; since the two goats were reckoned as one offering, the one was slain and the other was sent away. For, after the blood of the first goat, sprinkled upon the mercy-seat and altars, had brought the offending nation within the pale of the covenant again, then stood Aaron over the live goat with his hands upon its head, and there did he "confess over him all the iniquities of the children of Israel, and all their transgressions in all their sins, putting them upon the head of the goat" (verse 21). Thus was it symbolized that as the nation was being restored to fellowship in the kingdom by the blood of the slain goat, their sins were at the same time being left behind upon the living

goat. Thus did the second goat simply carry on to completeness that which was begun by the blood of the first, for the priest now sent the living goat burdened with these sins outpoured in confession, unto Azazel the evil one. "By the hand of a fit man into the wilderness" (verse 21) was the sin-bearer led away. The divine ordinance concerning this second animal was this, "The goat shall bear upon him all their iniquities unto a land not inhabited" (verse 22). A life had been surrendered to Jehovah's altar as an offering for the transgressions of the nation and yet a living being survived to carry away all sin and uncleanness.* In what wonderful completeness do we here find typified the spiritual reconciliation of the sinner with the total removal of all his sins. Further than this, in this ceremonial do we find a typical forecast of the character and work of our high priest who came to offer Himself; who, after His atoning sacrifice upon the altar of the cross, still survived to complete the work of redemption in removing our transgressions. This double sin-offering pointed unto the Son of God, "who was delivered for our offences and was raised again for our justification."

The supreme import of the national administration was concentrated in this day, which the Hebrews afterwards called the great day. That import was essentially *spiritual* and not legal. It may be well to remember just here, what has already been stated, that it is this *spirituality* of the law, and also the spirituality of the method of administering the law that separated Jehovah's government from that of Egypt, and all other heathen kingdoms.

Again, it is very clear that this same element of spirituality belonged to the day of atonement at its first establishment at Sinai. This day, in fact, as representing the most supremely solemn moment in Jehovah's administration, stood on the same spiritual plane with the day of the covenant, as representing Jehovah's inauguration as King. In that first great step in the revelation of this law, Jehovah spake in thunder from the summit of Sinai while the people, already sanctified by a three-days' ceremony, stood in awe at the foot of the mount and dared not approach because of the holiness of Jehovah's mountain throne. In

---

*Speaker's Com. *in loco*.

this second step, wherein Jehovah spake from the mercy-seat in the sanctuary, there were just the same indications concerning Jehovah's holiness and the sinfulness of His people. There could have been no long period of development between these two events, for the simple reason that they represented exactly the same truths concerning God and man from two different points of view. There is no advance in meaning to be found in the day of atonement beyond the meaning of the covenant spoken of in the Book of Exodus. Now, since the highest spiritual teaching in Leviticus is found in the ritual of this day, it follows that all reason for supposing a course of development in the pilgrimage feasts is thus precluded. The spirit of these feasts was one of rejoicing over Jehovah's mercies and bounties. But the atonement sacrifices were presupposed in these feasts; the rejoicing was made by those whose sins had been forgiven and borne away, and thereafter had come the temporal blessings of the year as the outward sign of spiritual restoration. This restoration in the atonement lay at the foundation of all the Hebrew's joy and hope. The feasts of rejoicing could never advance beyond this in spiritual import; that import they could possess and did possess when the day of atonement first marked the foundation of Jehovah's administration upon His love and mercy. It is therefore idle to suppose any development in the form of some part of this administration, when the supreme and final import of Jehovah's system of government was declared at the first in the establishment of the covenant at Sinai.

Further than this, it is now clear that this spiritual import of Jehovah's administration was summed up in its meaning as a prophecy of the coming of the Son of God, the chief administrator in the kingdom. Christ's priesthood, first of all, was shadowed forth in this great system of divine government; but beyond this there appeared a further indication of the time when He should assume the chief executive functions in the Father's realm; when He should become King of kings and Lord of lords. For Jesus Christ came, and "after He had offered one sacrifice for sins forever, sat down on the right hand of God; from henceforth expecting till His enemies be made His footstool. For by one offering He hath perfected forever them that are sanctified." *

---
* Hebrews 10: 12-14.

CHAPTER XIX.

THE NATIONAL ORGANIZATION.

(*Book of Numbers.*)

The National Assembly.

THE Sinaitic covenant established a government monarchical in *form*—for Jehovah was absolute sovereign. But in *spirit* this government was partly a democracy—for the covenant itself was ratified by the general assembly of the nation. Jehovah's personal rule as king over this unified commonwealth formed the theocracy. Herein was the great difference between the divine law and administration and that of Egypt. This covenant was the first great enactment in the history of the human race whereby the rights and privileges of the people as a body-politic were made the corner-stone of a form of government. The recognition of the national assembly was the crowning act in God's mercy shown at Sinai.

The foundation principle of the organization of the people was the recognition of this assembly. In the promise to Abraham, "a great nation" was set down in the terms of the contract. "My people" was the constant refrain in Jehovah's messages to Pharaoh concerning the tribes of Israel. "I will take you to me for a people, and I will be to you a God," was the encouraging promise uttered just as the conflict with Pharoah began. "Ye shall be unto me a kingdom of priests and an holy nation," was the voice of love that spake at Sinai after the deliverance from Egypt. The first of all the great institutions established was this of the national community. Jehovah stamped the people with the dignity of statehood, and then entered into covenant relationship with this commonwealth. As the covenant underlay the law, so was the assembly prior to the covenant.

In this national assembly there was the absolute equality of all before Jehovah in the matter of worship, and there was absolute justice for all in the administration of law.

The absolute equality of all was recognized in the covenant oath. The mass of the people as such entered into this obligation. The oath was moreover an act of worship in which each individual vowed allegiance for himself unto God. The priestly order was not yet established. No castes were recognized in the covenant. The caste-system of Egypt was disowned. Each man was to be made holy on his own account. Each man was hereafter to become a priest unto God for himself, in the ripeness of future time when the shadows of Sinai should have become the realities of Calvary.* What was the relation of the priesthood to this assembly? They were the *representatives* of the people. That is to say, we find in the theocracy elements of three different kinds of government, monarchy, democracy, and the representative system. Jehovah was king over the nation; the nation in mass-meeting had a certain authority accorded to it; the practical administration of Jehovah's supreme authority and of the assembly's limited authority was carried out through representatives.

In the national administration, thus far considered from the point of view of Jehovah's absolute sovereignty, we have found one system of representation. The prophet was Jehovah's representative as lawgiver, and the assembly's representative in the reception of the law, and that prophet was Moses. The king, foretold in Deuteronomy, was to be Jehovah's representative in the executive department; but this same king was to be elected by the assembly, also, as their representative. The priesthood was based upon this same system of representation and there were three gradations; for the *race* of Levi, the *house* of Aaron, and the *individual* high priest stood in the line of succession. The priests represented Jehovah in explaining His statutes, and they represented the people in the acts of public worship. They were like the people in nature, and must atone for their own sins. The principal part of this side of the representative system was found in the ritual of public worship before the sanctuary of Jehovah. But it must not be forgotten that the worshippers there were the community, composed of the great mass of individual Hebrews. The priest could mediate for him in the mere manipulation of the elements of the sacrifice,

---
* Heb. 8: 10.

but the free-born Hebrew must always appear in his own behalf before the door of Jehovah's dwelling-place.

Furthermore, after ratifying the covenant this assembly furnished the material for the construction of the sanctuary; they built it through their representatives; they accepted the priesthood which God sanctified, and in their corporate life as community they honored Him as their sovereign.

In the Book of Numbers we have the formal numbering, on two occasions, of this corporate community with the further organization of the people as a civil commonwealth. Here we find the second side of the representative system as it is connected with military affairs and the administration of justice. Equal justice to all before Jehovah is still the principle recognized in the national organization.

The time contemplated in this story of the corporate life of the people is the period of wilderness-wandering. It covers just six months more than the period of Aaron's administration of the religious worship. The movements of these years are contemplated from the point of view of the national assembly as a great army of God. They form the type of that church which shall follow Christ through the life militant into the life triumphant.

Every Hebrew over twenty years of age who was able to bear arms was enrolled in the census. But this enrollment was to be made "after their families, by the house of their fathers."* The basis of this polity was, therefore, the *house*. Political rights were accorded to the individual only as the member of a *house*. The next formal division was that of the family or collection of houses. Then in the order next highest came the tribe, or collection of families, while the assembly, or congregation, was the general mass-meeting of all the tribes.

The religious mark of citizenship was the rite of circumcision. This was the great seal of the covenant which each member of the community bore upon his person. The political mark of citizenship was the payment of a poll-tax at the taking of the census.† Beyond six hundred thousand fighting men were the Hebrews in number, according to the census taken at the beginning of their march.‡ Thus were they arranged according to tribes in the national

---

* Numb. 1: 2, 3. † Exod. 30: 11. ‡ Numb. 1.

encampment, under their standards and ensigns.* In a rectangular form was the camp spread out, with the sanctuary in the midst of all. Unto the door of this sanctuary came the assembly at the call of the two silver trumpets. No legislative authority was vested in the assembly. They simply accepted Jehovah's law, according to the terms of the covenant. Certain judicial powers were vested in the assembly, partly exercised in mass-meeting and largely exercised through their representative judges.

Thus was established one of the two great external institutions of the law—the Sabbath and the assembly. The national assembly was the foundation of the church of God. The national assembly-day of public worship was the second part in the making of a peculiar people, whose chief duty it was to worship Jehovah. This assembly-day found its highest culmination in atonement-day, although its simplest and most usual meaning was set forth in the weekly Sabbath. Taking this Sabbath as representing all public worship, we have the community and the sacred day as the corner-stones of the divine organization of God's people.

In this community, as the body politic, was lodged the only real authority that was vested in men; Jehovah's authority is supreme over all, but His authority was accepted by the free choice of the assembly, and in that act itself recognition was accorded to a certain sovereignty in the people of God. The priestly and judicial administrations were mediatorial; that is, they represented both God and the nation. There is no evidence here to support the systems of sacerdotalism that claim to rest on the theocracy. The priests had no authority as proceeding from themselves, but only as they represented the supreme authority of Jehovah and the limited authority of the community. As between God and men, there is no support in this covenant for the dogmas of the divine sight of bishops and the divine right of kings; but only for the divine right of the people to exercise certain privileges and prerogatives that are pleasing to Jehovah.

The Elders of the Congregation.

Judicial authority was vested in the national assembly. The constantly recurring command to the people was this,

---
* Num. 2.

Put away the evil from among you.* The people as a whole carried out nearly all death-sentences, especially in the case of the penalty of stoning.† But judicial *knowledge* in the decision of cases always was revealed from Jehovah. "The judgment is God's," cried Moses unto the nation.‡ To seek justice was to inquire of God. §

Between Jehovah and the nation in the administration of justice, a full-fledged representative system was recognized. This system was made up of three sets of officials. (1), Elders; (2), judges; (3), officers. The covenant at Sinai incorporated in the theocracy the patriarchal method of government among the tribes. Jehovah's supreme authority was to be carried down into the tribal life, so far as judicial matters were concerned, in the same manner in which those affairs had been administered by the ancient heads of the tribes.

"The elders" of 'Israel were the tribal leaders in the days of the exodus. At that time they were the only judges among the people,‖ nor did they ever lose their authority as *representatives-at-large* for the entire nation.¶ Seventy of these elders represented the people in the covenant-feast at Sinai, when they ate and drank in the presence of Jehovah.** There, as the "nobles of the children of Israel," they formed a kind of senate around Moses, as well as a judicial body. The great Sanhedrin of later days, in which was vested the highest judicial power, was based most probably upon the council of seventy elders who surrounded Moses.

"The judges" were selected from the elders by Moses at the suggestion of Jethro.†† These men represented the nation in assisting Moses. They were chosen by the people, though nominated by Moses, and their selection depended also upon their integrity. Thus did the people sit in judgment through these representatives, and yet when judgment was declared it was the expression of Jehovah's will. The princes of the tribes, "every one head of the house of his fathers," were the same as the "judges" appointed at Sinai before the covenant.

"The officers" existed before the exodus.‡‡ They performed duties in connection with the elders and judges, and

---

*Numb. 5: 2. †Deut. 13: 9; 17: 7. ‡Deut. 1: 17. §Exod. 18: 15. ‖Exod. 2: 14. ¶Numb. 7: 2; 17: 6; 34: 18. **Exod. 24; 9-11. ††Exod. 18: 21. ‡‡Exod. 5: 10.

therefore seem to have exercised judicial functions.* Upon the testimony of credible witnesses were men condemned before these tribunals, and the hand of the witness must be the first lifted in the infliction of the death-penalty.

Thus do we find that in the theocracy, Jehovah's supreme power was established over the Hebrew nation, and yet the patriarchal methods of government and of worship were still preserved. The patriarch of the tribe had been the chief priest, and now in God's government the people were still *represented* before Him through the priesthood. The patriarch had been the chief judge, and now the elders retained in their hands the administration of justice. The national unity and the national life were guarded by the theocracy. Jehovah was the eternal king and the only king. In the provision made for an earthly king, the latter was to be only temporary. Moreover, he was to be chosen by the nation and was to be Jehovah's representative for a time. In religious affairs, the access of each individual unto Jehovah was secured, not through his superior, but through his *representative*. In civil affairs, there was no respect of persons before the law. God's authority did not displace the customs and methods of government in existence among the tribes, but was administered through those forms. The state was not absorbed into the church in such manner that its ancient, individual character was lost. The claim of the papacy to absolute power over all civil governments finds no support in the covenant at Sinai. Nor does the other theory, that the church is only a part and parcel of the state, draw substantiation from the national compact between Jehovah and His people. The theocracy was dual in form, in so far as the source of sovereignty was concerned. Jehovah was the supreme ruler in all things; in so far as certain authority emanated from a human fountain, it came from the people alone, in solemn assembly before the holy sanctuary.

The Brazen Serpent.

When the organization of Israel as a holy community was made complete, then was the nation started upon the march. Canaan as the ultimate destination was set before the people. Guided and guarded by the visible tokens of Jehovah's

---
* Numb. 11: 16; 16: 18.

presence they moved forward. Out of the camp did they cast all diseased and unclean persons. The voice of Jehovah gave direction and announced new ordinances unto Moses from the mercy-seat. In the movements of the cloud, Jehovah gave definite signals for marching and for halting. By means of the manna He continued to feed them. And yet, the entire generation that had entered into the covenant at Sinai, failed to keep faith with Jehovah. "They failed to enter in because of unbelief." The story of this long test in the marchings in the wilderness and of the gradual failure of Israel to keep their plighted oath is given in detail in the Book of Numbers. In that story we see the organized nation on trial and we see them fail. And yet out of the midst of this old body-politic of Sinai there sprang a new body who were mustered in the plains of Moab ready to enter into Canaan. The nation as a covenant people did not die with those wanderers in the wilderness. It was preserved through the working of the national organization itself. For in that organization was the eternal power of the Godhead, and out of the death of the old members of the covenant Jehovah brought forth the new and stronger nation. Stronger in faith were they than were their fathers. The principle of a personal faith in Jehovah as the link between Him and the individual was clearly set forth in the symbol of the brazen serpent.

This symbol of Jehovah's deliverance of the individual who believeth in Him was set up near the close of the wandering. The long course of mumuring and rebellion on the part of the people and the consequent punishments visited upon them is set forth by the historian.* A plague carried off a great multitude when they lusted for flesh instead of manna. Korah, Dathan and Abiram, with many followers, rebelled against the rule of Moses and Aaron, and in punishment, some were swallowed up in the earth and others were consumed by fire. Then died fourteen thousand seven hundred more of a plague because of further murmurings. Yea, all that generation was condemned to die in the desert because they murmured concerning the land of promise. Even Aaron and Miriam spoke against their brother and were punished. Then at the rock of Meribah,

---

* Numb. 10-21.

both Moses and Aaron showed impatience and momentary distrust of Jehovah, and were forbidden to enter into the land of promise. In all these varied penalties for specific sins, Jehovah was teaching the Hebrews that the national covenant was made up, after all, of the sum of the individual oaths. He taught them that each man's salvation depended upon his individual covenant with God. The climax of this teaching was reached in the brazen serpent suspended upon the pole. Fiery serpents were sent in punishment for their murmurings. Healing from the serpent's sting was offered unto those who would look upon the serpent of brass. Simple faith in Jehovah as the healer was sufficient to re-establish the broken covenant. It was this divine saving power, exercised through the faith of the people, that brought the nation at last into the promised home. Thus was provision made in the national organization for the specific work of the Son of God in imparting new life to those doomed to death—in keeping the covenant for those who have violated it. "And as Moses lifted up the serpent in the wilderness, even so must the Son of Man be lifted up, that whosoever believeth in Him should not perish but have eternal life." *

The Spirit of God.

The Spirit of God is declared in the Book of Genesis to be the giver of light and life unto the whole world; † the subduer of evil and the promoter of integrity in men's hearts.‡ In the establishment of the theocracy, the Spirit was the agent through whom Jehovah directed all the affairs of divine government. First of all, upon Moses and the college of seventy elders rested the Spirit. For at the formal appointment of these elders as the assistants of Moses in the civil administration, "Jehovah came down in a cloud and spake unto him [Moses] and took of the Spirit that was upon him and gave unto the seventy elders; and it came to pass, when the Spirit rested upon them, they prophesied."§ It is here implied that the Spirit had rested upon Moses as God's prophet from the beginning of his work. It is further implied that the same Spirit was the living power within the national organization of the people, in so far as the administration of

---

*John 3: 15. †Gen. 1: 2. ‡Gen. 6: 3; 41: 38. §Numb. 11: 25.

civil affairs through the elders was concerned. On the other hand, the Spirit worked also through the priestly administration. The sanctuary itself was built by Bezaleel, who was "filled with the Spirit of God, in wisdom, in understanding, and in knowledge and in all manner of workmanship."* Then was the tabernacle and all that was therein anointed with the holy oil, a symbol of the Holy Spirit. Likewise, the priests were inducted into office by the use of the consecrating oil, all of these ceremonials prefiguring the coming of One who should be called preëminently the Messiah, or the Christ, that is, the Anointed. Christ's anointment was the Spirit in full measure, just as His types, the sanctuary and the priesthood, were sanctified symbolically with oil.

The agency of the Holy Spirit in directing the organized nation unto prosperity and blessing was set forth in the story of the prophecies of Balaam. This man was a practiser of heathen sorcery and soothsaying from Mesopotamia, whose fame had extended westward. Barak sent for him to come and utter magical curses against the further advance of God's people. Balaam had evidently learned something of the true God from the descendants of Nahor in the old home of Abraham, beyond the Euphrates. He knew and quoted some of the history of this nation sprung from Abraham. He had heard, possibly, of the miracles connected with the exodus, and now, like an earlier Simon Magus, desired to have the gift of wonder-working through the name of Jehovah. Perhaps he had some real reverence for the God of the Hebrews, but his love for the wages of unrighteousness was stronger. Most probably he saw that the call of duty and right was the spoken command of God, but he deliberately broke away from it. Then "the Spirit of God came upon him."† With such inward power came the Spirit that Balaam fell down and his eyes were opened, and in a vision he saw the Almighty; then heard he the words of God and spake them. The man's bodily powers were overcome, his will was subdued, his mind was enlightened, and he was compelled to foretell the coming power and glory of the Hebrew nation. When the Spirit departed from him, then returned his old obstinacy, and he devised the devilish scheme of inveigling

---

* Exod. 35: 31. † Numb. 24: 2.

the Israelites into open sin, but the result of this measure to Balaam was the loss of his life. In that great transaction on the mountain-top, Jehovah had shown through His Spirit what future He had in store for his people. Likewise had He shown that the trinity of divine power was working in this great organization leading it forward unto that time when

> There shall come a star out of Jacob
> And a sceptre shall rise out of Israel,

—when the wise men from Balaam's country, but not with Balaam's disposition, should come to worship Him who is born King of the Jews, and who gathers about Himself a church whereof this Hebrew nation was only a type.

CHAPTER XX.

Jehovah's Ideal for the Nation.

[*Book of Deuteronomy.*]

The Last Messages of Moses.

THE eleventh month of the fortieth year of Israel's wanderings after crossing the Red Sea, found the assembly of the tribes gathered in the plains of Moab by Jordan near Jericho. The first ten days of that eleventh month were spent by Moses in delivering his final messages unto the people. Then, beyond the view of Israel, on the summit of Mt. Nebo, the great leader was transferred to Abraham's bosom. The people of Israel spent thirty days in mourning for Moses, and afterwards, under Joshua's leadership, crossed over the river Jordan on the tenth day of the first month of the forty-first year after the exodus.*

Three distinct discourses unto the people, with certain words and acts of final blessing, comprehend the active work of Moses during these ten last days of his life, and the record thereof constitutes the Book of Deuteronomy. These addresses were made unto the national assembly in its organized capacity as the body-politic of Israel. The organization of that assembly at Sinai, and its subsequent test during thirty-eight years in the wilderness as the *local* governing power—these facts, as already well-known, formed the background of the discourses of Moses. Then, looking into the future, Moses set forth the ideals in political, religious, and social life which Jehovah had revealed as the special task to be wrought out by the Hebrew National Assembly in the home beyond the Jordan. That this may be made clear, let us examine in detail the three addresses.

Jehovah, God of Your Fathers.

The first address of Moses is contained in Deuteronomy 1: 1—4: 40. The people to whom he spake was Israel in its

---
* Deut. 1: 3; 34: 8. Joshua 4: 19.

organized character. "In the fortieth year, in the eleventh month, on the first day of the month, Moses spake unto the children of Israel."* They stood before him as the seed of Abraham,† the successors of the covenanters of Sinai,‡ and of the electors of the administration of elders, judges, and officers,§ and of the rebels of Kadesh-Barnea.‖ "The generation of the men of war" that came out of Egypt was already wasted away, and the second generation of Israelites listened unto the words of Moses. He appealed to their patriotism, to their national pride. As the successors of the national assembly at Sinai, they must take their place among the nations of the earth. In the name of Jehovah, Moses cried out, "This day will I begin to put the dread of thee and the fear of thee upon the nations that are under the whole heaven, who shall hear report of thee, and shall tremble and be in anguish because of thee." ¶

We have learned already that the period of the exodus saw both a religious and a political revolution. The Almighty God, as the only king of united tribes of men, revealed a new idea concerning the relation of the soul of man to the one supreme spiritual being, and a further new idea concerning the local authority lodged in the organized body-politic of the nation. It was a new dispensation among the nations of the earth, that a national assembly should have the power of self-administration in certain important affairs of the national life. It was this new political power which Moses discussed in these three addresses; it was the function of the national organization in the furtherance of Jehovah's plans for His people, of which he spake. Just as the religious life of the nation rested upon the voluntary offerings upon the national altar, so were the civil life and the civil progress of the nation to rest upon the voluntary obedience of the assembly unto Him who organized it. Now, in this first speech, Moses laid chief stress upon the character of Jehovah as the organizer of the national assembly. This thought was brought forward time and again in the phrase "Jehovah, God of your fathers." Unto Him must the national sentiment of obedience be directed. "Now, therefore, hearken, O Israel, unto the statutes and

---
*Deut. 1: 3.   †Deut. 1: 8.   ‡Deut. 1: 6, 7, 8.   §Deut. 1: 15, 16.   ‖Deut. 1: 19–38, 43.
¶ Deut. 2: 25.

unto the judgments which I teach you for to do them, that ye may live and go in and possess the land which Jehovah God of your fathers giveth you."* Every step in the long process whereby Jehovah created the national organization was recalled to the memory of the people.

(1) "God assayed to go and take Him a nation from the midst of another nation, by temptations, by signs, and by wonders, and by war and by a mighty hand and by a stretched-out arm." †

(2) "Jehovah thy God . . in Horeb said unto me, Gather Me the people together and I will make them hear my words. . . . And Jehovah spake unto you out of the midst of the fire. . . . And He declared unto you His covenant."‡

(3) "These forty years Jehovah thy God hath been with thee." . . . "And because He loved thy fathers, therefore He chose their seed after them."§

Jehovah has been the source of their origin as a nation and of their strength as a nation. When they have forgotten Him and have rebelled against Him, then have they been weak. Therefore the only hope for the future of the nation is faithfulness unto Jehovah, even as He hath been faithful unto His people. "Take heed unto yourselves lest ye forget the covenant of Jehovah your God. . . . Jehovah thy God will not . . . forget the covenant of thy fathers which He sware unto them." ||

The one great fact which is set forth in this address is this: that the national covenant at Sinai has been already completed and has been in operation nearly forty years. The terms of that covenant are known to this assembly. The law is known likewise, but the people need admonition concerning their attitude to that law. Some of the modern critics suppose that the law as an expanded code was not given at Sinai, but was developed by the nation from the outline given in Deuteronomy. It appears very clear, however, that the utterances in the Book of Deuteronomy presuppose all the details of the covenant at Sinai; they presuppose the organization of the assembly with its representative elders and judges and its representative priests. The life of the organization already completed, saith Moses in this

---

* Deut. 4: 1. † Deut. 4: 34. ‡ Deut. 4: 10, 12, 13. § Deut. 2: 7; 4: 37. || Deut. 4: 23, 31.

first address, depends upon keeping in contact with Him who made the organization. The covenant already sworn to must be preserved by eternal obedience. Jehovah, God of their fathers, must be kept as their God by means of that great national compact. The unity and the life of the nation depends upon their keeping the law already given. "Jehovah . . . is God in heaven above and upon the earth beneath; there is none else. Thou shalt keep, therefore, His statutes and His commandments which I command thee this day, that it may go well with thee and with thy children after thee, and that thou mayest prolong thy days upon the earth which Jehovah thy God giveth thee forever." *

There is a further link with the past history of Israel in the use of the double name, "Jehovah, God of your fathers." Moses uses the compound name to indicate the God of the covenant and the God of creation. "Ask now of the days that are past, which were before thee, since the day that God created man upon the earth. . . . Did ever people hear the voice of God speaking out of the midst of the fire as thou hast heard and live? . . . Unto thee it was showed that thou mightest know that Jehovah He is God; there is none else beside Him."†

Thus do we find in this address a vital connection existing between the substance of Deuteronomy and the substance of Exodus, Leviticus, and Numbers. The organization effected in the period covered by those three books is here viewed in connection with the character of Jehovah, God of their fathers, who instituted that national organic life. Again, we find a vital connection between the Book of Deuteronomy and the Book of Genesis. The same God is the author of creation and of national government, and that God is the Jehovah of the Hebrews.

National Ideals.

The second address of Moses is recorded in Deuteronomy 5–26. More clearly than in the first address is it here made certain that Moses spake to the national assembly as the body-politic in the administration of civil affairs. They represented the continuity of the nation. "Jehovah made not

---

*Deut. 4: 39, 40. † Deut. 4: 32, 33, 35.

this covenant with our fathers, but with us, even us who are all of us here alive this day."* Moreover, the assembly before him represented the old tribal organization which was recognized and preserved in the covenant. "Jehovah spake unto all your assembly in the mount. . . . And it came to pass . . . that ye came near unto Me, even all the heads of your tribes and your elders. And ye said . . . Go thou near and hear all that Jehovah our God shall say, and speak thou unto us all that Jehovah our God shall speak unto thee, and we will hear it and do it."† The authority with which Moses spake came not only from Jehovah, but also from the assembly. They had chosen him as their representative before God. They had bound themselves as an entire body of people to hear and obey what he should speak. That same political body of united tribes was now standing before him, still directed by their chosen elders and judges, and unto this little republican commonwealth did Moses address himself concerning the inner life and the future hopes of the nation.

(1) The first principle of the national law is love. This declaration occupies the record in the seven chapters, Deut. 5–11. The decalogue is repeated before the people and its spirit is summed up thus: "Thou shalt love Jehovah thy God with all thine heart, and with all thy soul and with all thy might." ‡ Jehovah's words must be lodged in the heart, must be bound as frontlets between the eyes and written on the door-posts and upon the gate-posts.§ This inward tribute of love toward God is called for as an expression of gratitude for God's love toward the nation. "Because Jehovah loved you and because He would keep the oath which He had sworn unto your fathers hath Jehovah brought you out . . . . . from Pharaoh." ‖ The law delivered to the nation at Sinai was the gift of Jehovah's love; the people needed this code of regulations for the inner life just as much as they needed deliverance from Egypt. The law has done more toward the establishment of Israel as a separate nation than was accomplished in the miracle at the Red Sea. Great moral and religious principles are of more worth as national treasures than the memory of the defeat of the Pharaoh's host. The ten commandments and the other

---

*Deut. 5: 3.   †Deut. 5: 22–27.   ‡ Deut. 6: 1–9.   § Deut. 6: 1–9.   ‖ Deut. 7: 7–8.

statutes of the law are the highest expression of Jehovah's love. They reveal the secret of the way unto a holy life; they are the formulated principles that regulate the invisible kingdom of the Redeemer. The law is the legal summary of that covenant which Jehovah's mercy has led Him to complete with Israel; it is one of the attributes of His character that He will be faithful to the terms of that compact. The provisions of the great covenant imply that Jehovah will plant this people in a land of great fruitfulness, wherein they shall eat bread without scarceness.* He will drive out heathen nations before Israel, and the yoke of their fear will He lay upon all the tribes of the earth. In the face of other people will He manifest himself as Israel's benefactor and deliverer, as "God of gods and Lord of lords, a great God, a mighty and a terrible." † All this external manifestation of His power in their behalf, both in the past and in the present, is based entirely upon Jehovah's love for His chosen. These are His ways of blessing His children. But all these mercies are a part of the terms of His covenant; they are the spirit of the written form of His love. Therefore, these temporal blessings must come upon the people through the administration of the covenant law. The assembly, as the sworn agents of administration, must work their part in securing these national benefits. The law must take hold upon their hearts and lives. They must put themselves in sympathy with Jehovah's government by loving Him. The national oath to keep the covenant implies love to Jehovah. Just as love was the ground motive of God in His work of building up the nation, so must love toward Him prompt all the acts of the people. They must live as an holy people; they must not tolerate idolaters when they come into Canaan; they must enter not into covenant with the heathen nations; in all matters must they be an exclusive people, living apart from contamination. If this nation shall observe with sincerity all the charges, commandments, testimonies, statutes and judgments delivered through Moses, then shall their strength be as that of the everlasting hills. "There shall no man be able to stand before you; for Jehovah your God shall lay the

---

*Deut. 8. †Deut. 10: 17; 11: 23.

fear of you and the dread of you upon all the land that ye shall tread upon." *

The ideal here proposed is that of a great people, whose external power is manifest, but whose internal strength is invisible. Great outward freedom shall rest upon moral principles. The strength of this nation must begin to spring up in the hearts of the people. The love for Jehovah and His law is declared to be the only foundation for national prosperity.

(2) Unity in the national worship. In Deuteronomy 12: 1–16, 17, Moses speaks to the assembly as a body of worshippers. From his new point of view he refers to the religious laws given at Sinai. Those laws are here presupposed. The people already are familiar with them. But a great crisis is just before the people. They are about to pass from a nomadic state of existence to a life among the fertile fields of Canaan. There will they be scattered over a broad expanse of land. The tribes will be widely separated. But they must have only one national sanctuary. They must remain as a unit in the worship of their Redeemer. "There shall be a place which Jehovah your God shall choose to cause His name to dwell there."† The regulations concerning sacrifices are repeated here by Moses in connection with the specific injunction that they must be offered at this religious capital of the nation. If a dreamer shall arise to teach rules of worship contrary in spirit to these laws now enjoined, let the assembly stone him. Their unity and their purity must be guarded by the use of force against all open teachers of apostasy.‡ The laws concerning the clean animals to be used for food are again enjoined as necessary to the dignity of the children of Jehovah, and as essential means in preserving unity in the religious life.§ The law of charity to the poor and the law of grateful tribute of the firstling of the flock unto Jehovah are likewise enforced as bonds of national unity.‖ As a climax to these renewed precepts concerning unity of worship, Moses names again the three great festivals. The previous legislation concerning these is made the basis of the present regulations, that they must be all celebrated at the central sanctuary. The national assembly shall there meet as a solemn

---

* Deut. 11: 25. † Deut. 12: 11. ‡ Deut. 13. § Deut. 14. ‖ Deut. 15.

assembly. The highest expression of the unity of the nation shall be these festivals around the one holy place. "Three times in a year shall all thy males appear before Jehovah thy God in the place where He shall choose."*

(3) The national administration must be subject to Jehovah. Deuteronomy 16: 18—18: 22, refers to the representative system established at Sinai. Here find we crowning proof that Moses addresses in all these speeches the national assembly concerning its functions as the agent of Jehovah's sovereignty. This assembly must enforce both the civil and religious ordinances of the law. Its system of judicial administration must be preserved; but Jehovah must still share in the selection of the judges. If the crime be a religious one, then the assembly itself must be judge and executioner, appealing unto Jehovah, through the priests and Levites, in all cases of difficulty. The system of representation by chosen judges and chosen priests may be further expanded in the choice of a king. Even then, Jehovah must bear a part in choosing the individual who is to represent both Himself and the people in the executive office. Again, the priests and Levites are mentioned as possessing administrative functions, representing the assembly before Jehovah. Finally, Moses foretells the selection of a prophet like unto himself. "Jehovah thy God will raise up unto thee a prophet from the midst of thee, of thy brethren, like unto me; unto him ye shall hearken."† Here have we a prophecy of the Christ who shall fulfill all the purposes of the theocracy. He shall come from God and yet He shall represent Israel. He shall bring with him divine authority, and yet He shall perform all the administrative functions of priest, king and prophet. Just as Moses is the head of both of the lines of divinely-appointed men who administer civil and religious affairs in the assembly, so will He gather into His personality all the administration of affairs between man and God. "The government shall be upon His shoulders and His name shall be called . . . . the Prince of Peace."‡

(4) In all social relations the nation must be just and humane. Moses concludes his summary of national ideals concerning the life of the people of Israel in Deuteronomy 19–26.

---

* Deut. 16: 1-17. † Deut. 18: 15. ‡ Isa. 9.

Here we find injunctions concerning social purity, filling out the entire round of statutes that began with ecclesiastical and civil affairs. Be it remembered, that Moses continues to hold the national point of view in setting forth these social principles. The nation is a unit; therefore must the national life be unified by the observance of strict precepts of integrity and honor. Human life must be held sacred in the enforcement of strict justice, and also in the provision for mercy in the cities of refuge. Moderation must be shown in the treatment of faint-hearted men and of prisoners taken in battle. A gentle humanity must mark their treatment of all men and of all beasts. Freedom from contact with any evil thing must be carefully guarded. The national honor must be maintained among all men. The fragments of the harvest must be left in the field for the gleaner, and even the ox that treadeth out the corn must not be muzzled. Precepts many are set before the nation as guides unto their inward growth in all the graces of an exalted humanity. All of these ideals are fitly rounded into one compact model of law and truth, which the nation must follow as Jehovah's chosen people among the tribes of earth. "Jehovah hath avouched thee this day to be His peculiar people, as He has promised thee . . . . . . to make thee high above all nations which He hath made, in praise and in name and in honor."*

The Everlasting Covenant.

The third address of Moses is contained in Deuteronomy 27—30. He concerns himself here with the renewal of the covenant between Jehovah and the national assembly. "Ye stand this day, all of you, before Jehovah your God; your captains, your tribes, your elders, and your officers, all the men of Israel; your little ones, your wives, and thy stranger that is in thy camp, from the hewer of thy wood unto the drawer of thy water: that thou shouldest enter into covenant with Jehovah thy God." † All the elements that make up the nation stand before him, under the direction of their civil administrators. They renew the solemn oath given at Sinai, but the sacrifices then offered are not repeated here. The blood of that first covenant sacrifice serves

---

* Deut. 26: 19. † Deut. 29: 10-12.

to sanctify this new oath. No new terms are stipulated in the contract, but the national organization is simply called upon to renew the solemn professions of obedience sworn to by the assembly at Sinai. The tribes of Israel as a national unit under their tribal leaders ratify the obligations assumed by their fathers. They recognize that the preservation of that national unity depends upon the covenant made with Jehovah. It must be an everlasting covenant in order that the nation may abide forever.

Not only in the plains of Moab, in his own presence, does Moses make the people swear anew unto the terms of the covenant, but the larger part of this address is occupied with injunctions concerning a further ratification when they shall have passed over Jordan. The voice of the elders of Israel is added unto the commandment of Moses* as a ratification of his authority. Likewise, the priests speak also in confirmation of what Moses enjoins. All the authority that was lodged in the national organization itself, first through the elders as the civil representatives and then through the priests as the religious representatives, is added to the authority from Jehovah whereby Moses calls this last time upon Israel: "On the day when ye shall pass over Jordan . . . . thou shalt set thee up great stones and plaister them with plaister: and thou shalt write upon them all the words of this law . . . . in Mount Ebal, ... and there shalt thou build an altar unto Jehovah thy God, ... and thou shalt offer burnt-offerings . . . . and peace offerings, . . . and rejoice before Jehovah thy God."† Moses further enjoins that the nation shall stand on Mount Ebal and on Mount Gerizim, in renewing the covenant, according to their tribal divisions. It shall be the Abrahamic covenant merged into the covenant of Sinai. From the beginning the nation has been a unit through the covenant, and only through the same compact shall it continue as a nation forever. The spirit of the covenant stipulations shall be repeated by the people in the form of the curses and the blessings attached to God's law as penalties and rewards.‡ The climax of penalty is reached when Moses foretells the complete dissolution of the nation and their return back into Egypt, if they

---

*Deut. 27: 1. † Deut. 27: 2-8. ‡ Deut. 27 and 28.

keep not God's law. As God created the national organization through the agency of the covenant, so will He un-make the organization and scatter the dissolved members thereof through the land of bondage whence He once led them, if they keep not the terms of that great national compact.* And yet, the permanence of the nation is not surrendered entirely to the action of the assembly. Their obedience will hasten, their rebellion will postpone, the final unity of God's people. Even from the nations of the earth into whose bosom the curse for disobedience shall drive the fragments of this dissolved organization, even from the places of their bondage shall He finally call forth a people to keep His covenant. A great national restoration shall at last, far off, follow the penalties that come upon those generations that shall be stiff-necked before God. The calling of the spiritual Israel from the midst of Jews and Gentiles by the prophet like unto Moses is here distinctly foreshadowed.

Some discussion has arisen concerning the law here mentioned by Moses. It must seem clear that this can be none other than the entire legislation of the Pentateuch given unto Israel through Moses. The law here enjoined is the bond of national unity. It is sworn to in the plains of Moab by the assembly for itself, and also as the representative of the patriarchs and the representative of posterity.† The nation, as it takes the solemn covenant again before Moses, is a unit in the present, the past and the future. The bond of that unity is called by Moses "the words of this law."‡ In spirit it must be the same law imposed upon Abraham and upon the assembly at Sinai. The people swear unto the words as Moses speaks them in Moab; they are to write them upon stones in Ebal; they are to utter the sanctions of that law as summed up in its blessings and curses; and, moreover, they must continually keep its precepts written in their hearts.§ Further, as to its constituent parts this law has already been mentioned as Jehovah's charges, commandments, testimonies, statutes and judgments. This law can be only the written form of all Jehovah's sovereign acts in establishing the nation. It can be only the national legislation, enacted

---

*Deut. 28: 15–68. †Deut. 29: 13, 14, 15. ‡Deut. 27: 3. §Deut. 30: 14.

from the beginning of the history of this people until this present hour.

The Three Legal Codes.

Some modern critics have made a division of the laws of the Pentateuch into the covenant-code, the priest-code and the Deuteronomic-code, and assert that these codes were drawn up during widely separated periods in Israel's history.* Some hold, further, that the Deuteronomic-code was the only part of the law developed at the time of the exodus and that this is "the law" enjoined by Moses in Moab. But the historical facts disprove the claims of this theory. If we regard the covenant-code as that part of the law connected with the formation of the nation at Sinai, the priest-code as connected with the organization of religious unity in worship and the Deuteronomic-code as connected with the permanence of the nation and of its religious unity, then all these parts of the law must have been in the mind of Moses as he called for a renewal of the covenant vows. The establishment, the organization, the permanence of the nation were the very interests involved in this final transaction in Moab. Without an explicit statement to the contrary, we are forced to recognize the law here brought forward as designating the legal enactments connected with the entire history of the nation up to this time, and recorded in Genesis, Exodus, Leviticus, Numbers and Deuteronomy.

All the essential facts connected with the old tribal organization before the exodus were made a part of the terms of this national oath in Moab, for that old tribal organization still remained intact. The covenant-terms with that early tribal basis of the nation were recorded in the Book of Genesis and were known to Israel in Moab. All the essential facts connected with the inauguration and continuation of the wider national life at Sinai and afterwards, were here involved in this new covenant. Again, let it be remembered, those facts were imbedded in the history as well as in the mere legislation of Exodus, Leviticus, Numbers and Deuteronomy. The new covenant itself was based upon an intelligent knowledge of all those facts and laws on the part of the nation. That knowledge was drawn by this second

---

* W. R. Smith: "Old Testament in the Jewish Church."

generation after the exodus from the book of the law which contained a written account of all their national life. That law was the external bond of national unity and of national permanence. Just so surely as this history in the Pentateuch makes declaration that the twelve tribes were descended from Abraham and Jacob and that they were compacted into national unity before crossing the Jordan into Canaan, with the same certitude is it stated that the Pentateuch was at that time written out in one "book of the law" as the sign and seal of that completed statehood. The Pentateuch was the national constitution and it was made complete at the same time with the organization of the nation itself.

CHAPTER XXI.

AUTHORSHIP AND INSPIRATION OF THE PENTATEUCH.

Moses Wrote the National Constitution.

ALREADY has it become apparent that the Pentateuch, as containing all the stipulations of the national covenant, was presented in its unity to the assembly in the plains of Moab. The 31st chapter of Deuteronomy declares that Moses wrote this constitution.

The work of Moses as a writer of national records dates back to the passage of the Red Sea. The song which Miriam and the other women sang is called the Song of Moses. All the attendant circumstances and the internal character of the song itself indicate that Moses wrote it on the very day of deliverance. It was the birthday of the nation, and as such did Moses celebrate it. "Thou in thy mercy hast led forth the people which thou hast redeemed."* After the first victory wrought by the sword over a heathen nation in the wilderness, God commanded Moses to write an account of the defeat of these Amalekites "in the book and rehearse it in the ears of Joshua." † Evidently the reference here is to a well-known national record-book which was then in course of composition at the hand of Moses. Another entry in the national chronicle is spoken of in connection with the people after their departure from Sinai: "These are the journeyings of the children of Israel, which went forth out of the land of Egypt with their armies under the hand of Moses and Aaron. And Moses wrote their goings out according to their journeys by the commandment of Jehovah." ‡ In the making of the covenant at Sinai, all the terms of agreement were written down by Moses. Jehovah spake the ten commandments unto the people, and at the end of forty days wrote them with His own finger upon the tables of stone. Then "Moses wrote all the words of Jehovah, ... and he took the book of the covenant

---
*Exod. 15: 13.   †Exod. 17: 14.   ‡ Numb. 33: 1, 2.

and read in the audience of the people."* This book of the covenant is embraced in Exodus 20: 22–23: 33, and deals with the establishment of the national assembly of the Hebrews as one of the nations of the earth. Certain maxims and laws from the time of the patriarchs were incorporated in the legal judgments set forth by Moses as national statutes.

After the covenant had been sworn to, and after Moses had spent the first period of forty days in Jehovah's presence on the mount receiving directions for the administration of worship, he returned to the people with the two tables of stone only to discover their apostasy. Then Moses brake the tables and returned to ask Jehovah for the restoration of the nation. "If thou wilt forgive their sin; and if not, blot me, I pray thee, out of thy book which thou hast written. And Jehovah said unto Moses, Whosoever hath sinned against me, him will I blot out of my book." † This book must have been the book of national records wherein were enrolled all the people and all the tribes of Israel. The sum of all the men capable of bearing arms had been taken at the time of the exodus,‡ and the sum of all the men, by families and by names, was again taken by Moses and Aaron before the march into the wilderness.§ The book containing this register of the national assembly was evidently written by Moses at Jehovah's commandment. It was Jehovah's book, for it contained the names of His people. To be blotted from the roll therein inscribed meant the loss of a place among God's people both now and forever. Further than this, at the end of the second conference of forty days with Jehovah, after Moses had received minute instructions concerning the civil and religious administration of God's government, "Jehovah said unto Moses, Write thou these words: for after the tenor of these words I have made a covenant with thee and with Israel." ‖

Concerning the composition of the Book of Leviticus, the phrase "Jehovah spake unto Moses," or "Jehovah spake unto Moses and Aaron," occurs no less than thirty-six times in the book itself. This legislation concerning worship came through Moses. Its minute specifications could not be remembered without a written record. Moreover, it is asserted that "these are the statutes, and judgments, and

---
* Exod. 24: 4–7. † Exod. 32: 32, 33. ‡ Exod. 12: 37. § Numb. 1: 2, 3, 17, 44. ‖ Exod. 34: 27.

laws which Jehovah made between him and the children of Israel in Mt. Sinai by the hand of Moses."* The necessary implication involved in all these assertions is that Moses wrote down all the religious legislation of Jehovah. A similar statement is made at the close of the Book of Numbers concerning the origin of the laws and statutes therein recorded,† and, moreover, in the book we find the phrase, " Jehovah spake unto Moses" or "unto Moses and Aaron" set down in formal manner about seventy-eight times. The record-book of their journeyings was thus not the only chronicle kept by Moses, but the inference from all these facts is clear that he kept also a detailed record of God's laws as they were uttered.

We have seen that the first thirty-chapters of Deuteronomy are the very words of Moses himself. They form an inspired commentary on the previous national history. He declares that Jehovah has constituted him as *teacher* of all the national laws.‡ How could he teach definite statutes unless they were already written out ? Moreover, the people themselves were to teach them to their children, were to talk of them, were to *write* them on the door-posts and gate-posts. In the times to come, when they shall set up a king, this monarch " shall write him a copy of this law in a book out of that which is before the priests, the Levites; and it shall be with him and he shall read therein all the days of his life."§ A written national constitution given through Moses for the guidance of the people and their chosen rulers is here spoken of as a book well-known.

In the closing days of Moses we are told that " Moses wrote this law and delivered it unto the priests the sons of Levi, which bare the ark of the covenant of Jehovah, and unto all the elders of Israel. And Moses commanded them, saying, At the end of every seven years, in the solemnity of the year of release, in the feast of tabernacles, when all Israel is come to appear before Jehovah thy God in the place which He shall choose, thou shalt read this law before all Israel in their hearing." ‖ A formal renewal of the covenant every seven years is here contemplated, and that renewed covenant must be made after a clear understanding of the national constitution. This book is now completed and

---
*Levit. 26: 46. †Numb. 36: 13. ‡Deut. 5: 31. §Deut. 17: 18, 19. ‖ Deut. 31: 9, 13.

given into the charge of the civil and religious administrators, the elders and the priests. Doubtless, the priests had been the keepers of the book during the wilderness journeys and none but Moses had access thereto in order that he might make additional entries. "And it came to pass when Moses had made an end of writing the words of this law in a book, *until they were finished*, that Moses commanded the Levites, which bare the ark of the covenant of Jehovah, saying, Take this book of the law and put it in the side of the ark of the covenant of Jehovah your God that it may be there for a witness against thee."*

This book, which Moses completed in Moab, contained the foundations of the national organization. The permanence and the religious character of Israel were intimately connected with that book. It was the sign and seal of the Hebrew religion and government. The principles of all their past history were therein recorded. It must have been the same national record-book which we have seen growing under the hand of Moses along with the organization of the theocracy. It must have contained not only one, but all of the three so-called codes. It must have contained not only codes, but national acts and chronicles. It must have contained all the matter written in Genesis, Exodus, Leviticus, Numbers and Deuteronomy.

Of course, we except from this statement the last three chapters of Deuteronomy. These were added by a later hand in the formal collection and arrangement of the canon of the Jewish Scriptures. The Jews have a tradition that the scribe Ezra made such an arrangement, and made also slight verbal additions and changes in the holy books.†

Concerning this national constitution, it will be sufficient here to make brief mention of the evidence concerning its existence from that time forward. Unto Joshua this book written by Moses was given by Jehovah as His own governmental constitution for the direction of the nation.‡ In the time of the judges the national apostasy was due, as the record implies, to the indifference of the people to their national law. The reformation of Samuel was based upon the teaching and the enforcement of the divine constitution. The reformation in the time of Josiah sprang from the

---

* Deut. 31: 24-26. † Tertullian. ‡ Josh. 1: 1-8; 14, 18 and 21.

new-discovered "Book of the Law of Jehovah by Moses."* The writings of psalmists and prophets were based upon a minute knowledge of all the books of the Pentateuch as the covenant-book of the nation. Likewise, when our Lord spake to the Jews of the law of Moses, He evidently spake from this national point of view. He denounced national sins and national apostasies as departures from the real teachings of him who set forth in written form the national constitution. Pharisaic evil-doing, said the Lord, was going about to dissolve the national organization which Moses had been instrumental in forming through the agency of his law. The law of Moses, as thus referred to, could mean naught else than the entire Pentateuch.†

The Culmination of Moses' Work as Prophet.

The national constitution was the last and greatest work of Moses. In this book of the law was the activity of Moses to be perpetuated. As he had spoken Jehovah's words unto the people, so was this book to continue the utterance of the same divine commands and promises until the coming of the Prophet like unto Moses. When He did come, His mission was to sanction and fulfill the law as Moses had written it. Let us here recall the facts connected with Moses' life-work as prophet.

The primary function of Moses as prophet was to declare Jehovah's will. "See, I have appointed thee a god to Pharaoh: and Aaron, thy brother, shall be thy prophet. Thou shalt speak all that I command thee. And he shall be thy spokesman unto the people, ... and thou shalt be to him instead of God." ‡ Thus were his credentials assigned him as Jehovah's representative at the Pharaoh's court. Thus was he to stand as Jehovah's agent to make demands, to utter warnings and to wield infinite power. In this work as God's messenger or representative, Moses passed through three distinct stages of activity. First of all, he was appointed to declare Jehovah's purposes unto the Pharaoh and to substantiate his assertions by working "signs and wonders!" The stretching out of the hand of Moses and the hand of Aaron over the river and over the land of Egypt was the

---

* II. Chron. 34: 14.   † Vid. Introduction to Speaker's Com. on Pentateuch.   ‡ Exod. 7: 1, 2; 4: 16.

stretching out of Jehovah's hand. The miracles that were wrought at the command of Moses displayed the infinite power consigned to his direction. The rather did they show that the first activity of Moses as God's representative was in the great work of making known His power by redeeming Israel "with a stretched-out arm and with great judgments."* In the drama of the exodus, God wrought out before the eyes of all nations the greatest series of miracles of judgment ever manifested. This was unquestionably the period wherein God brought to a climax His miracles in the sphere of external nature, as indicating His punishment of those who render Him naught but defiance. Another age of miracles was the period of the Hebrew prophets, but many of God's wonders in this later time were manifested in healing lepers like Naaman as well as in punishing priests of Baal. Later still, the life of Jesus was spent in working wonders, but these were mostly wrought upon infirm bodies and demonized souls. The farther we advance in the history of God's wonder-working the more do we find Him effecting an approach towards the souls of men with the miraculous agencies that purify and bless and heal. But the period of the exodus was the one age of the world when God made the earth, air and sky, the rivers and the seas, and all that moves and lives, the sun, the animal world from every insect up to the first-born of men, all of these to speak forth His power and to stamp a curse upon the overgrown superstitions of earth. Never again were miracles of this character to be wrought upon such a scale until the end of all things earthly. For such wielding of miraculous power, the entire training of Moses had fitted him. Miraculous agencies had surrounded his life from the beginning. By a miracle had he been drawn out of the bulrushes to be trained up in the Pharaoh's palace. Divine power accompanied him through all his years of banishment in Midian, and the miracle of the burning bush opened up his commission to bring Israel out of bondage. Humanly speaking, no other man of that time would have been able to understand and to use the divine agencies which wrought deliverance for the Hebrews. God could have prepared another man for the work, but He did not, and we know well that the back-

---

* Exod. 6: 6.

ground of divine interference in Moses' life was a part of the preparation of this leading man of the first great age of miracles.

The second stage of the work of Moses began in the wilderness when he sat as judge to make Israel "know the statutes of God and His laws."* The function of legislator was added to his function as judge, and thus did he become the mediator between God and the people. Jethro suggested "God shall be with thee; be thou for the people before God," † and Moses heeded and assumed his double office as representative of Jehovah and representative of the people. As the minister of Jehovah he declared the ordinances and the laws whereby the people were to be guided, and as the deputy, or agent of the people, he brought causes unto Jehovah for final adjudication. When Jehovah began to deliver the great series of statutes from Sinai, it was through Moses that He spake to the people. In like manner, the people sent Moses into God's presence to hear His words for them, for when they saw the thunderings and the lightnings and the noise of the trumpet and the mountain smoking, they said unto Moses, "Speak thou with us and we will hear; but let not God speak with us, lest we die." ‡ Thus did Moses enter upon the work of *enlightenment* as distinguished from his previous career as *miracle worker*. Of course, he wrought in both ways at the first and continuously unto the end; but the predominance of the one element at different times seems to justify this division into different stages of activity. This lofty position as mouth-piece for God, as an ear-piece for the people, was dwelt upon by Moses in his latest addresses unto Israel. In the renewal of the covenant in the plains of Moab he reiterated the history of his induction into the office of *teacher of ordinances;* he recalled the fact that the people commanded him into Jehovah's presence to hear and to make report; that Jehovah commanded him, "Stand thou here by Me, and I will speak unto thee all the commandments and the statutes and the judgments which thou shalt teach" the people. §

Again do we assert that Moses was the one man of his time whom God trained for this work of legislation. In the universities and the armies of Egypt had Moses learned all

---
*Exod. 18: 16. †Exod. 18: 19. ‡ Exod. 20: 18, 19. § Deut. 5: 22 and 33.

that men then knew of civil and military law. He was the only man of whom we have record who could understand a great system of law, and with intelligence set it before the people. In the mere matter of hearing and explaining the divine covenant and of carrying into effect the national organization, Moses was the one and only man of his age fitted for the work.

The third and highest stage of the work of Moses was his *writing* of the law. He was the teacher not merely of his own age, but teacher of the ages yet to come. His work of enlightening future generations as well as his own was effected through the written copy of the law. After the writing, the book was given to Joshua as God's book, as God's law. In the first stage of his prophetic work, Moses wrought *miracles* as God's representative; in the second stage, he *spoke* God's Word as His representative, and in the third stage he *wrote* God's Word as His representative. Now, it must be admitted that the human agency involved in these three manifestations of supernatural power and wisdom, was an agency thoroughly in sympathy with the divine works. This sympathy would involve intelligence. The human agent must have been divinely instructed in the specific understanding of all that he did. The ultimate purpose of all these revelations may have been made known to him only through a glass, darkly, but the present intention and application must have been known to him in their full scope. The contention here made is that Moses was the only man of that age endowed with the special fitness adequate to the completion of such divine works. None other man of his time would have successfully led the advance in Jehovah's war against all the gods of Egypt. None other man would have received and put in operation such a complete system of divine laws when the minds of men were prejudiced in favor of codes of an opposing spirit. None other man of that period would have been able to incorporate Jehovah's institutions into the forms of human language so distinct and so complete that Jehovah could accept that language as His own. Superadded to all these individual necessities of circumstance that compel the inference that Moses must have wrought each individual part of the works of this great age of revelation, there is the further logical necessity that the same man must have been Jehovah's agent in all of these manifestations. The man who stretched out his arm as the sign that Jehovah's lightning would strike the fetters from the hands of the Hebrew slaves, must of necessity have been the same man who heard and spake the ordinances that made the liberated nation also subject to Jehovah. The man who invoked Jehovah's power to strike down the Pharaoh's tyranny was of necessity the same man who interpreted Jehovah's wisdom in the establishment of a self-regulating community. And, then, the man who had played the leading part in all this great drama from the Nile to the Jordan was the one man who could have made a permanent record of the entire series of events. We are not discussing the limits of the divine power, for that is without limit or boundary. We speak here of the methods always used by Jehovah in the exercise of His power. Among the Hebrew prophets, later than the time of Moses, the man who wrought miracles was also the man who came to speak a message which he himself had received from God, and the man who did both of these was also the writer of his own messages to the people of his own time and of succeeding times. These three stages of miracle-working, declaration by word of mouth and writing a permanent record, constitute the elements of complete unity in the functions of the prophet. Where we find this completeness, the same man always did the entire work. In like manner was Moses the one man whom God prepared for the completion of the great system of revelation made in the age of the exodus.

At this point we may sum up the argument concerning the Mosaic authorship of the Pentateuch. In this argument there are just three steps. The first contention made is that the Pentateuch is a complete unity, and necessarily the work of one man. This contention is involved in the discussion set forth in the main body of this volume. We have maintained that the writer of the original records of these five books was of necessity the man who gave them final and permanent literary form, with the exception of certain slight verbal alterations by a later scribe.

The second contention is that this book was made complete in the age of the exodus, before the permanent occupation of Palestine. The book, in its five parts in complete literary form, is contemporary with the organization of the nation. The institutions and the record are made permanent together. This is the clear statement of the Pentateuch itself, as we have already endeavored to show. If we accept its credibility as history we must needs accept this historical oneness of the nation and the book. We can recall in how many particulars the narrative of the Pentateuch is interwoven with Egyptian life. The institutions of Egypt form the great background. The entire book must have been written with that background in the clear view of the writer. In the foreground of the Pentateuch is the Jordan and Palestine. From beginning to end of the five books the crossing of the Jordan and the permanent settlement in Palestine are contemplated. It is self-evident that the writer of the Pentateuch looks forward to the promised home. It is evident that when he lays down his pen at the close of the five-volumed work, the wilderness and the desert are still about Israel, and their rich inheritance still is beyond the river.

The third and final claim in the argumentation is that Moses was the sole individual of the age of the exodus who was at all equal to the task of writing this great national record. We have seen that the patriarchal organization of the Hebrew tribes was incorporated into the civil organization of the nation at Sinai. The sacrifices practiced by the patriarchs, with certain regulations and laws, formed a part of the religious and civil organization formally established at Sinai. Moses, as God's agent, completed that national organization and framed its laws. He must have known the history of the patriarchs, for he did obey the command of Joseph concerning his bones, and he did know all about the patriarchal organization, administration of justice, and religious rites. We are not concerned here with the question as to how Moses learned that history. He may have obtained it through tribal traditions, or there may have been tribal records. Moses undoubtedly knew all the history set forth in the Book of Genesis. He made use of the facts involved in that history when he was establishing the national covenant. That history had to be known by the people in entering into the covenant at Sinai. A complete record of God's dealings with His people in Egypt and at Sinai involved a record of what He had done for them in patriarchal times. No other man before or since the age of the exodus could have had such complete knowledge of the entire patriarchal period as Moses. No other man before or since could have had such necessity laid upon him to write the history of that period as it has been recorded in the Book of Genesis.

Furthermore, as the chief actor in all the scenes of national deliverance, he was the most thoroughly-equipped man for the writing of that history. There was the supreme motive, likewise, that the permanence of this newly-formed nation depended upon obedience to the expressed ordinances of Jehovah. Those statutes must be written out then and there. Our necessary inference is that they were written out by the only man who had completely entered into the shrine of God's presence to learn His purposes and His laws. Moses was the one man of all the throng who spake with God, who saw the glory of God, and who had that glory so stamped upon his own face that Israel could not look upon him. From that living presence of the divine glory came he forth with the heavenly voice ringing in his ears and the heavenly pattern before his eyes, not only to interpret Jehovah's plans, but to perform that loftiest of all acts permitted to man—to transfer to human speech in written form the very thoughts and laws of God Himself. Through Moses, God expressed His will in Human speech as the necessary prelude to the manifestation of His nature in the human flesh of His Son.

The Inspiration of the Pentateuch.

Thus far have we considered the Pentateuch as a great body of divine revelation. Within these five books is incorporated a great system of teaching concerning the character of God and the character of man; and this system is imbedded in the narrative history of races and individuals extending over a period of hundreds of years. In calling the Pentateuch a body of revelation, we simply connote the fact that God has herein opened up the mysteries of the supernatural world to the knowledge of men through the teaching agency of material facts; that He has herein communicated divine ideas unto finite minds through the medium of visions, voices, symbols and angels. All of these are only methods of His self-manifestation or means of the divine revelation.

This system of revelation likewise has a great aim and purpose distinctly declared. This aim is to make Israel holy even as Jehovah is holy. Through the agency of the moral and spiritual ideas revealed God has sought, and continues seeking, to make His chosen like unto Himself. Aside from its method and its aim, however, let us hold distinctly in view the fact that the Pentateuch is a great body of revelation—a system of supernatural truth which men could not reach unless God had broken through the bonds of the unseen and had spoken it in terms unmistakable.

A second characteristic of the Pentateuch is its historical credibility. Each and all of its parts have been examined in connection with contemporary records, and upon every line of these five books have we found stamped the marks of truth. We have found the entire book to be a true history of real events. From its consecutive unity, from its self-consistency, from its entire accordance with contemporary events, we receive the Pentateuch at its face value as a narrative history. Moreover, our judgment is sustained by the divine wisdom of our Lord Himself, for He accepted the Pentateuch and He taught it as worthy of entire credence. Upon His sanction alone are we made confident that the Pentateuch is a part of the Old Testament canon, and, as such, is a true and unimpeachable record of facts.

From the statements and implications of the Pentateuch as a credible history have we drawn out our reasons for believing Moses to be the writer of this book. The name and character of the author are interwoven with the historical character of the book itself. That is to say, the authorship of the Pentateuch is a historical question. Certain scholars bring forward word-lists from the narratives on different subjects in the course of the history, and they assert that these different words and phrases imply different authors. This claim is fortified by the additional assertion that these passages are marked by difference in linguistic style, and that sometimes there is found a parallel narrative concerning the same subject.* But we hold that difference in subject-matter and difference in point of view will account for all these variations in the style and language. The claim that different documents have been woven together by some editor after the time of the exile is a flat denial of the historical credibility of the Pentateuch. We maintain that, upon the face of it, the book claims to be a unity in theme and in authorship. When these scholars attempt further to find the Pentateuch and the psalter to be results of national development in government and religious ceremonial,† they deny the truth of the historical statements of the Pentateuch. They invalidate the character of the narrative as a body of revelation and bring it down to the level of human wisdom and tribal folk-lore. The whole history, from beginning to end, cries out against such an assault upon its credibility.

The matter of the inspiration of the Pentateuch brings us into a wider field. Here have we before us the inspiration of the entire Bible. · The question of divine revelation, concerned as it is with the theme and the credibility of the statements made in the sacred narrative, has been left behind as a matter already solved, and now are we busied concerning the origin of the *written record* of revelation. We have accepted as authentic historical facts the truths of revelation, many of these being such facts long before their history was committed to writing. Now must we investigate the manner and the means of that writing.

In one passage we find "all Scripture" characterized as "God-breathed."‡ Again, the holy prophets are called the mouth-pieces of God,§ and they also, as scripture-writers, are said to have been "moved by the Holy Ghost.∥ Further than this, the written record made by Moses is called the very mouth-piece of God."¶ All these claims mean naught else than this, that the written record of divine revelation is essentially God's work and not man's, for it is God's Word and not man's. These claims mean that the written record was inscribed by human penmen so completely under His direction that the process of literary com-

---

* Canon Driver: Introd. to the Literature of the O. T. Dr. Charles A. Briggs: The Higher Criticism of the Hexateuch. † Briggs: The Higher Criticism of the Hexateuch. ‡ II. Tim. 3: 16. § Luke 1: 70. ∥ II. Peter 1: 21. ¶ Joshua 1: 7-9.

position was controlled by divine wisdom superadded to human wisdom.

This conclusion is sustained by additional testimony from the *quality* of the sacred narrative. The quality of the Bible as prophecy, in addition to its quality as credible history, bespeaks the finger of God in its literary composition. Its quality of freedom from error in every part, even in those sections where questions of chronology, natural science and contemporary history are dealt with, distinguishes the Bible from all other books. In these respects, human historians make mistakes and contradict themselves in their own writings. No contradiction of the facts of nature, nor of science; no self-contradiction between its parts, has yet been pointed out in the Bible, with the sole exception of those errors in the text which have resulted from human mismanagement in the handling of the books since their composition. These qualities extend to the minutest part of the Bible record and even permeate the very words used to communicate the supernatural truth. This inerrancy is denied by the above-mentioned scholars, on the ground that they can point to errors in the Bible narrative. But not a single error have they yet demonstrated; not one statement have they pointed out as a mistake on the part of the original writers. Things not clearly understood are numerous, but of positive errors, none have come to the surface. Not one of these scholars can say, "Here is a matter concerning which I know the truth, while the original writer did not know it, and I can prove both propositions." The claim for the absolute inerrancy of the Bible stands unimpeached by a single demonstrated fact to the contrary.

This overwhelming testimony brings the conviction that even in the matter of giving literary permanence to His revelation God wrought a miracle. As a written record the entire Bible is just as clearly the result of miracle as a part of its contents are the result of miraculous visions. If we call the sudden appearance of the risen Lord unto Saul at Damascus by the term miracle, so do we apply the same term *miracle* to Paul's continuous work of writing down on parchment all of God's revelations to him. In the first case, the Son of God was the Revealer of new truths to Saul himself; in the second case the Spirit of God was the continual guide in such manner as to make the writing a series of divine messages unto all ages. Therefore, using the terms found in the Bible itself, we agree to call the Bible record "inspired," denoting the fact that it is the very word of God and not of man. Likewise we say that the writers were "inspired" authors—that is, under the complete guidance of God's Spirit. Then we use the general term "inspiration" to express the fact that God's Spirit so superintended the process of writing, that God's thoughts and plans stood transcribed upon the pages in a literary form of absolute inerrancy. When the Scripture speaks, it is God that speaks. God's authority is clad in the garments of human language and dwells among men as the only infallible rule of faith and practice.

We have learned certain facts concerning the work of Moses as prophet that indicate just here the character of the origin of the Pentateuch. The first stage of Moses' activity was that of miracle-working exercised upon external nature. The second stage was miracle-working in a wider and higher sphere. All the self-manifestations of Jehovah at Sinai, not merely the thunderings, but the Voice that spake all the statutes—these were a very high order of the miraculous. They displayed the hand and the wisdom of God in the midst of human affairs in a manner never before witnessed. God's communications to Moses were nothing less than a continuous miracle. But more miraculous still was the work of Moses in making permanent record of those revelations. Herein was a continuous miracle of yet more marvelous character. Herein Moses found his loftiest sphere of work, and herein God wrought His greatest miracle, until that other transcendant wonder of later centuries when the Word became flesh. God's sanction rested upon the written record of His revelation in addition to the sanction accorded unto the facts revealed.

Somewhat has been said concerning Bibliolatry in connection with this claim of the divine origin of the Pentateuch and of the whole Bible. But it must not be supposed that we hold up the letter of God's word as also a worker of miracles. The book is itself the result of miraculous agencies, but the mere printed page is not, in turn, competent to work further miracles. The axe which Elisha made to swim upon the surface of Jordan did not become an instrument of miraculous cutting power, and probably had to be sharpened with the rest. The body of Lazarus was gifted with no miracle-working touch, with no exemption from another hour of death after the Lord called him forth from the tomb. God wrought a miracle in producing the inspired Book, but when it stood complete, the record was then subject to the ordinary laws that govern all human records, just as the life of the risen Lazarus was again subject to the ordinary conditions of human existence. The paper leaves will not turn a rifle ball, nor will the touch of them avert the contagion of disease. The language is altogether of the speech common to mankind, and can be turned into many vernaculars.

The crowning work of Moses was just this work of making God's law current in the speech of men. First among the sons of men was he to have his writing so superintended by the Holy Spirit that the result was an inspired book. The book itself was guarded by the watchful providence of God, but it was surrendered to human agencies for transmission. As a matter of fact, these human agencies have made mistakes. The copyist's pen has sometimes slipped and the wrong word has been substituted for the original term. By means of the supernatural knowledge imparted through the use of the Pentateuch, God inspired other men to the miraculous work of writing other parts of His revelation. The remaining parts of the Old Testament and all of the New were, in large measure, founded upon the Pentateuch. Copyists continued to make errors, for copyists are not inspired—but the book is inspired because the Spirit of truth dwelleth therein, even as our spirits dwell in these houses of clay. At length the canon was closed and the sacred writing, begun by Moses, was completed by John; the Spirit of God was domiciled forever in His linguistic tabernacle, even though the parchment of the original human penman might wax old and decay after the manner of all things material.

Finis.

www.ingramcontent.com/pod-product-compliance
Lightning Source LLC
Chambersburg PA
CBHW022111230426
43672CB00008B/1341